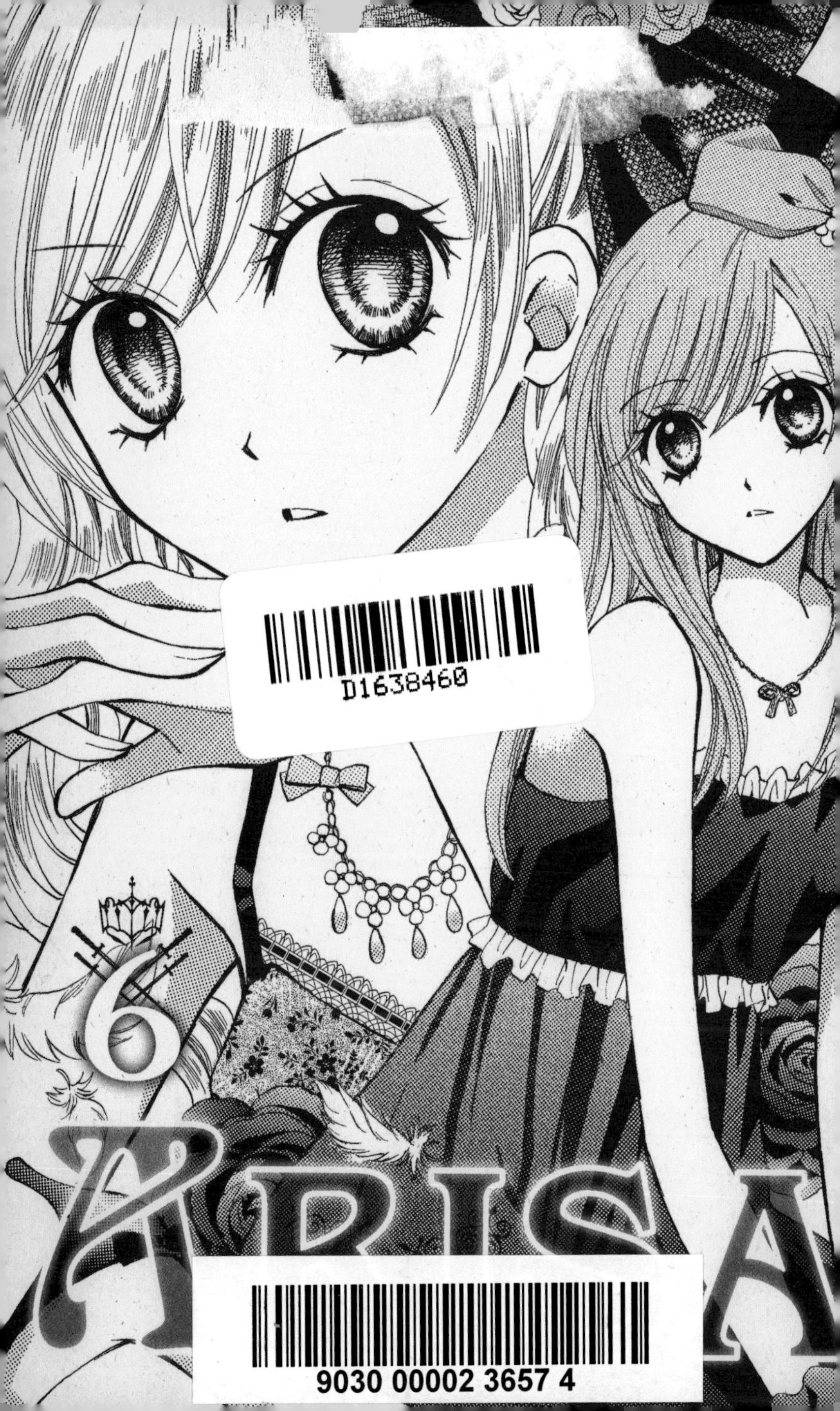
6
ARISA

Contents

コンテンツ

ARISA

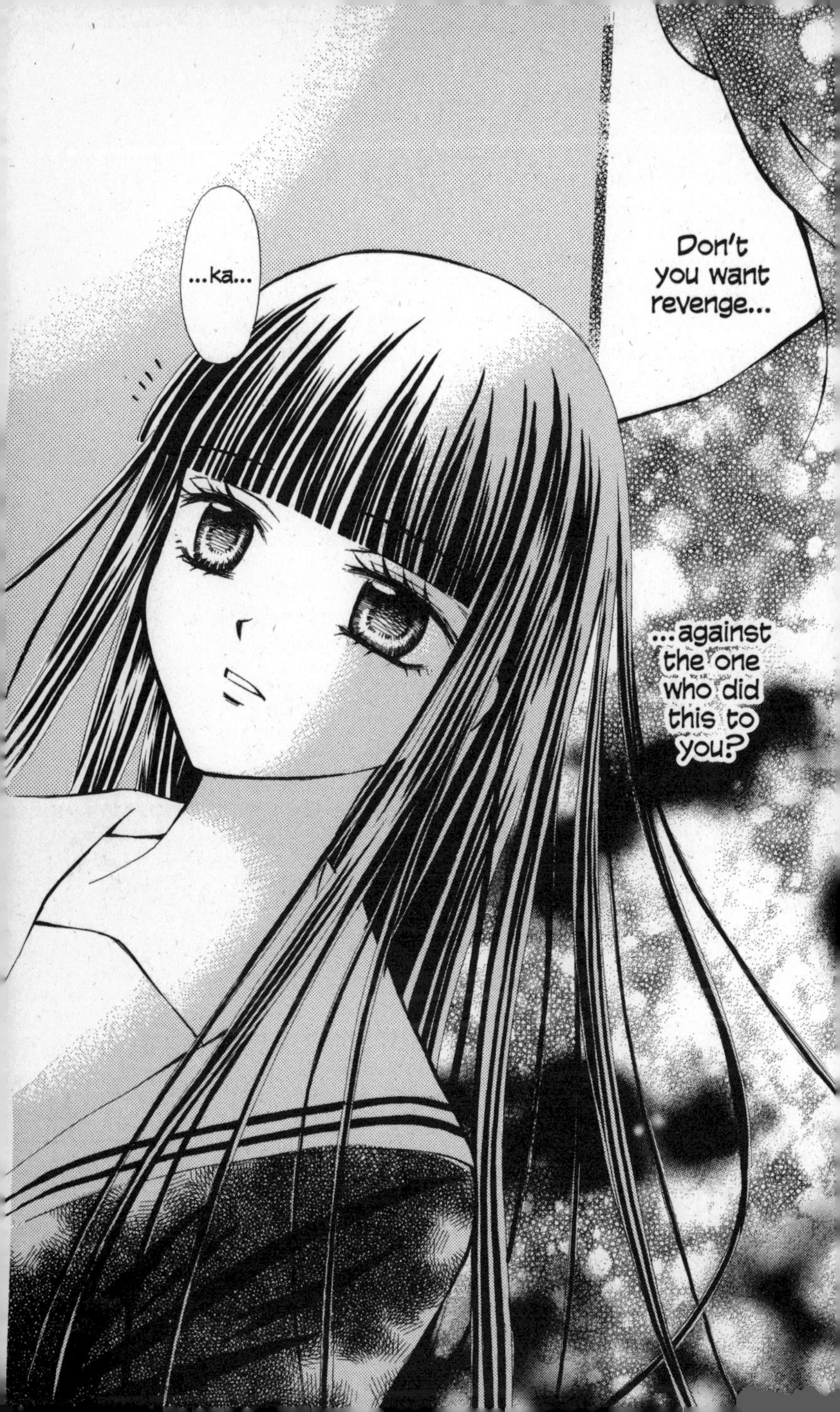
Don't you want revenge...
...ka...
...against the one who did this to you?

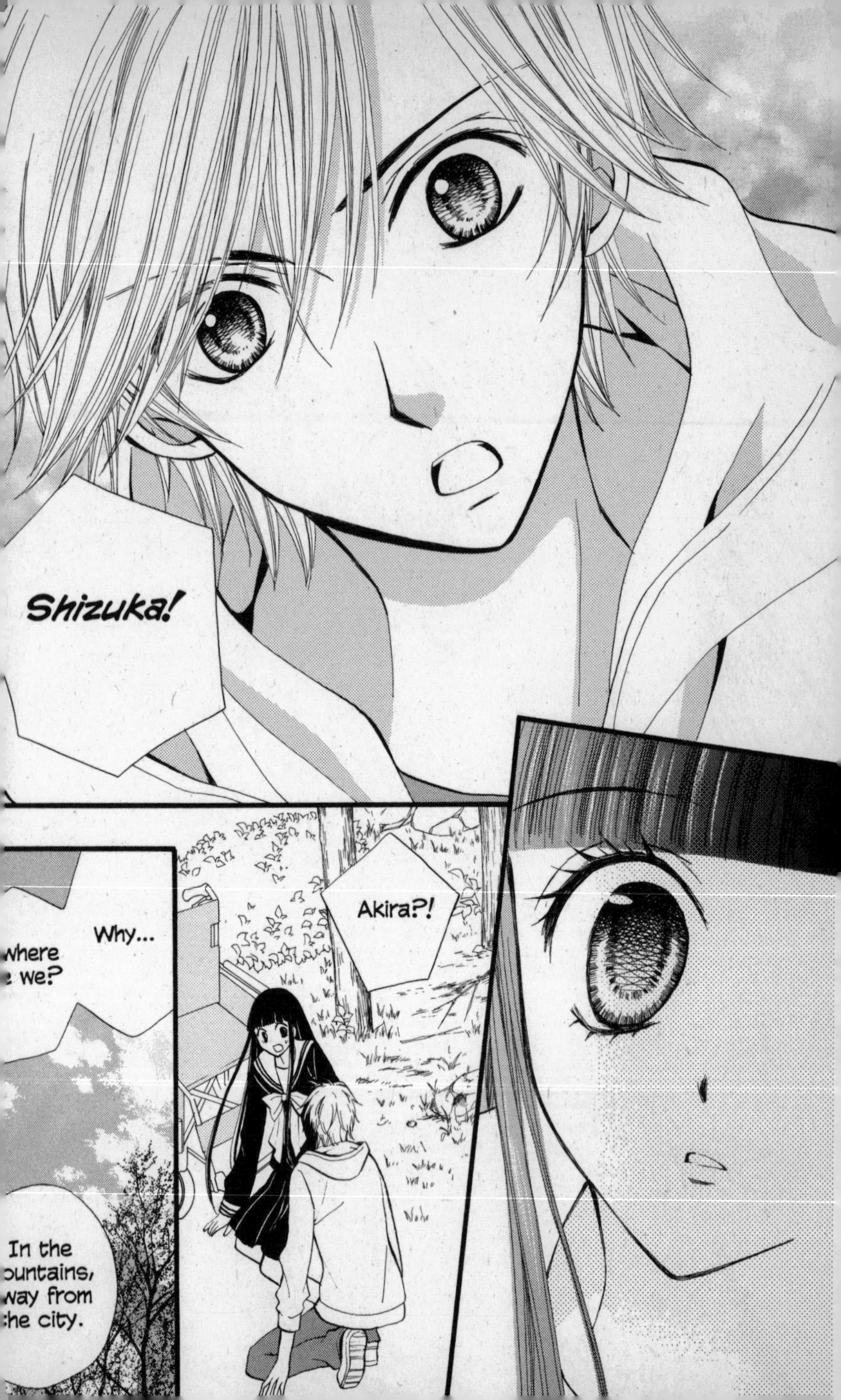
Shizuka!
Akira?!
Why...
where e we?
In the ountains, way from he city.

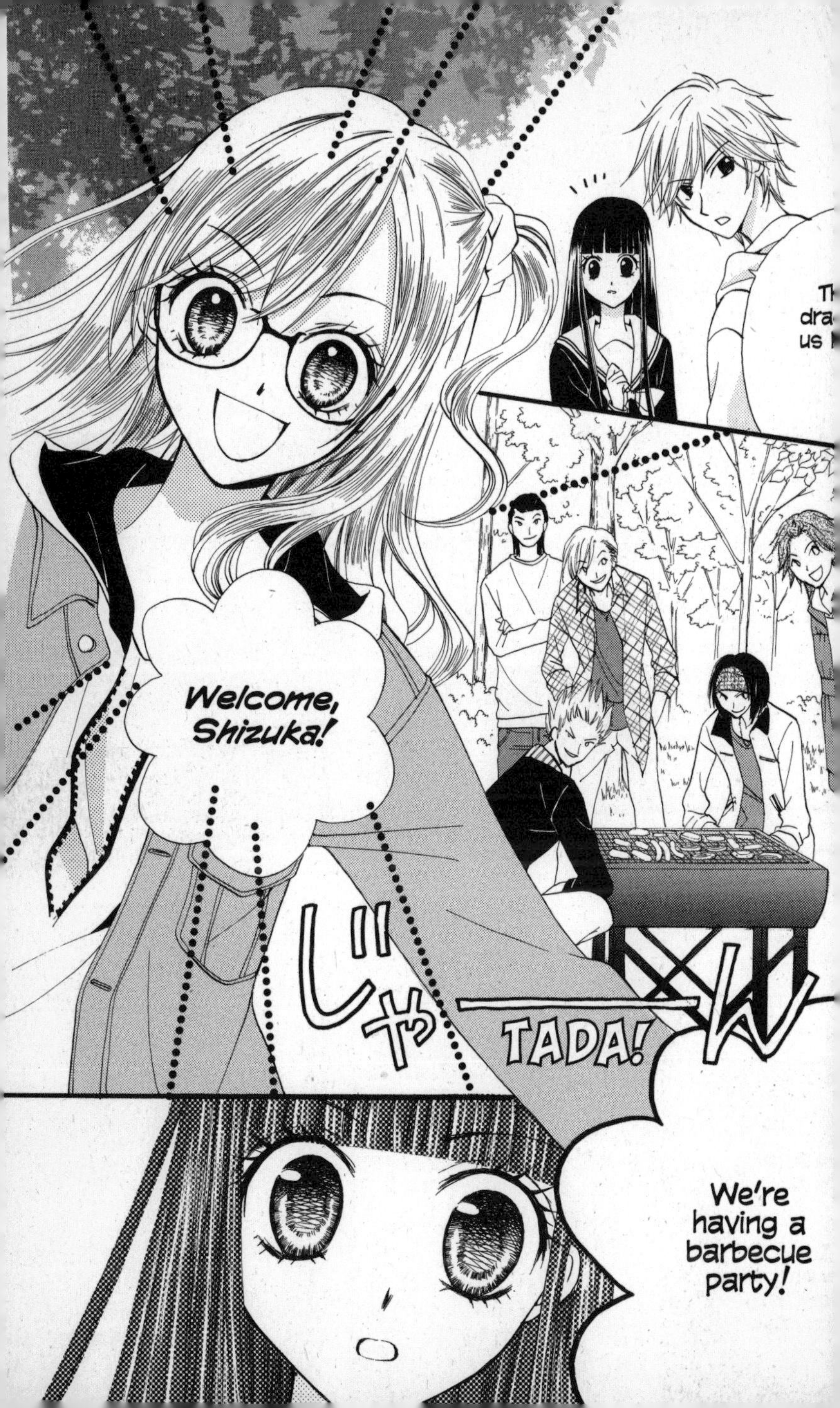
じゃーん
TADA!
Welcome, Shizuka!
We're having a barbecue party!

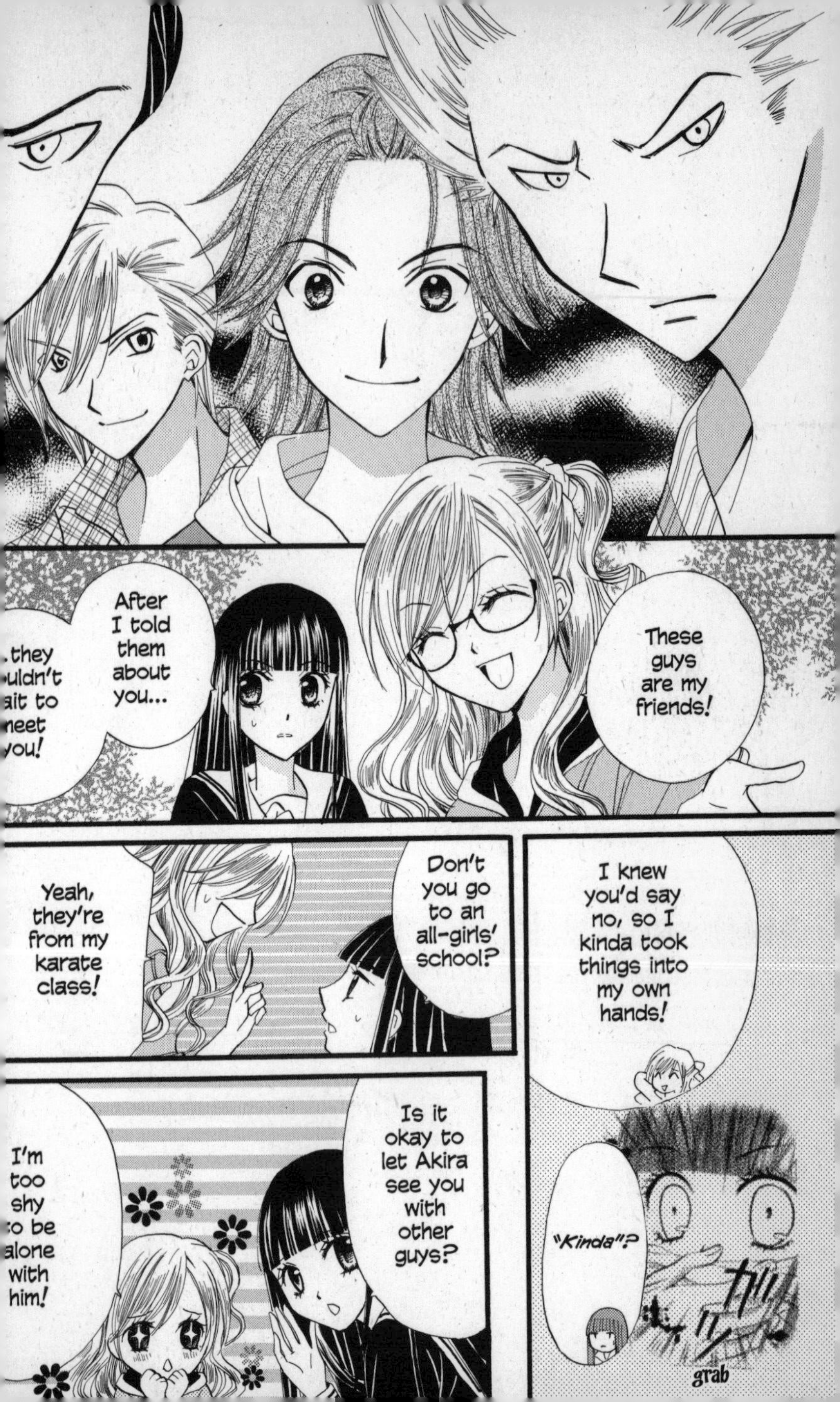

These guys are my friends!
After I told them about you...
. they uldn't ait to neet you!
I knew you'd say no, so I kinda took things into my own hands!
"Kinda"?
grab
Don't you go to an all-girls' school?
Yeah, they're from my karate class!
Is it okay to let Akira see you with other guys?
I'm too shy :o be alone with him!

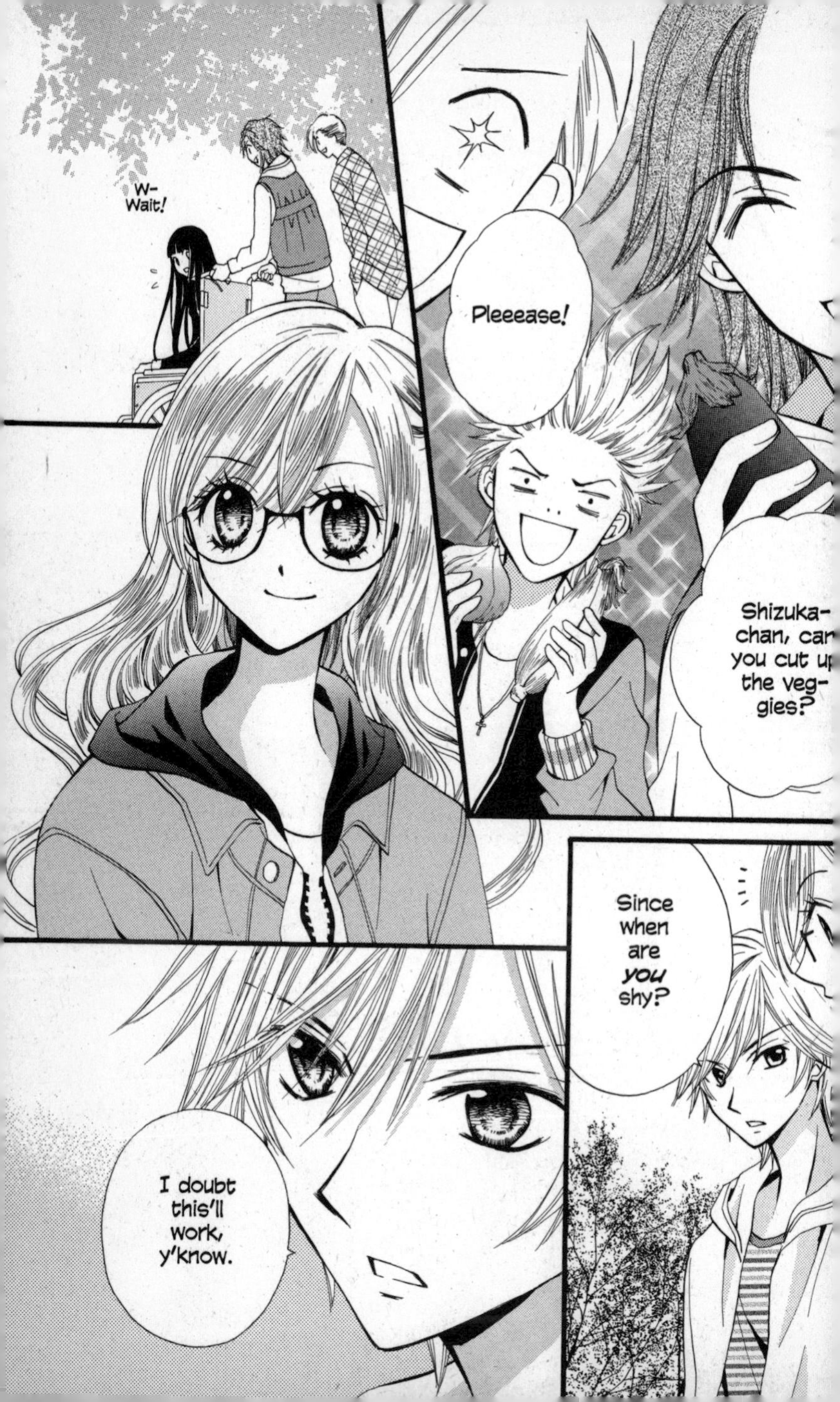
Shizuka-chan, can you cut up the veggies?
Pleeease!
W-Wait!
Since when are *you* shy?
I doubt this'll work, y'know.

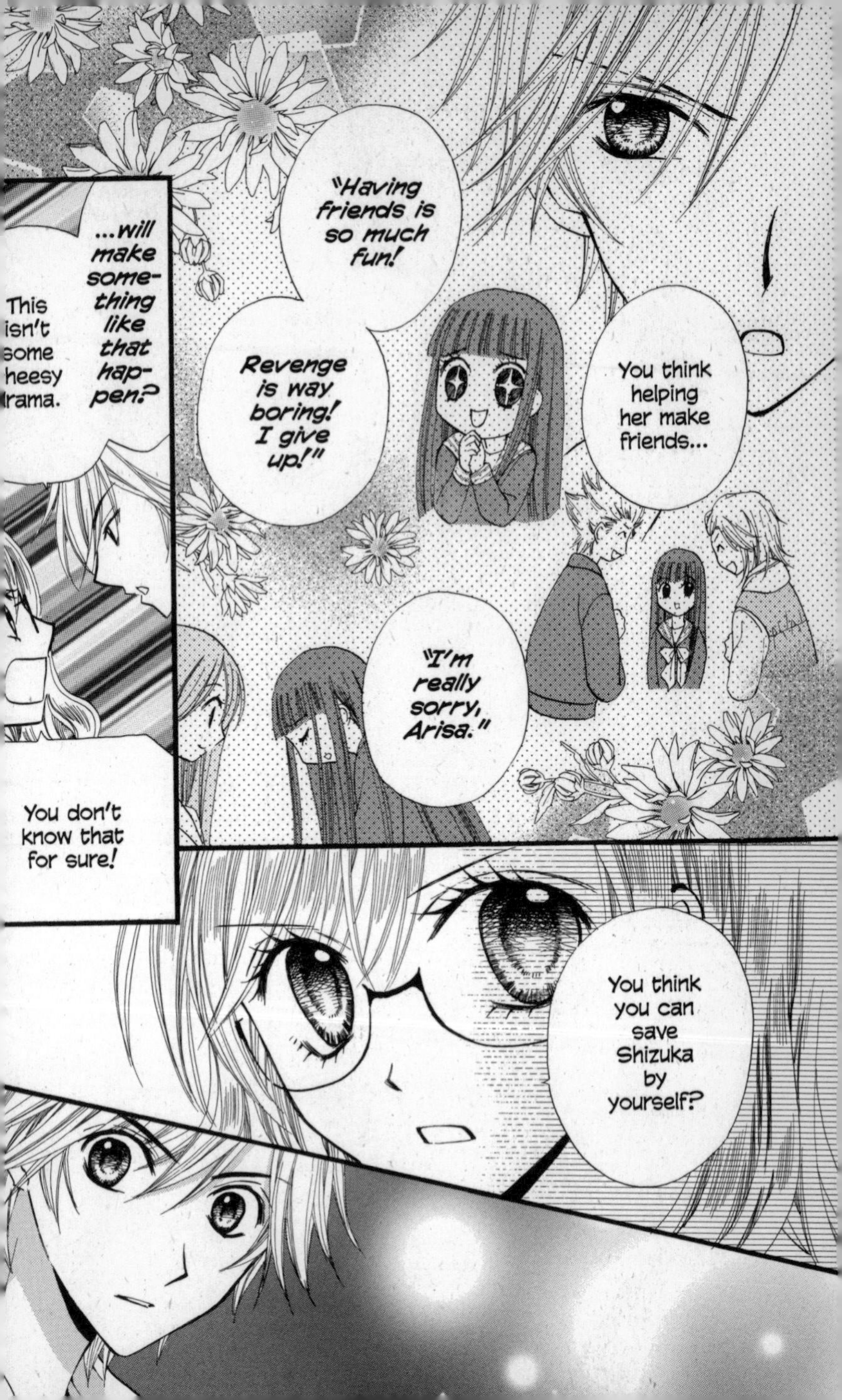
You think helping her make friends...
"Having friends is so much fun!
Revenge is way boring! I give up!"
"I'm really sorry, Arisa."
...will make some-thing like that hap-pen?
This isn't some heesy rama.
You don't know that for sure!
You think you can save Shizuka by yourself?

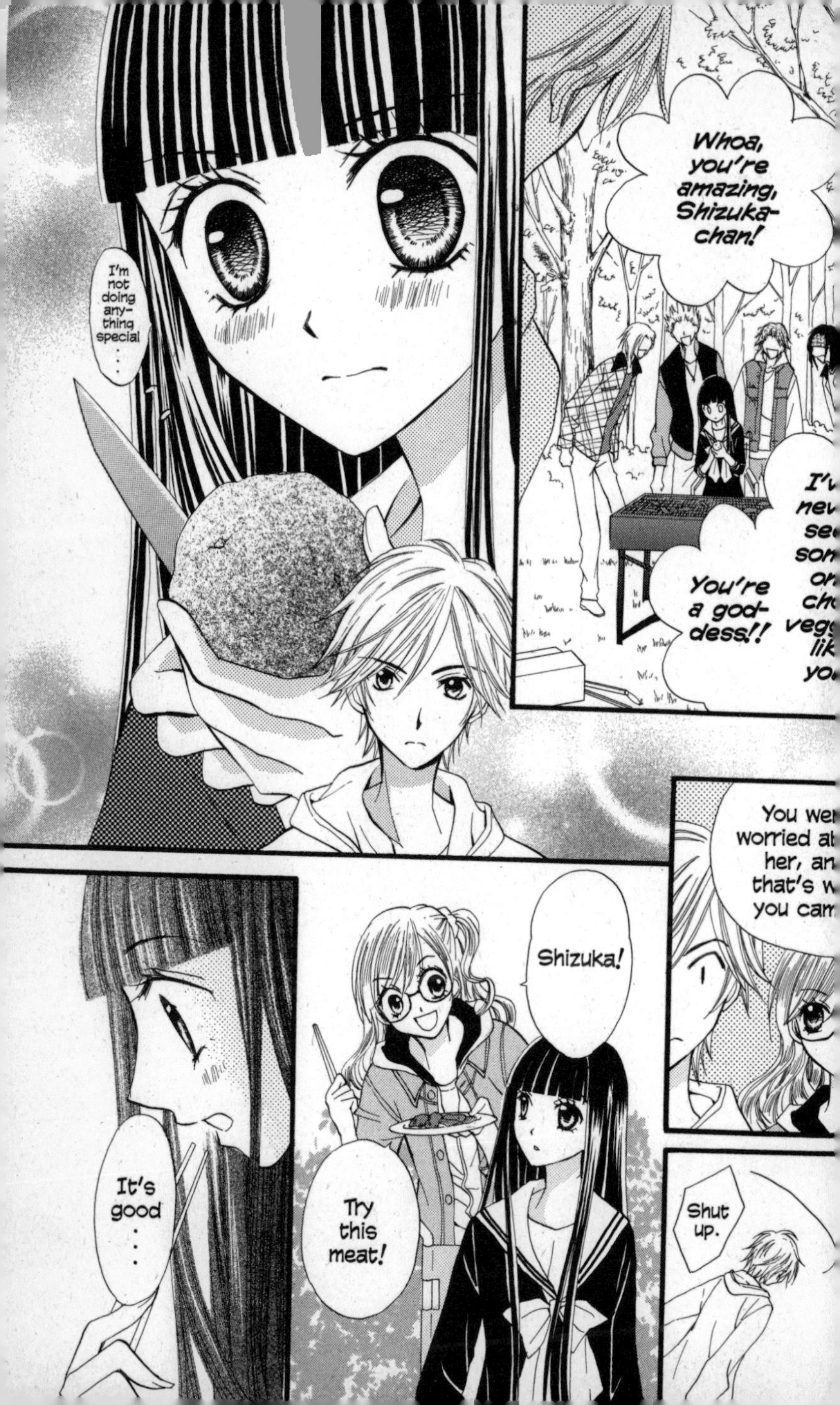
Whoa, you're amazing, Shizuka-chan!
I'v nev se som or ch vegg lik yo
You're a god-dess!!
I'm not doing any-thing special . . .
You wer worried a her, an that's w you cam
Shut up.
Shizuka!
Try this meat!
It's good . . .

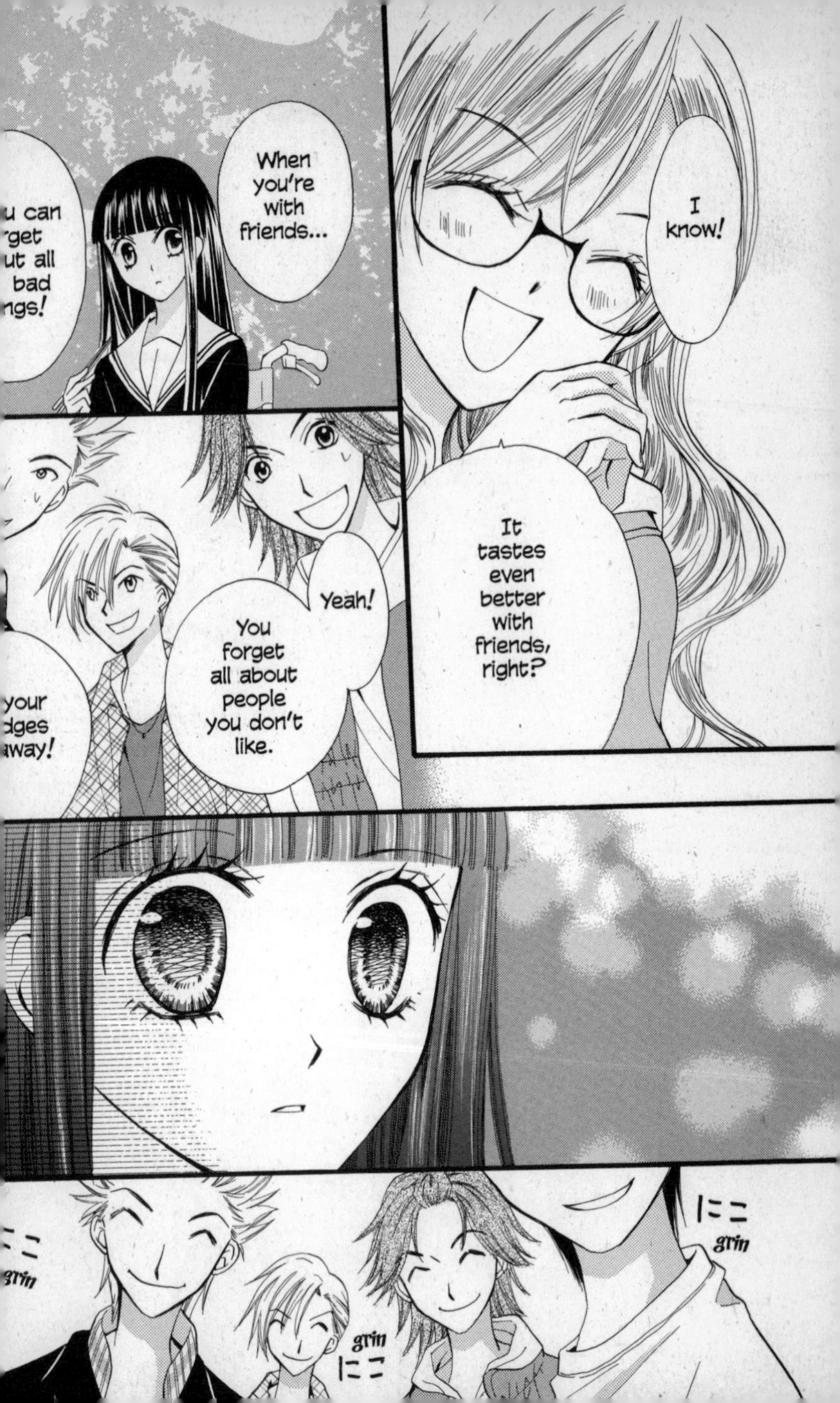
I know!
It tastes even better with friends, right?
When you're with friends...
u can rget ut all bad ngs!
Yeah!
You forget all about people you don't like.
your dges away!
にこ grin
grin にこ
にこ grin

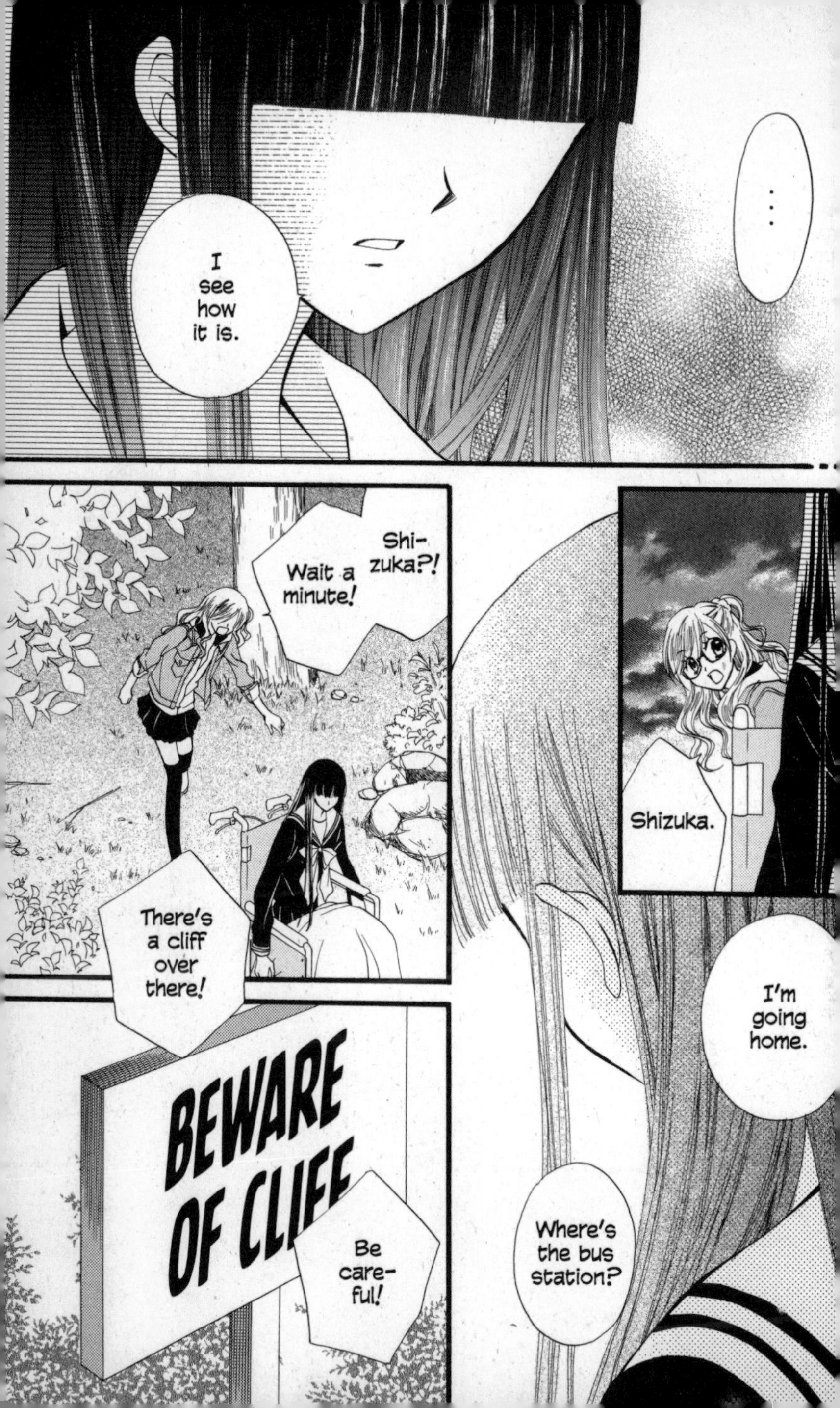
...
I see how it is.
Shizuka.
I'm going home.
Where's the bus station?
Shi-zuka?!
Wait a minute!
There's a cliff over there!
BEWARE OF CLIFF
Be care-ful!

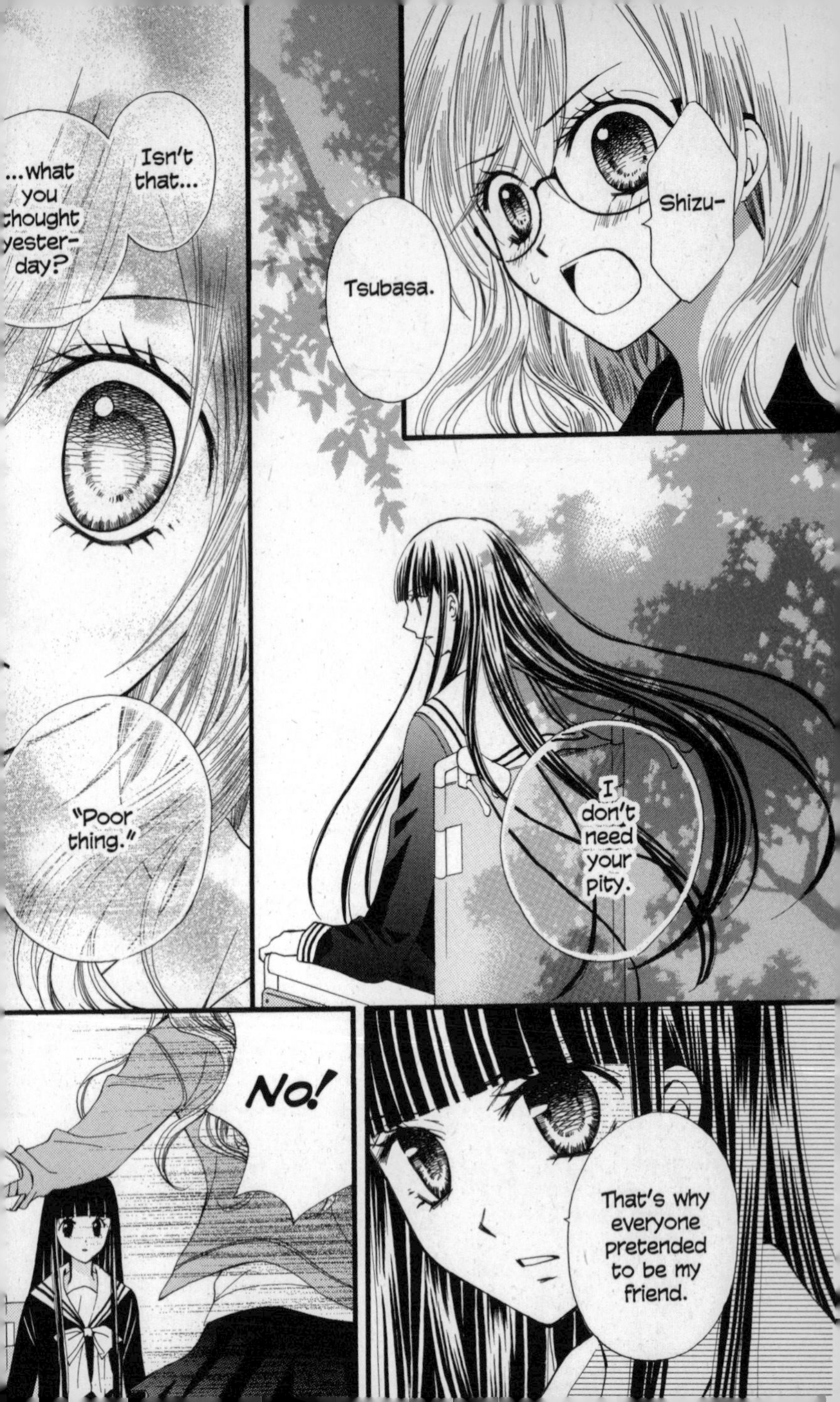

Shizu-
Tsubasa.
I don't need your pity.
Isn't that...
...what you thought yester-day?
"Poor thing."
That's why everyone pretended to be my friend.
No!

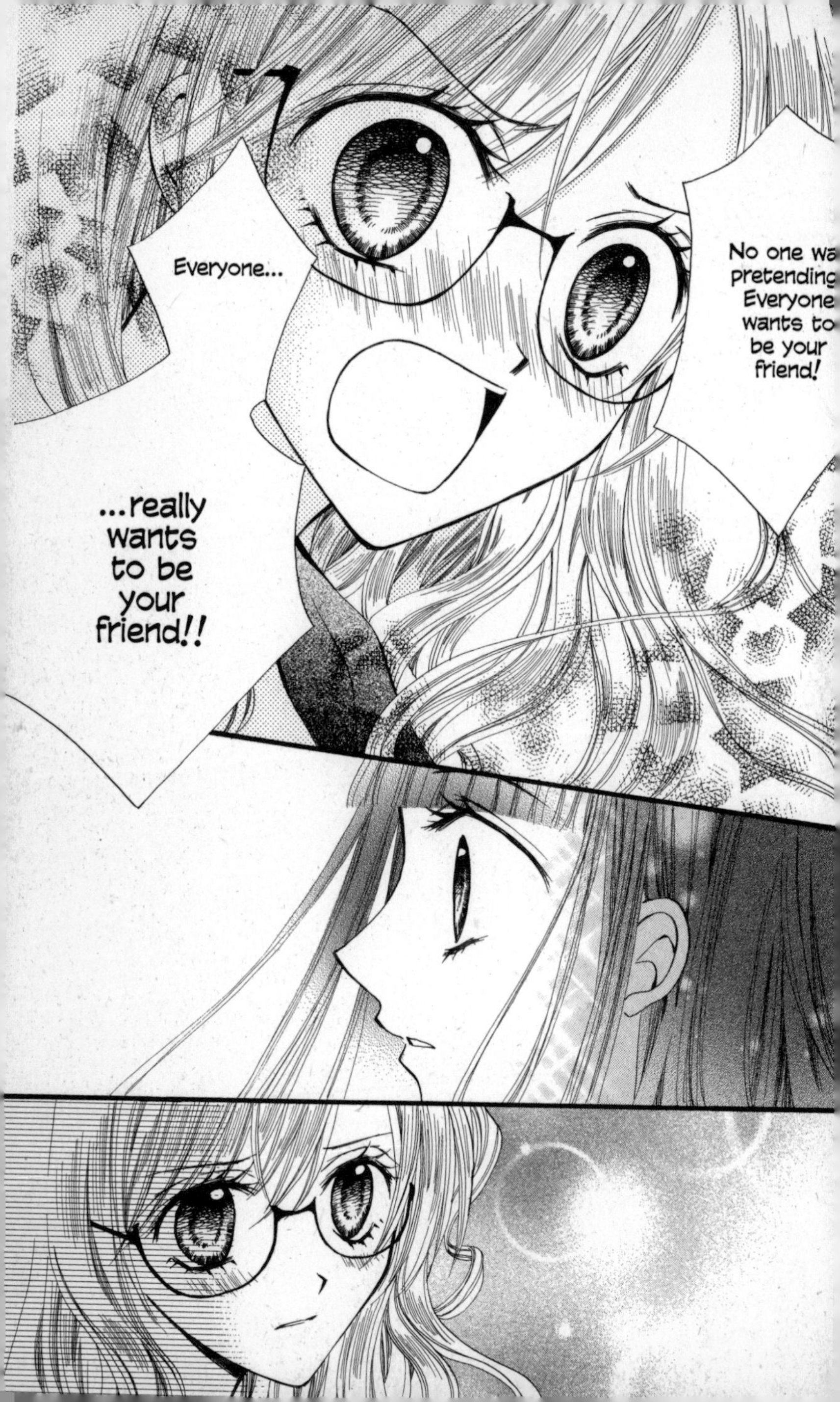
No one wa pretending Everyone wants to be your friend!
Everyone...
...really wants to be your friend!!

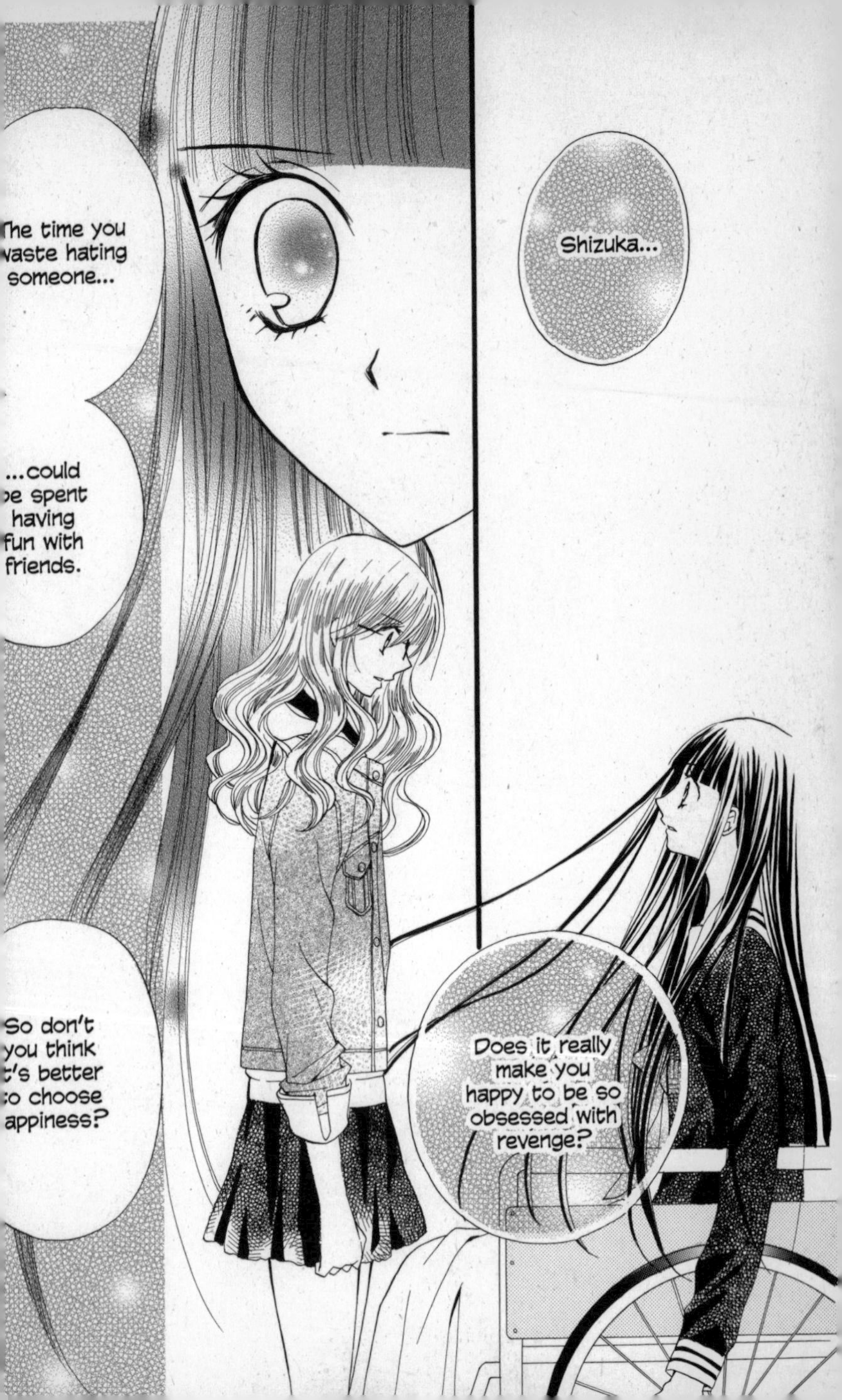

Shizuka...
Does it really make you happy to be so obsessed with revenge?
The time you vaste hating someone...
...could pe spent having fun with friends.
So don't you think t's better to choose appiness?

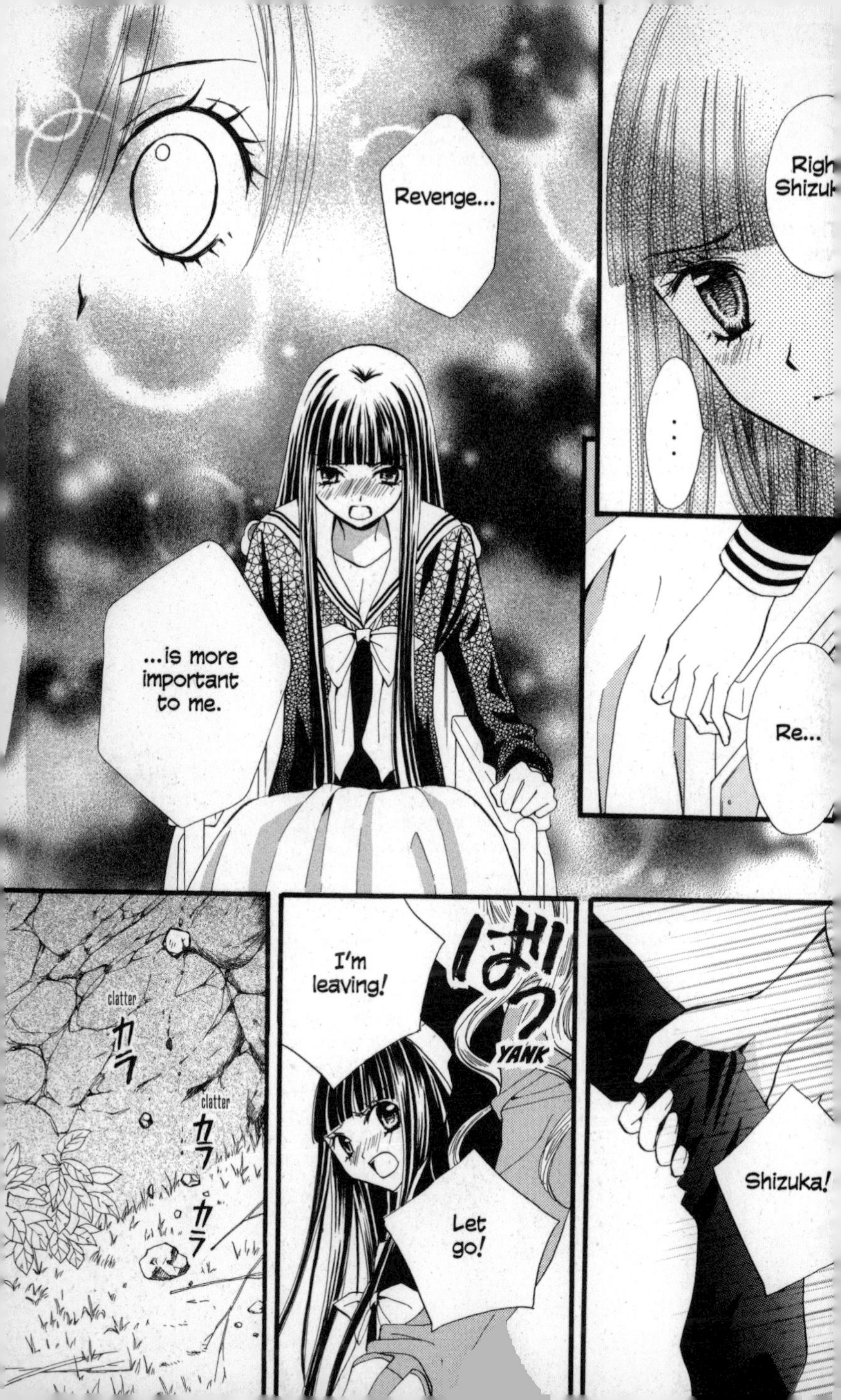

Righ
Shizuk
...
Re...
Revenge...
...is more important to me.
Shizuka!
I'm leaving!
ばっ
YANK
Let go!
clatter
カラ
clatter
カラ
カラ

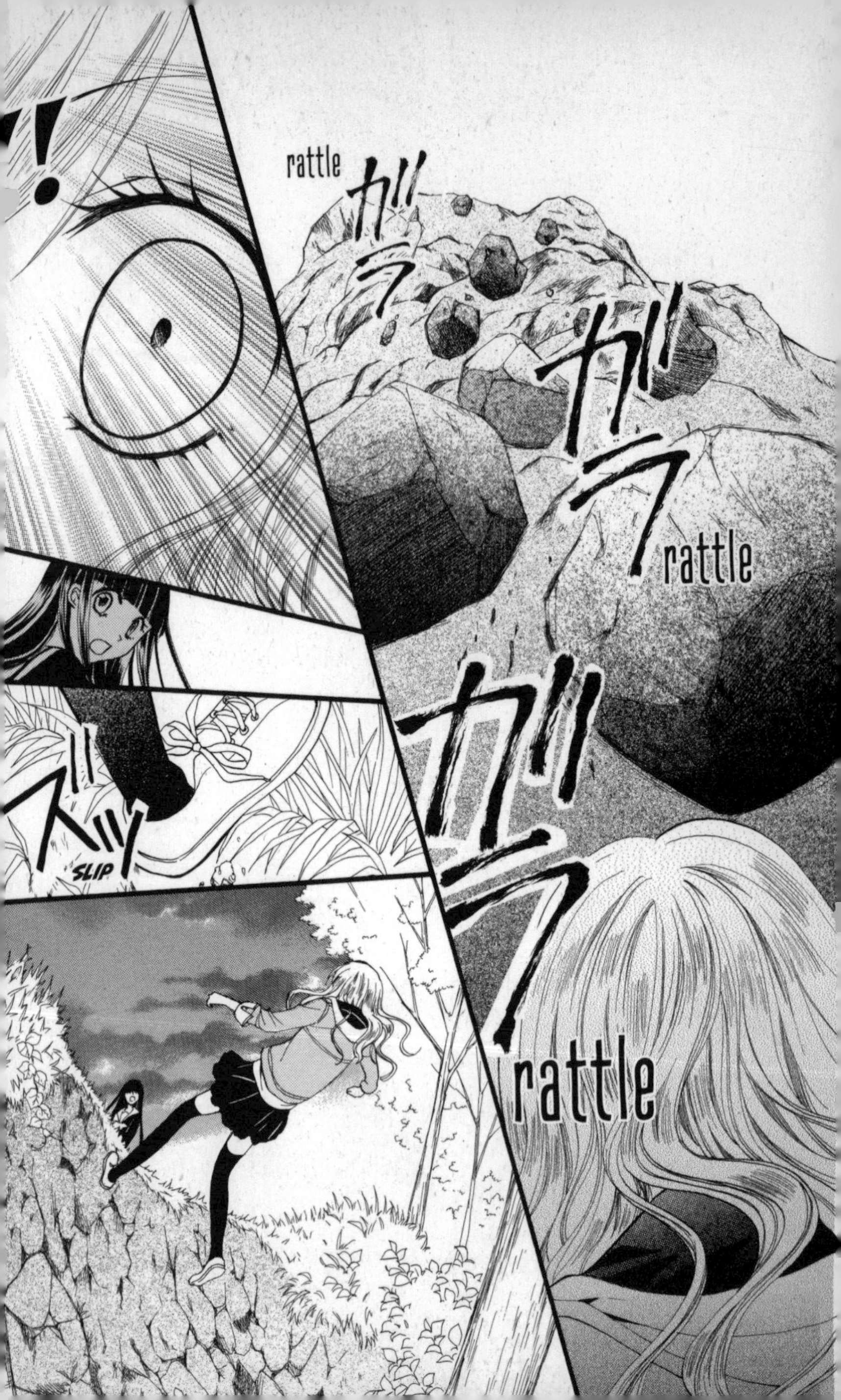

ガラ
rattle
ガラ
rattle
ガラ
rattle
!
ズリッ
SLIP

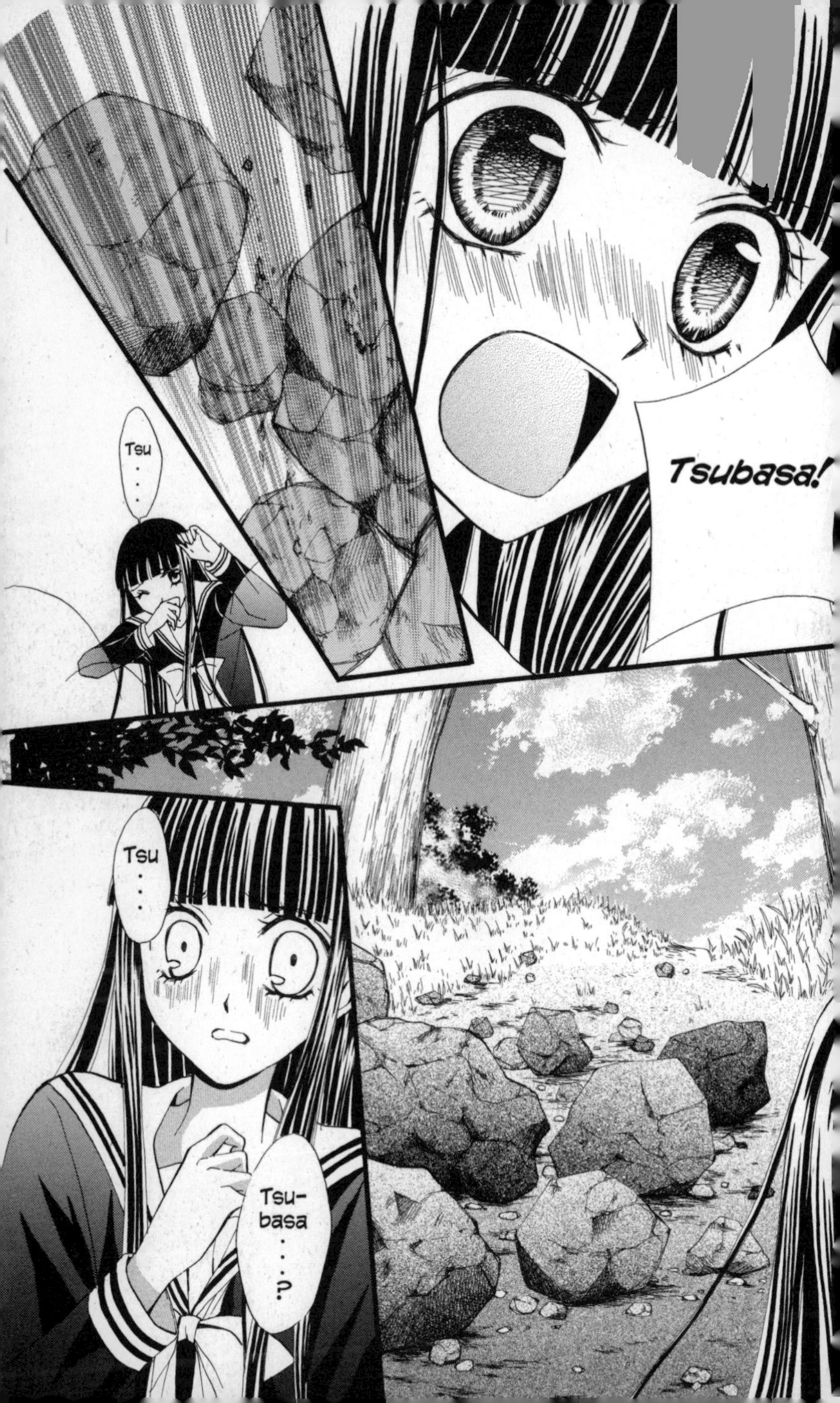
Tsubasa!
Tsu . . .
Tsu . . .
Tsu-basa . . . ?

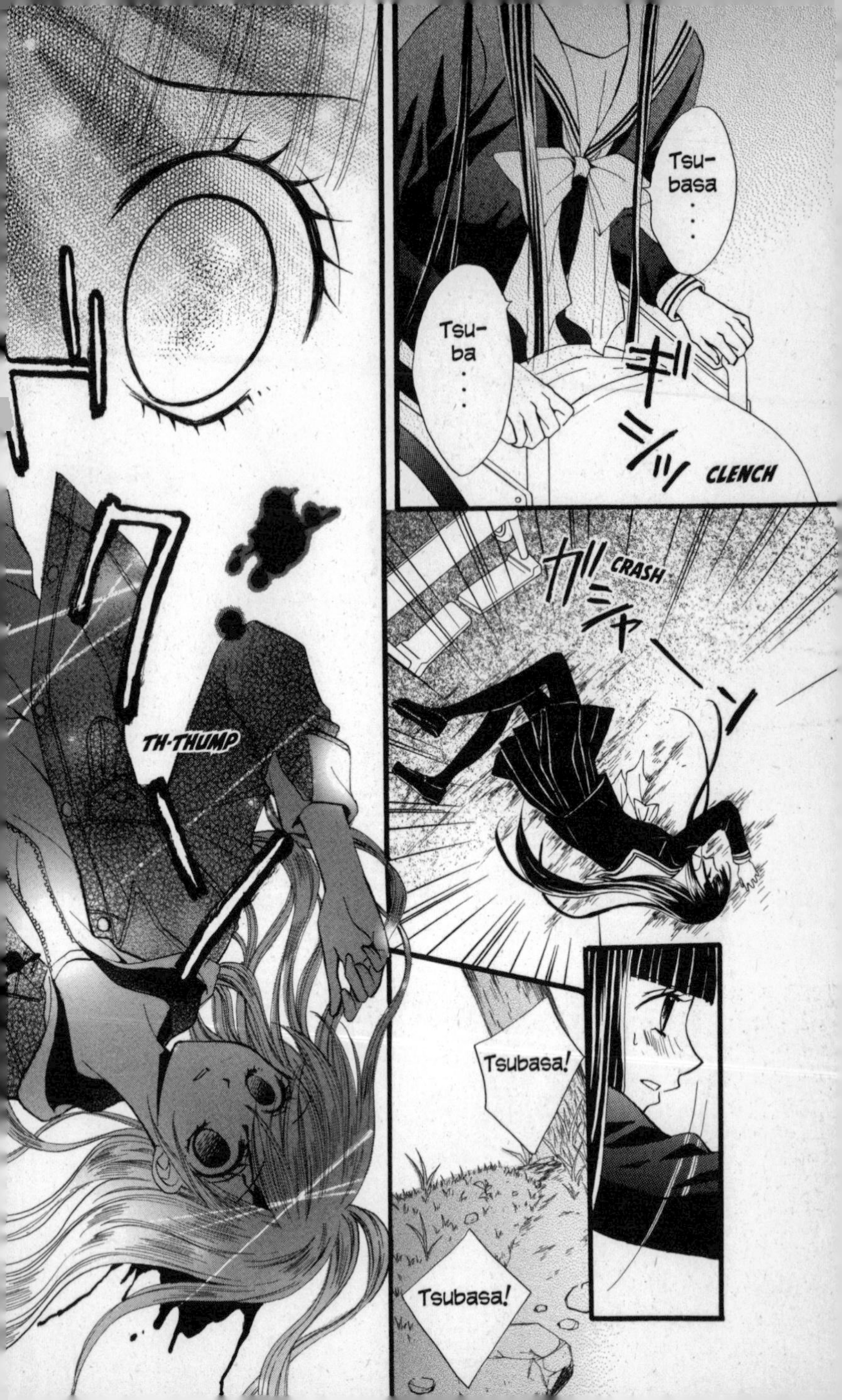
Tsu-basa . . .
Tsu-ba . . .
CLENCH
CRASH
Tsubasa!
Tsubasa!
TH-THUMP

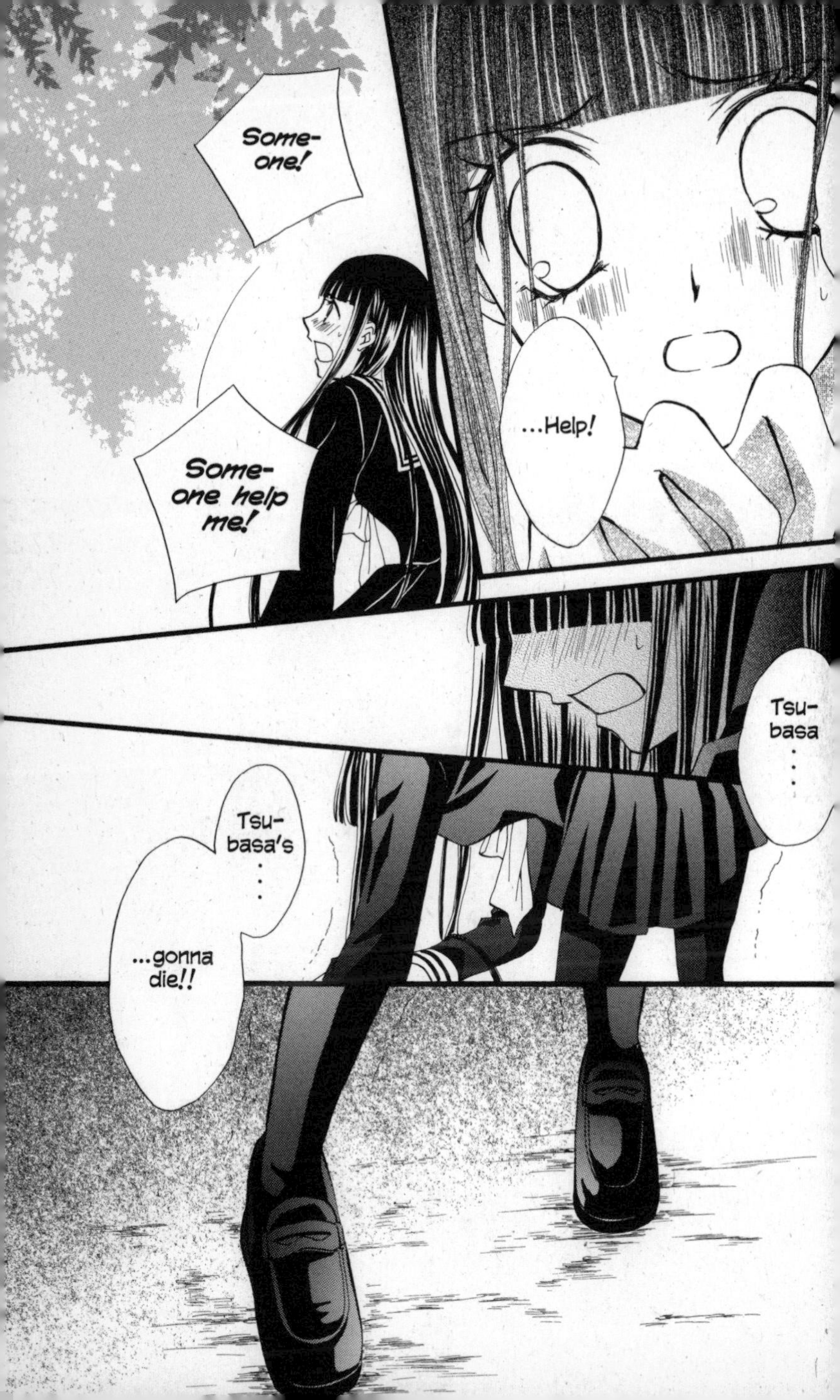

...Help!
Some-one!
Some-one help me!
Tsu-basa . . .
Tsu-basa's . . .
...gonna die!!

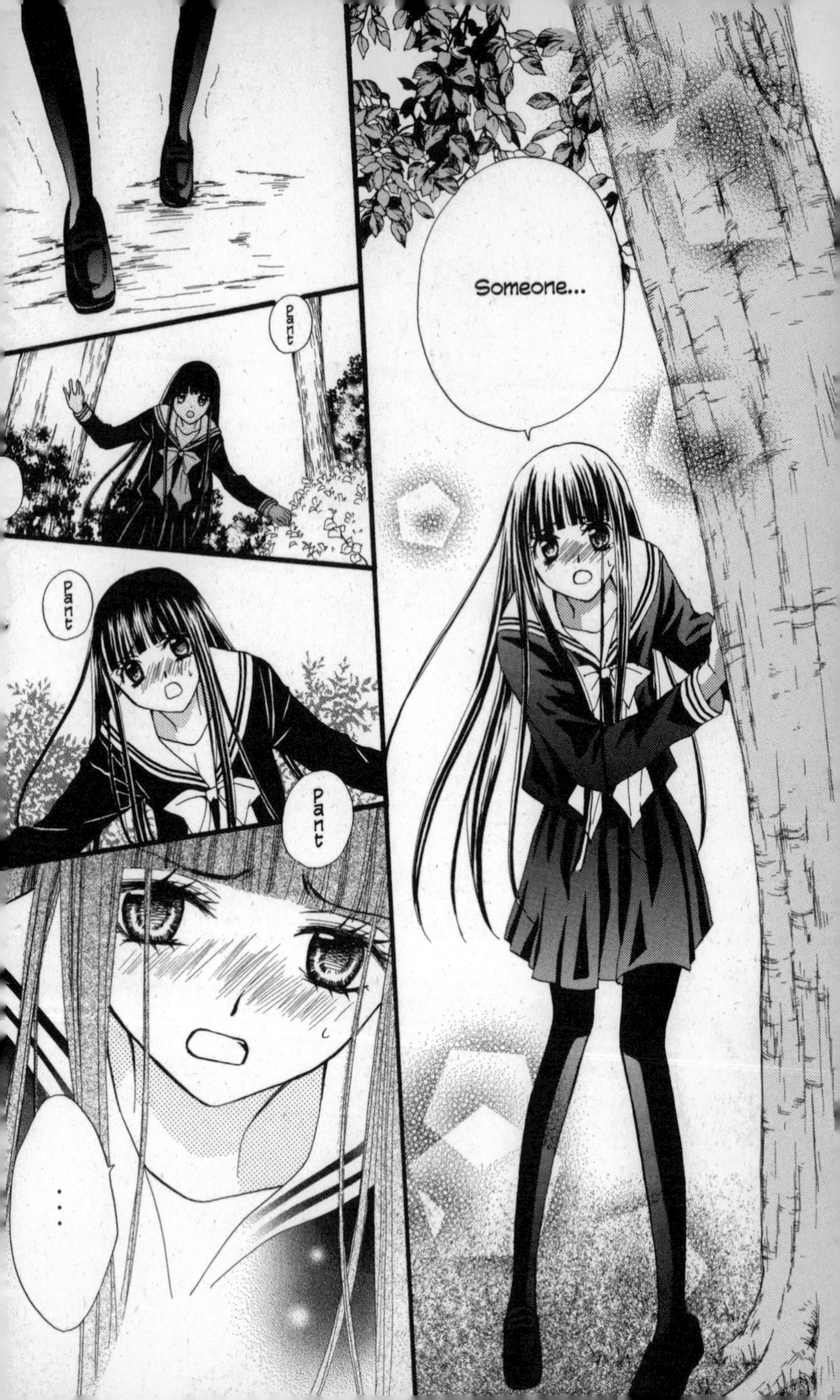

Someone...
Pant
Pant
Pant
...

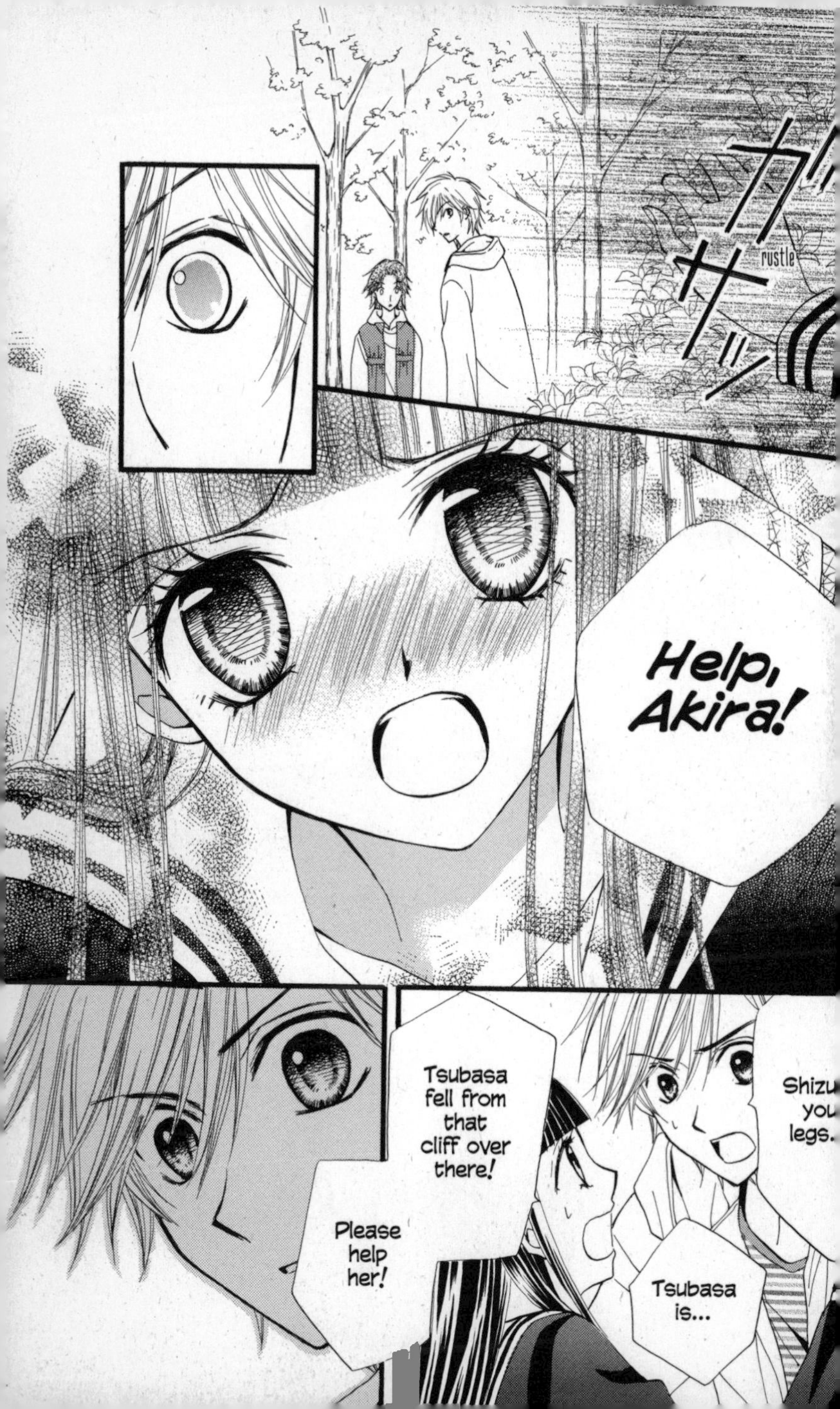
rustle
Help, Akira!
Shizu you legs.
Tsubasa is...
Tsubasa fell from that cliff over there!
Please help her!

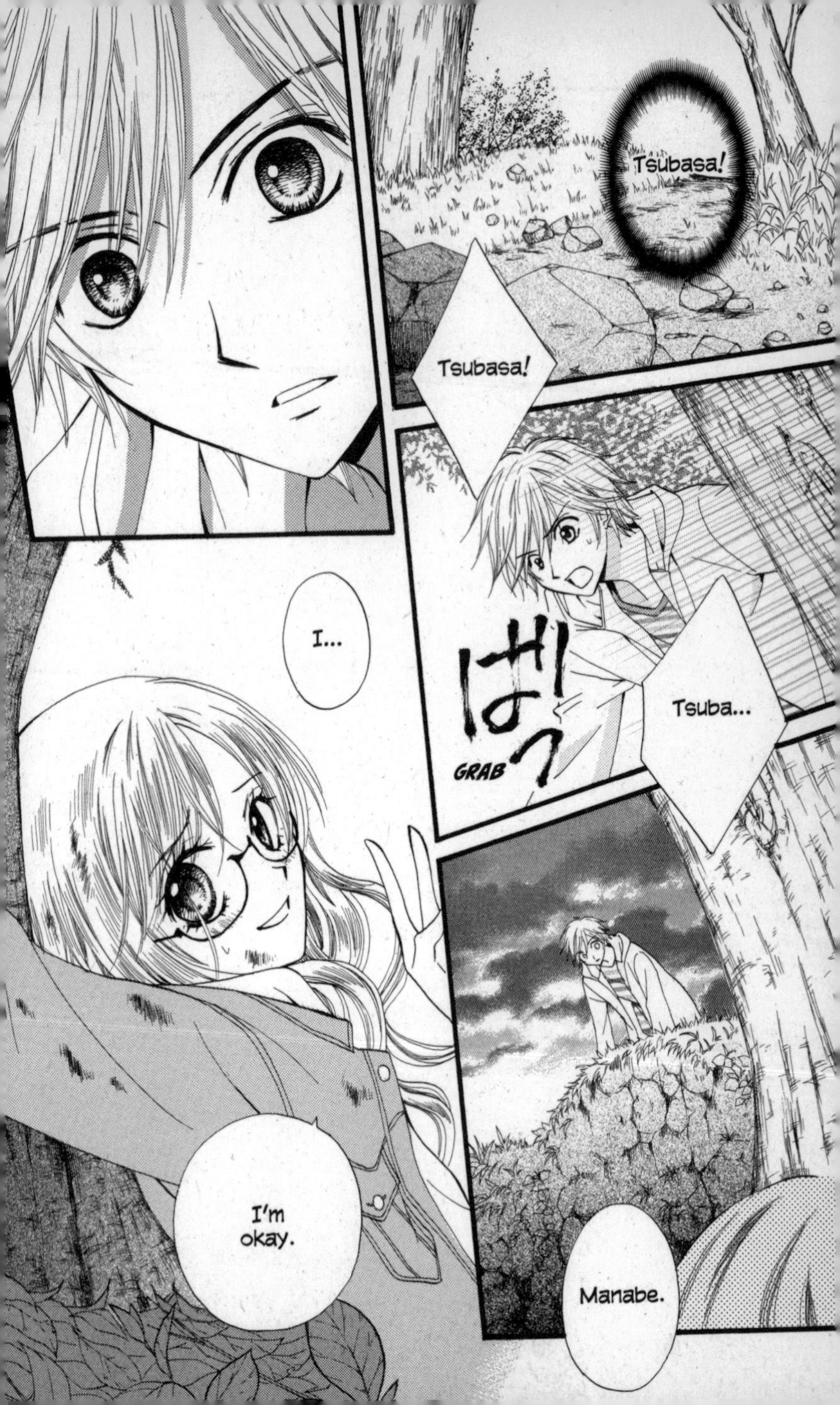
Tsubasa!
Tsubasa!
はっ
GRAB
Tsuba...
Manabe.
I...
I'm okay.

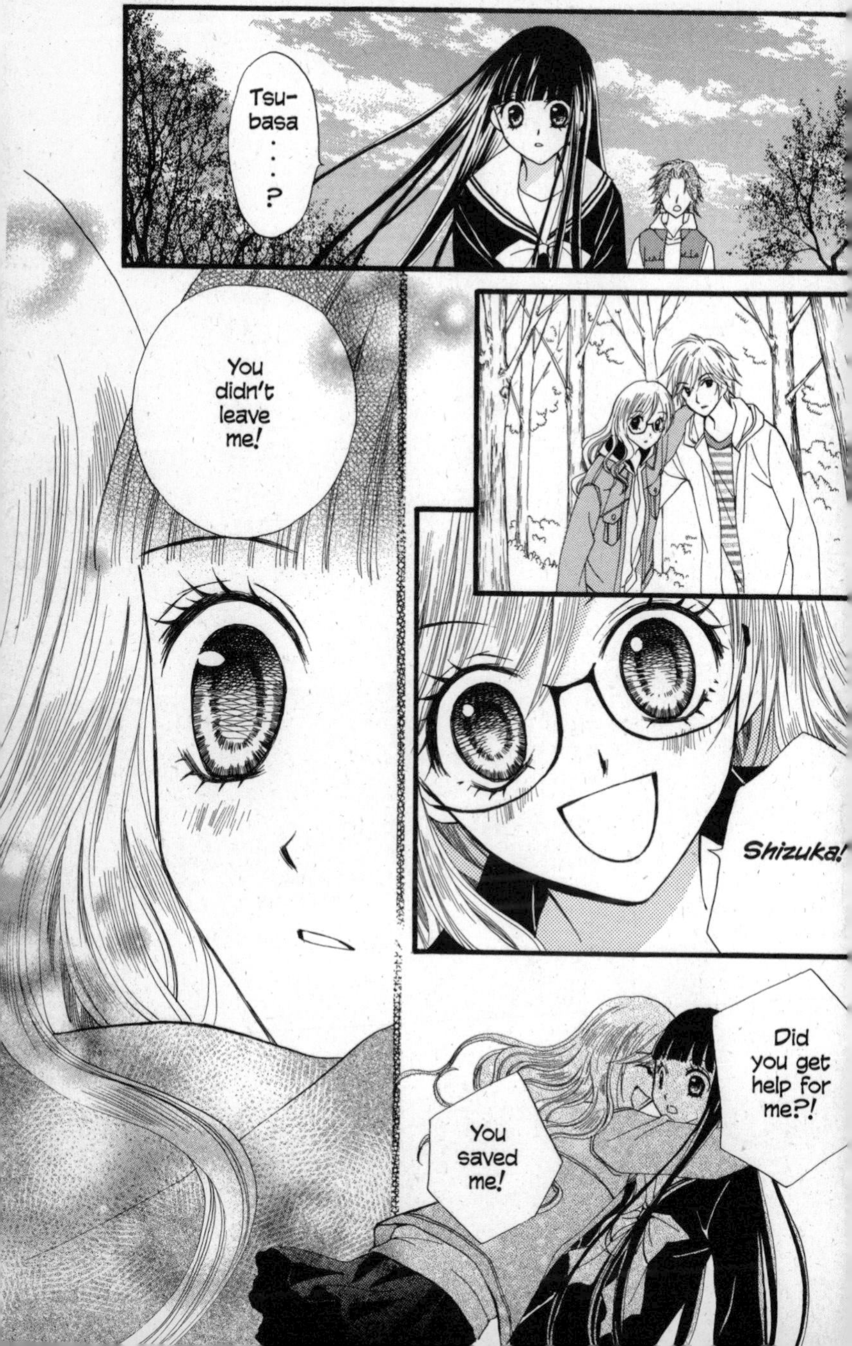
Tsu-basa . . . ?
Shizuka!
Did you get help for me?!
You saved me!
You didn't leave me!

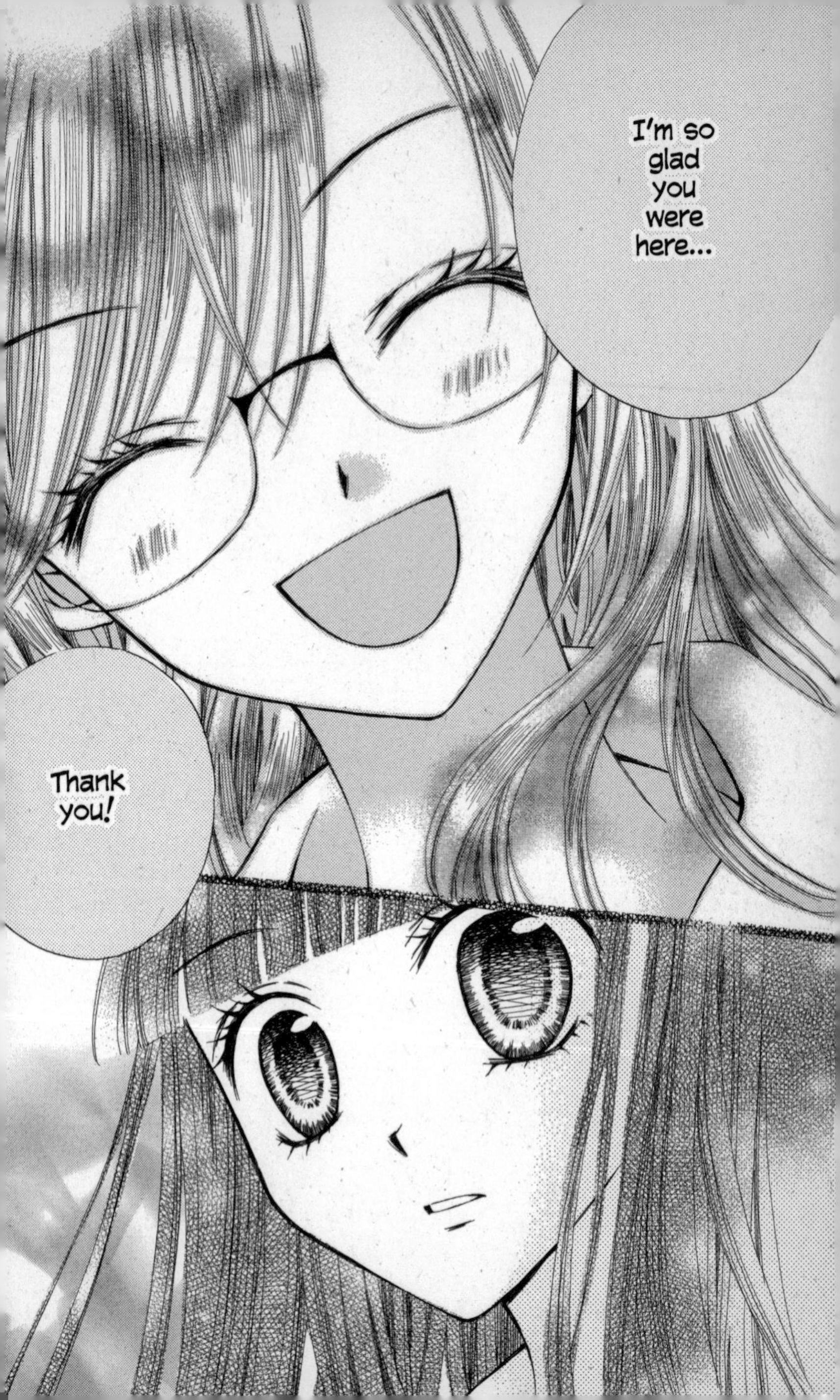
I'm so glad you were here...
Thank you!

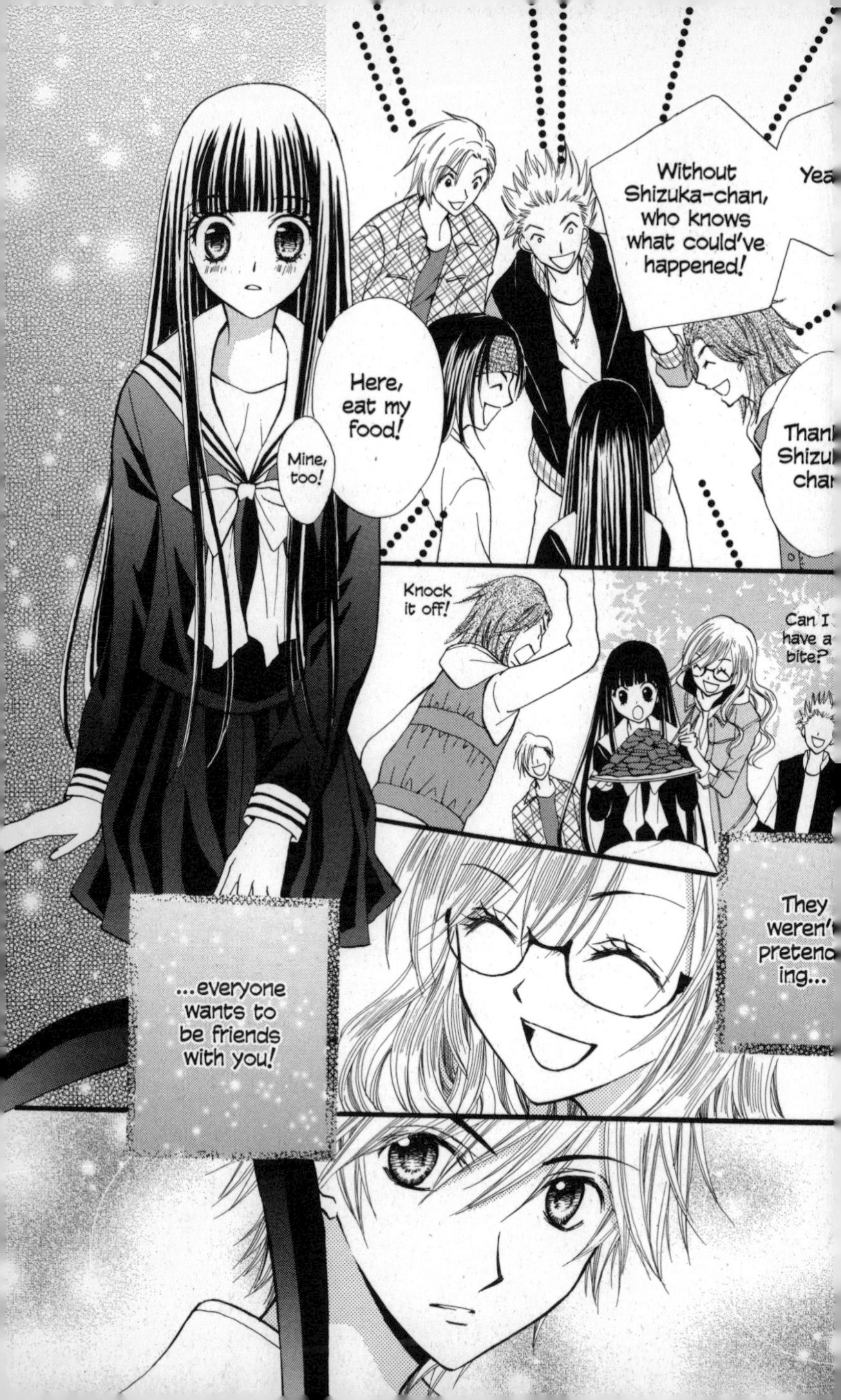

Yea
Without Shizuka-chan, who knows what could've happened!
Than Shizu cha
Here, eat my food!
Mine, too!
Can I have a bite?
Knock it off!
They weren' pretend ing...
...everyone wants to be friends with you!

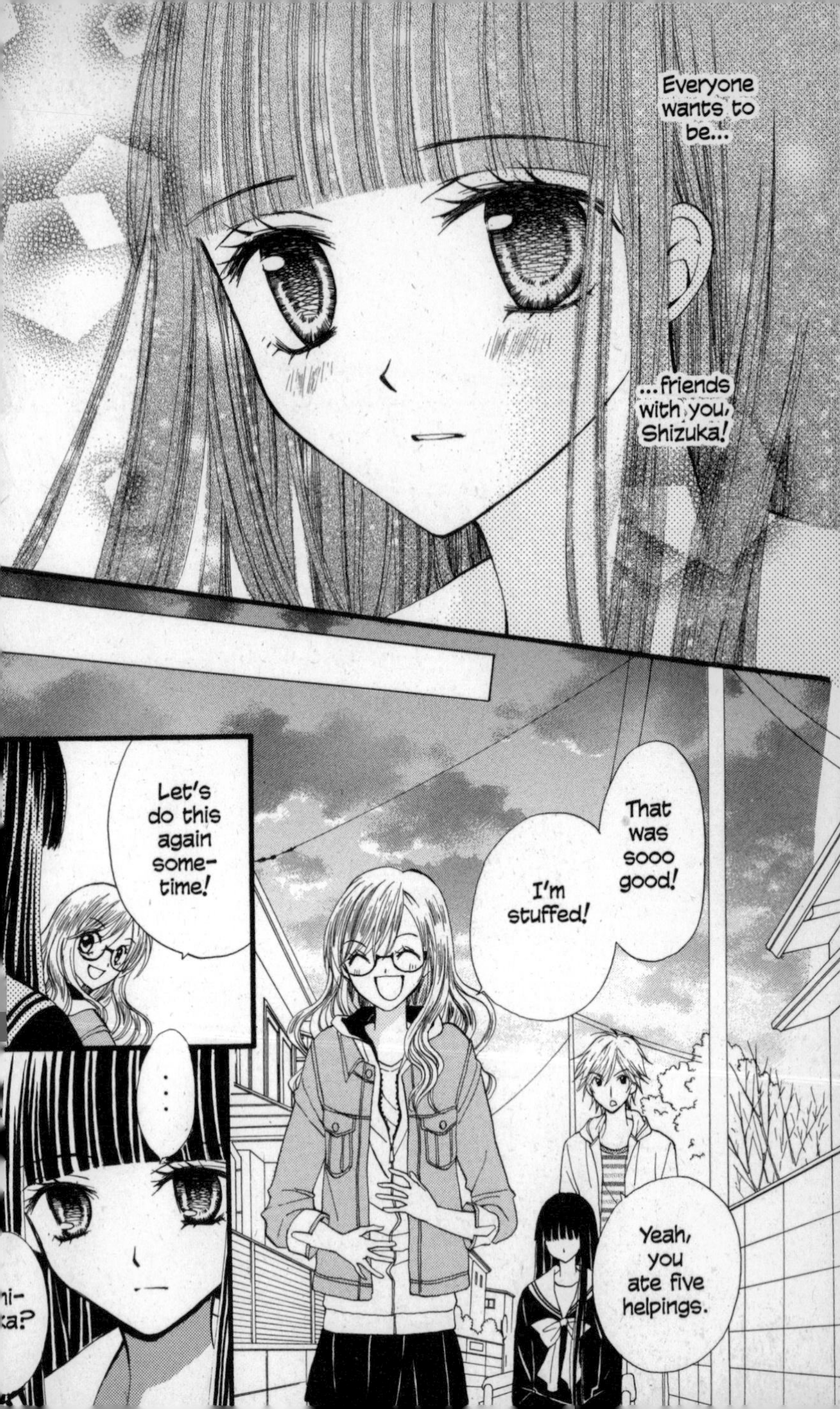
Everyone wants to be...
...friends with you, Shizuka!
That was sooo good!
I'm stuffed!
Yeah, you ate five helpings.
Let's do this again some-time!
...

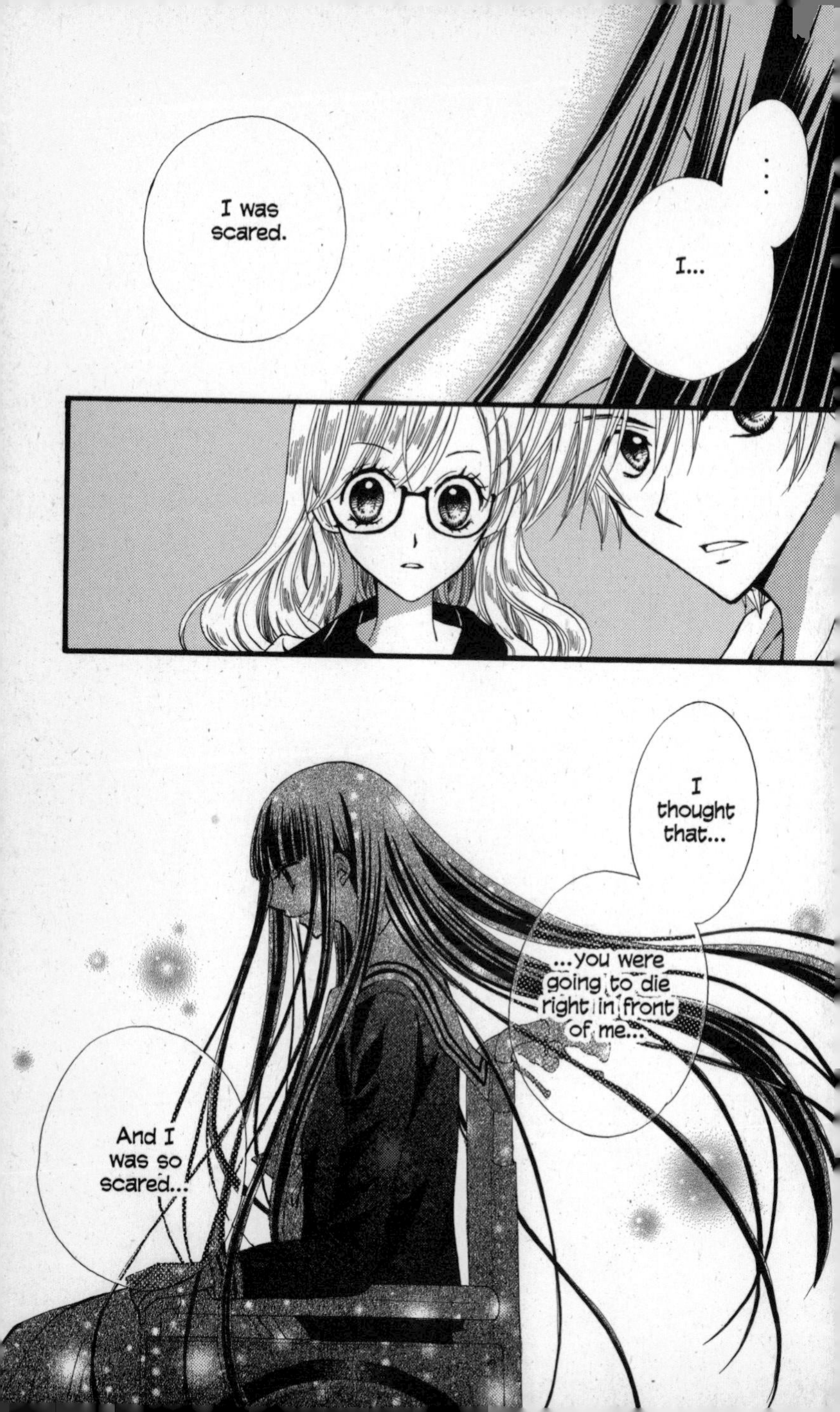
...
I...
I was scared.
I thought that...
...you were going to die right in front of me...
And I was so scared...

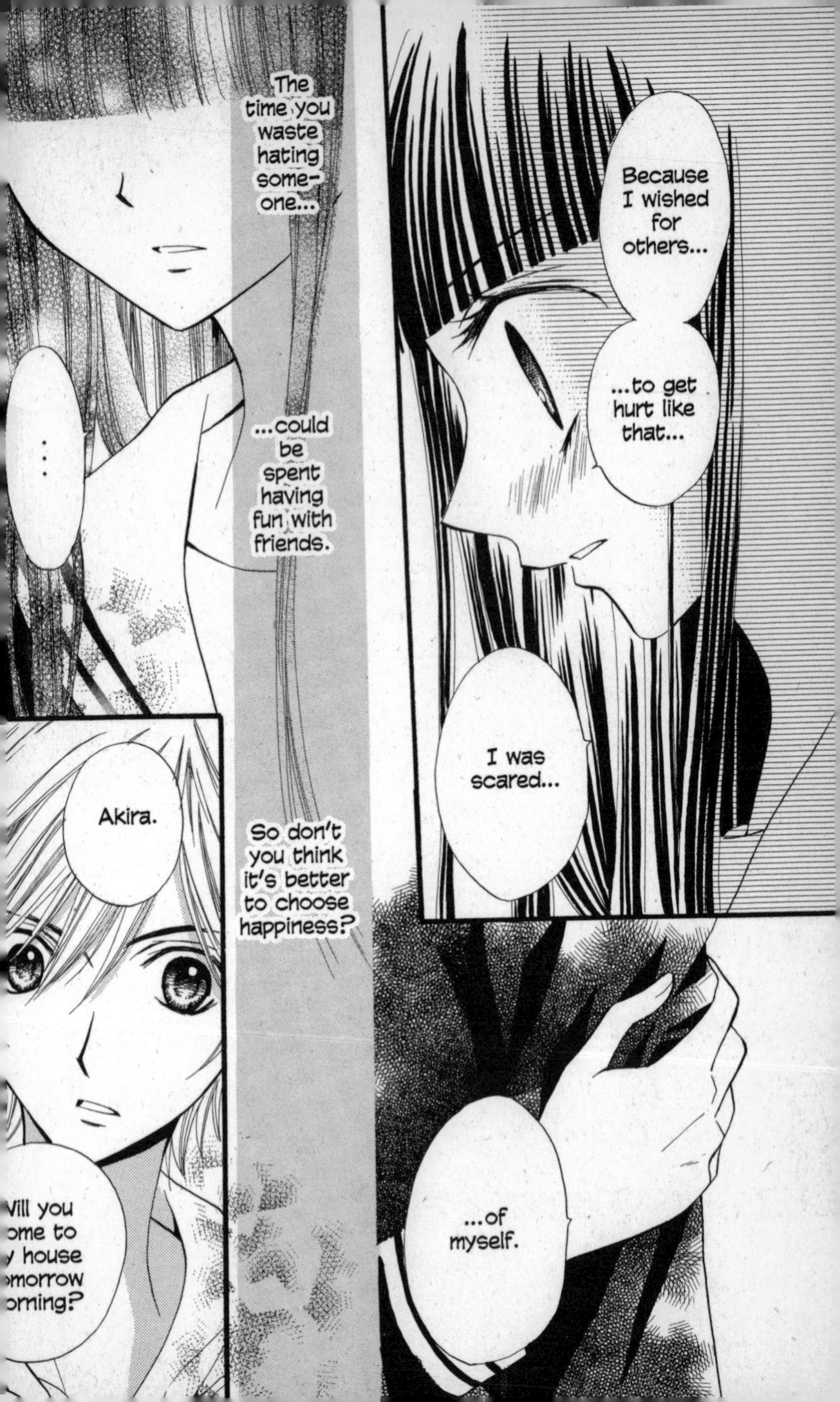

Because I wished for others...
...to get hurt like that...
I was scared...
...of myself.
The time you waste hating some-one...
...could be spent having fun with friends.
...
So don't you think it's better to choose happiness?
Akira.
Vill you ome to y house omorrow orning?

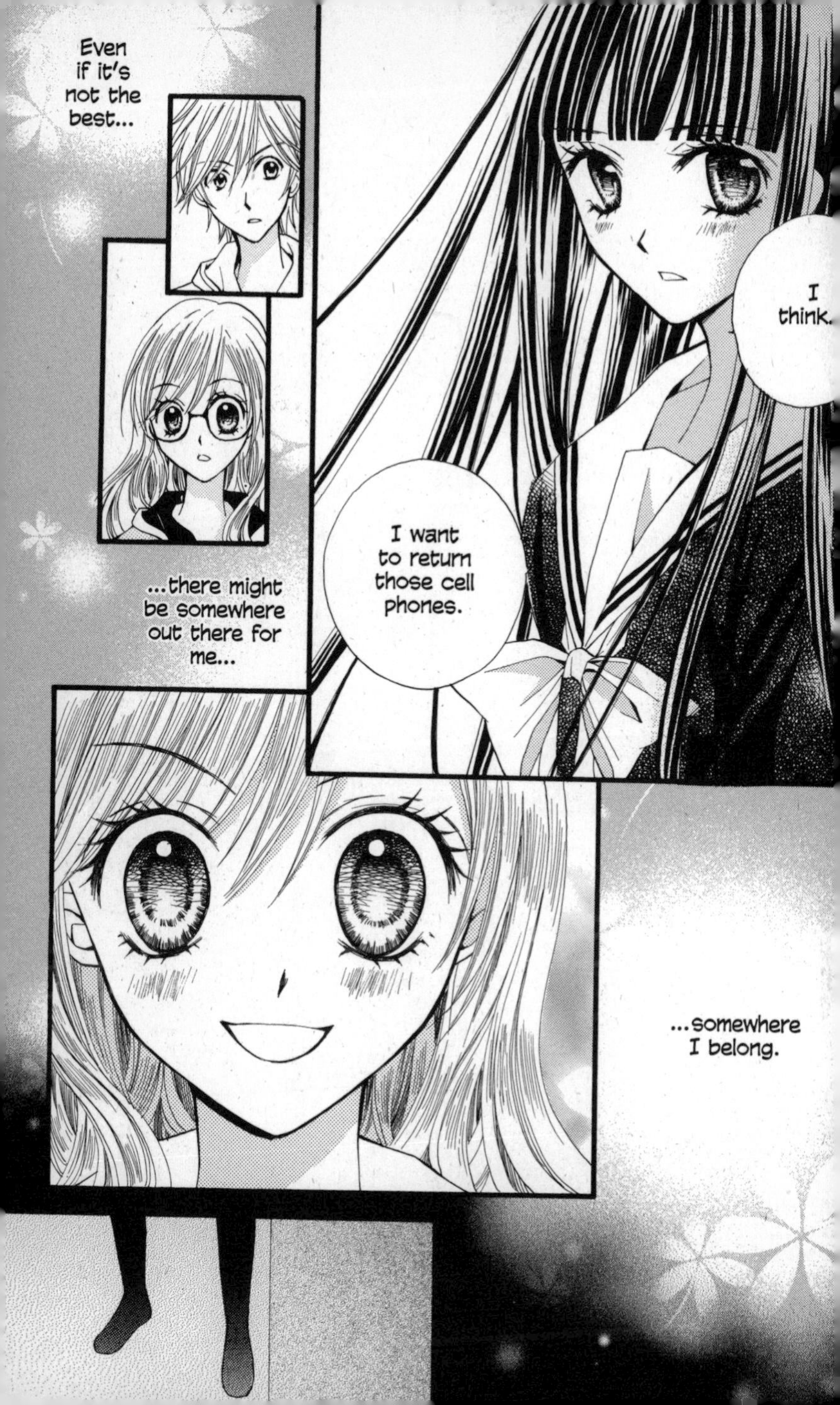
I think.
I want to return those cell phones.
Even if it's not the best...
...there might be somewhere out there for me...
...somewhere I belong.

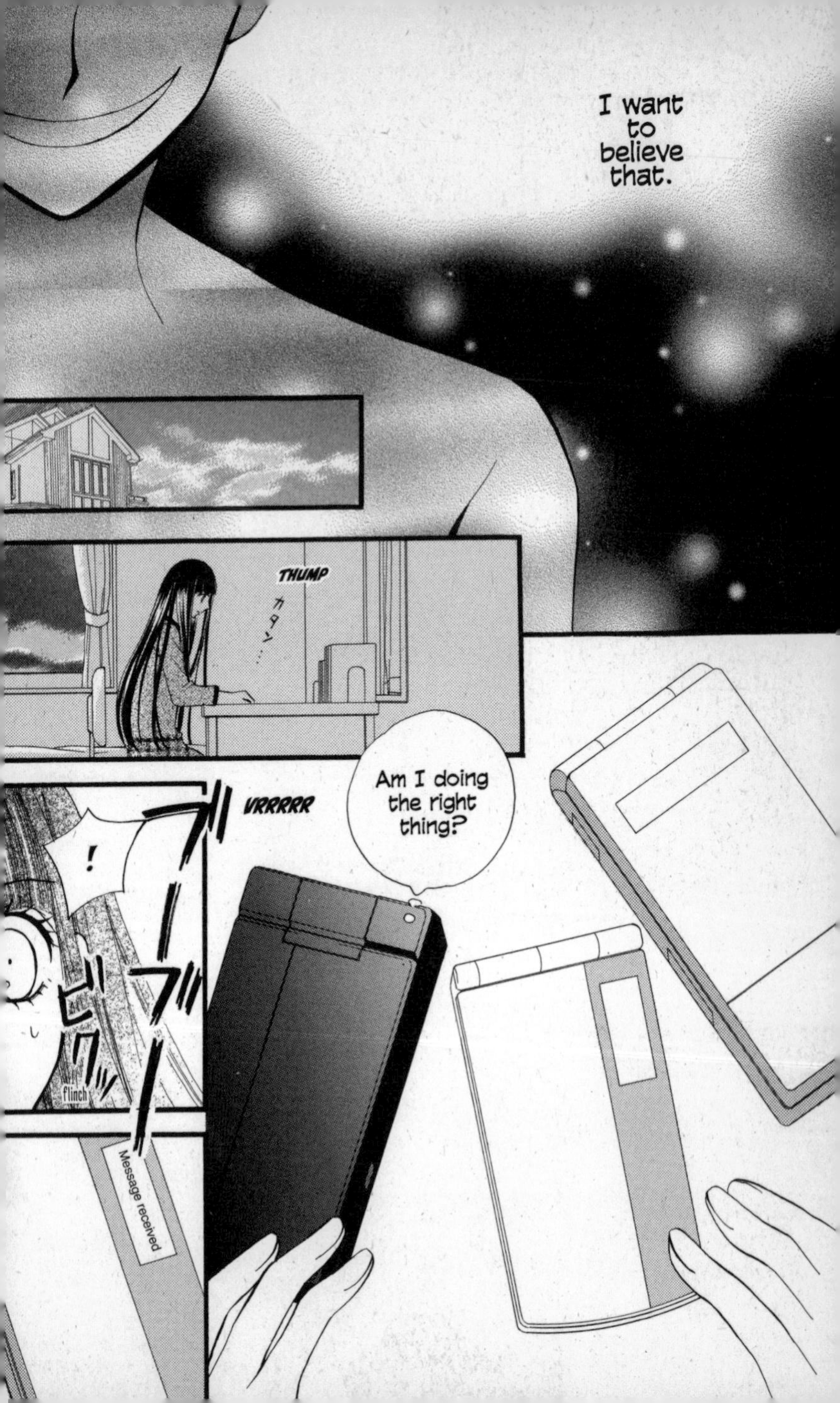
I want to believe that.
THUMP
カタン…
Am I doing the right thing?
VRRRRR
!
ビクッ
flinch
Message received

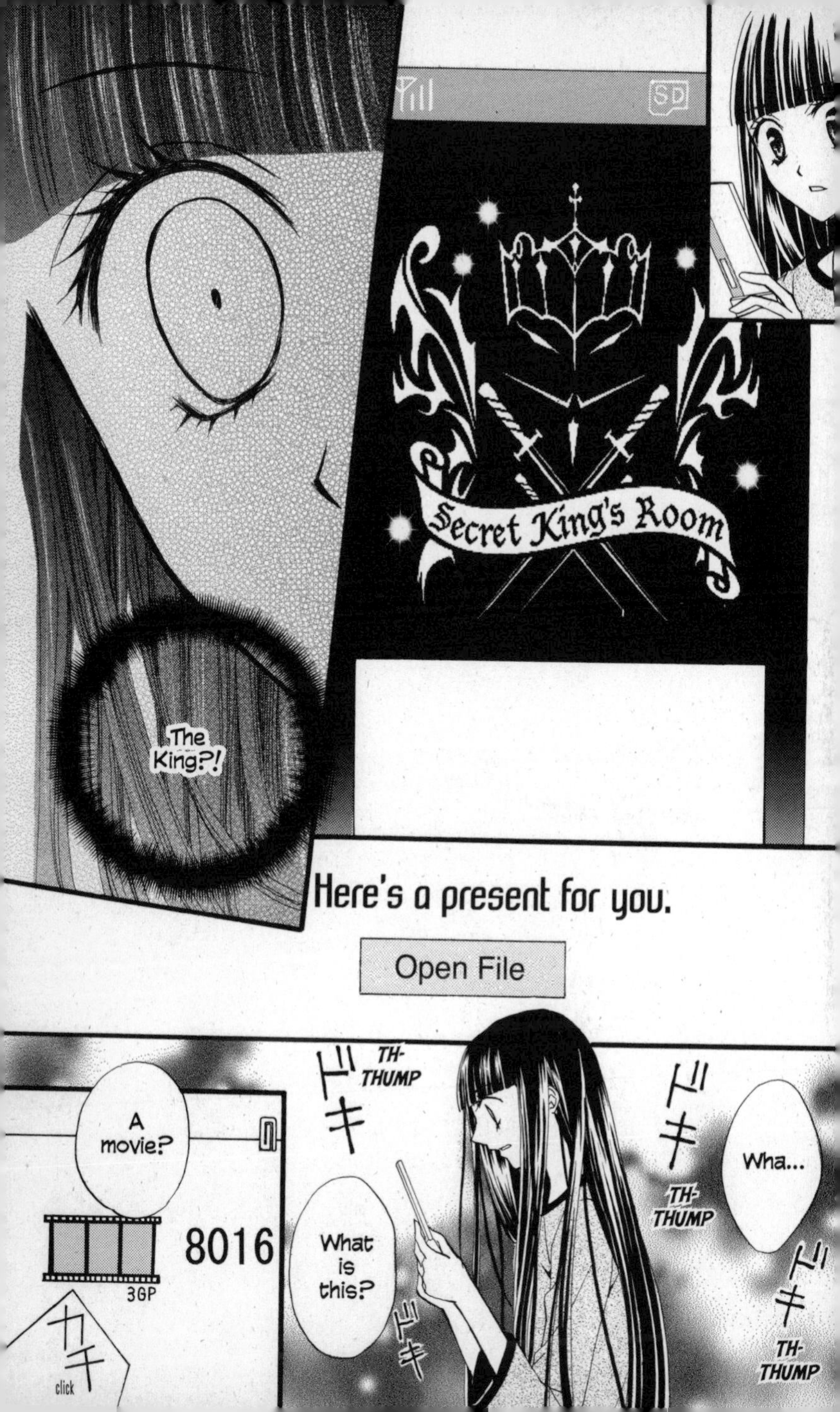

Secret King's Room
Here's a present for you.
Open File
The King?!
ドキ
TH-THUMP
Wha...
ドキ
TH-THUMP
ドキ
TH-THUMP
What is this?
ドキ
A movie?
8016
3GP
カチ
click

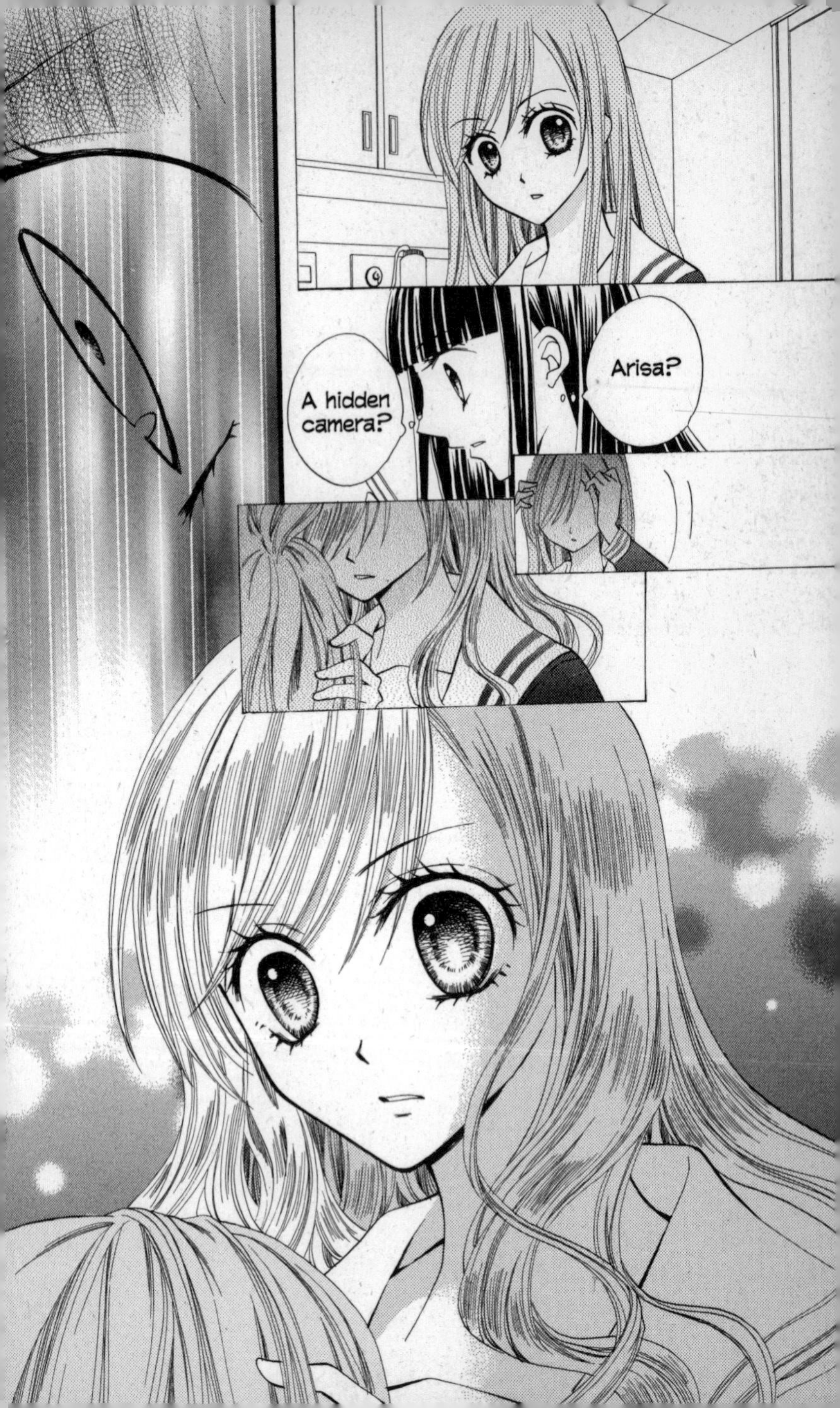
Arisa?
A hidden camera?

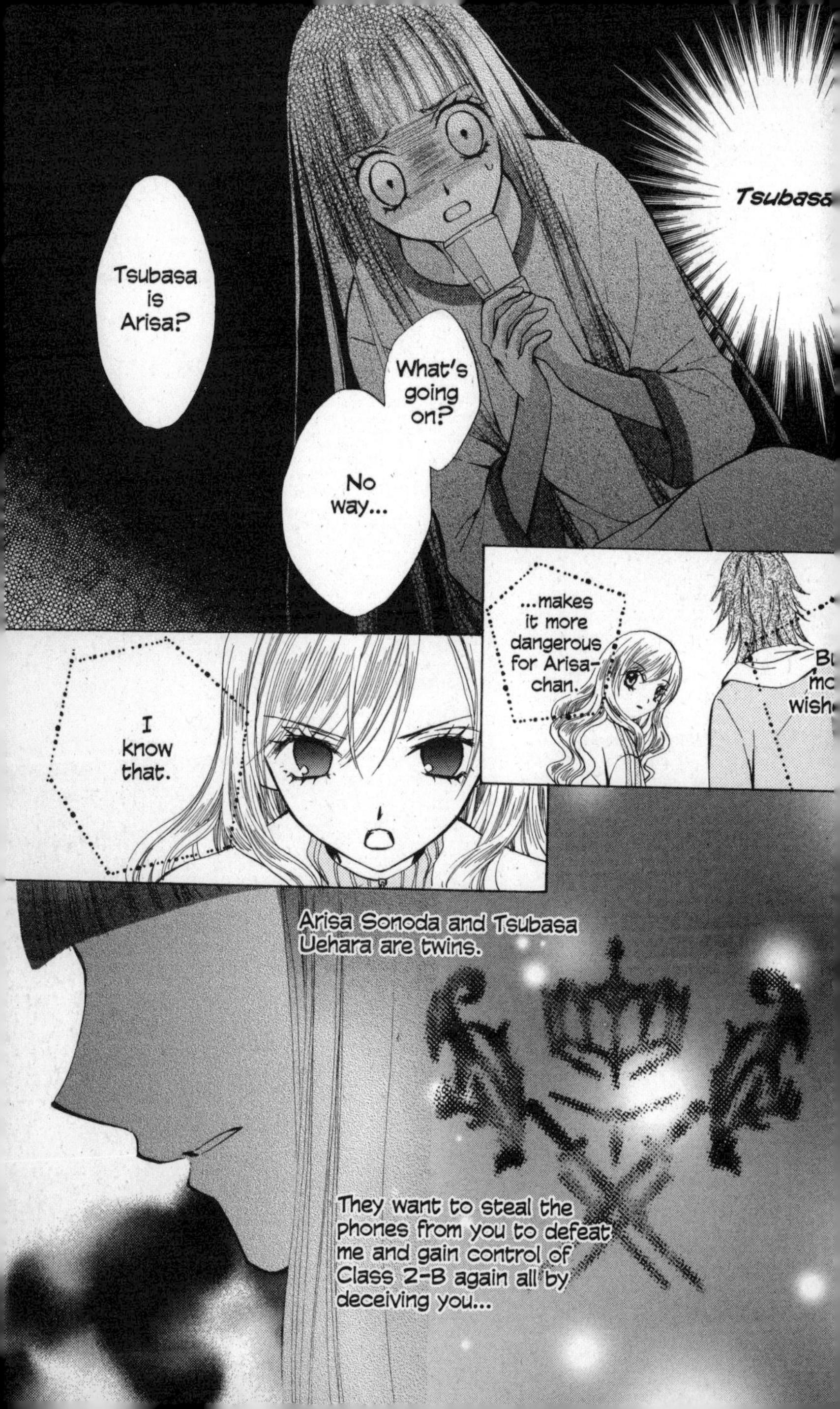
Tsubasa
What's going on?
No way...
Tsubasa is Arisa?
...makes it more dangerous for Arisa-chan.
I know that.
Arisa Sonoda and Tsubasa Uehara are twins.
They want to steal the phones from you to defeat me and gain control of Class 2-B again all by deceiving you...

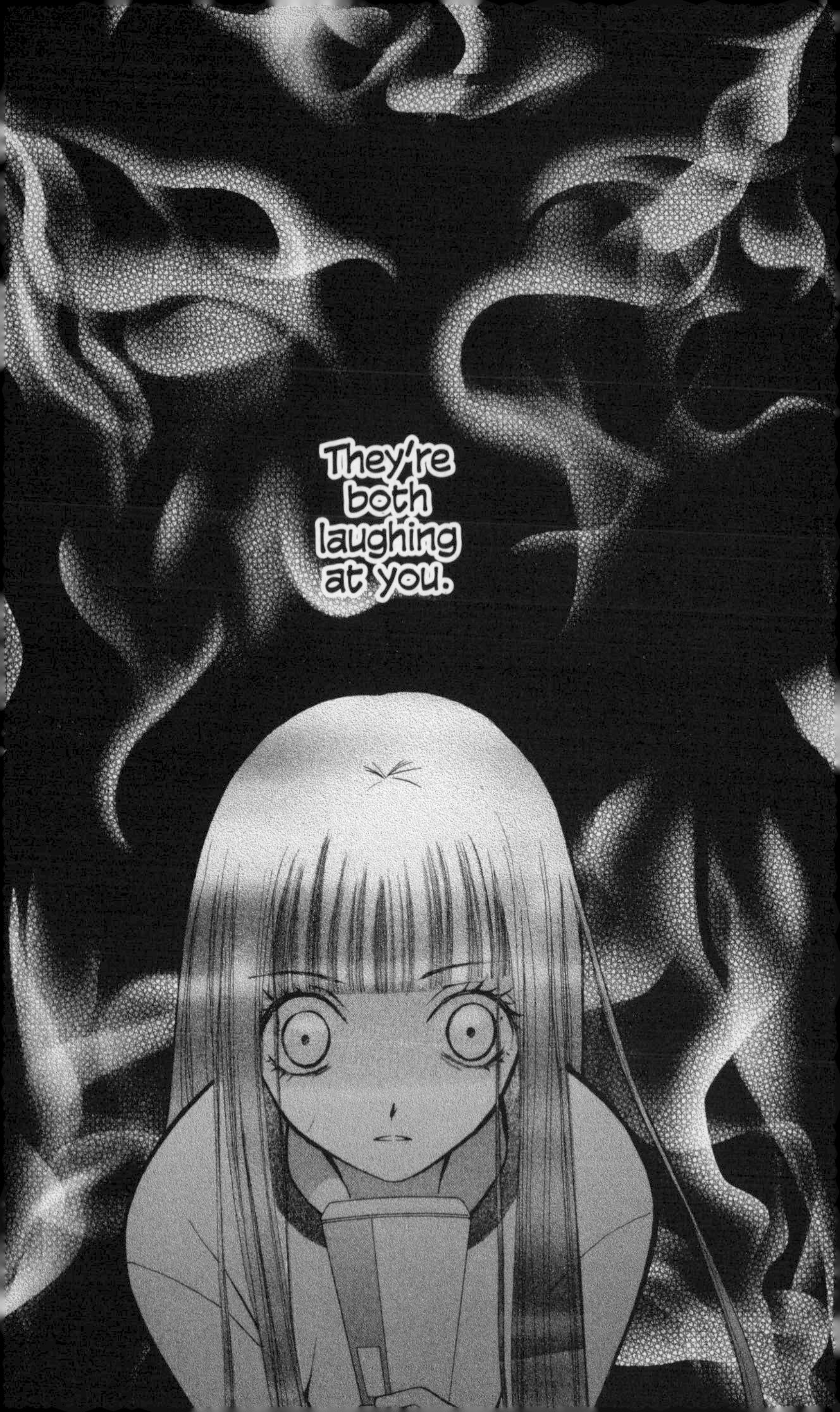
They're both laughing at you.

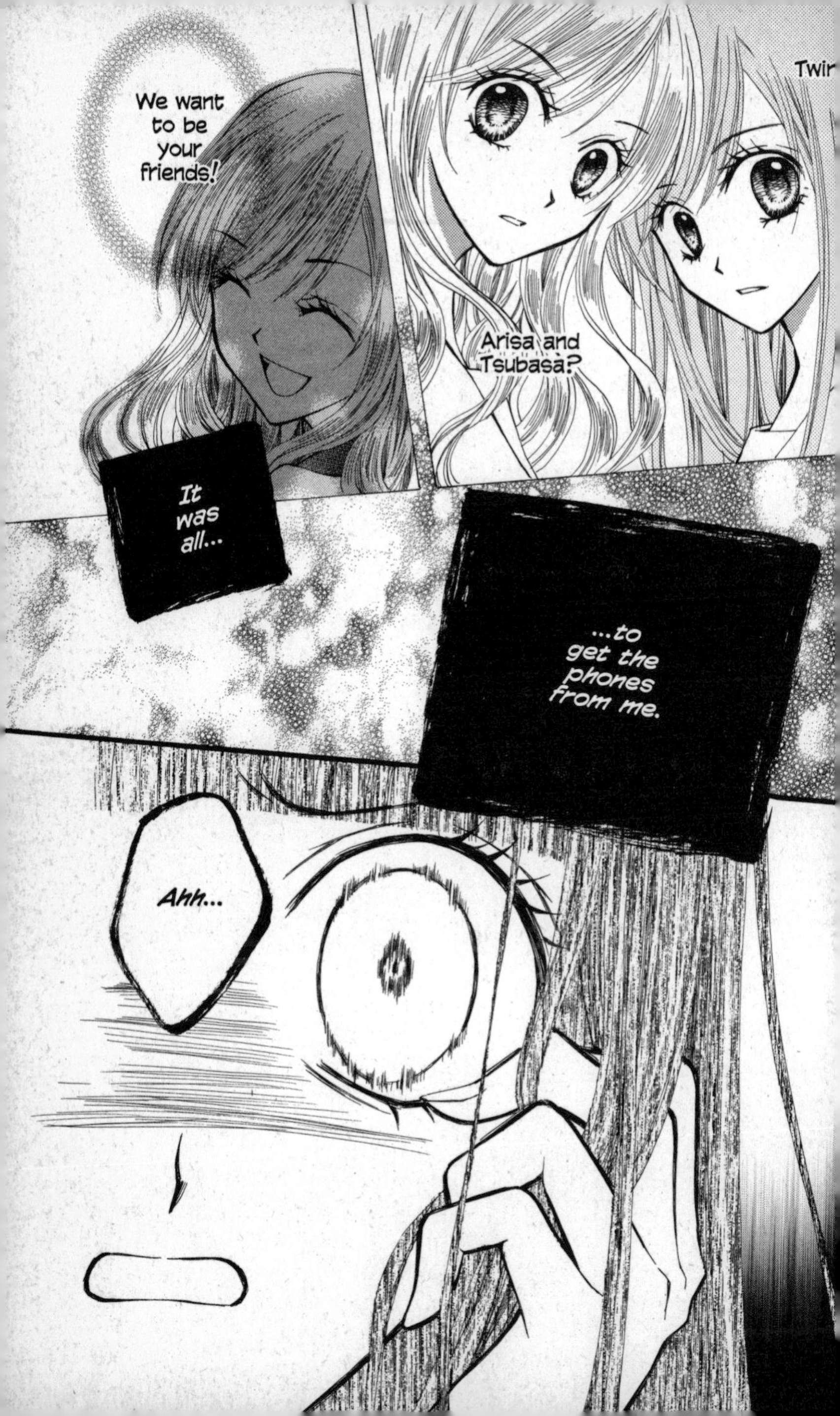
Twir
Arisa and Tsubasa?
We want to be your friends!
It was all...
...to get the phones from me.
Ahh...

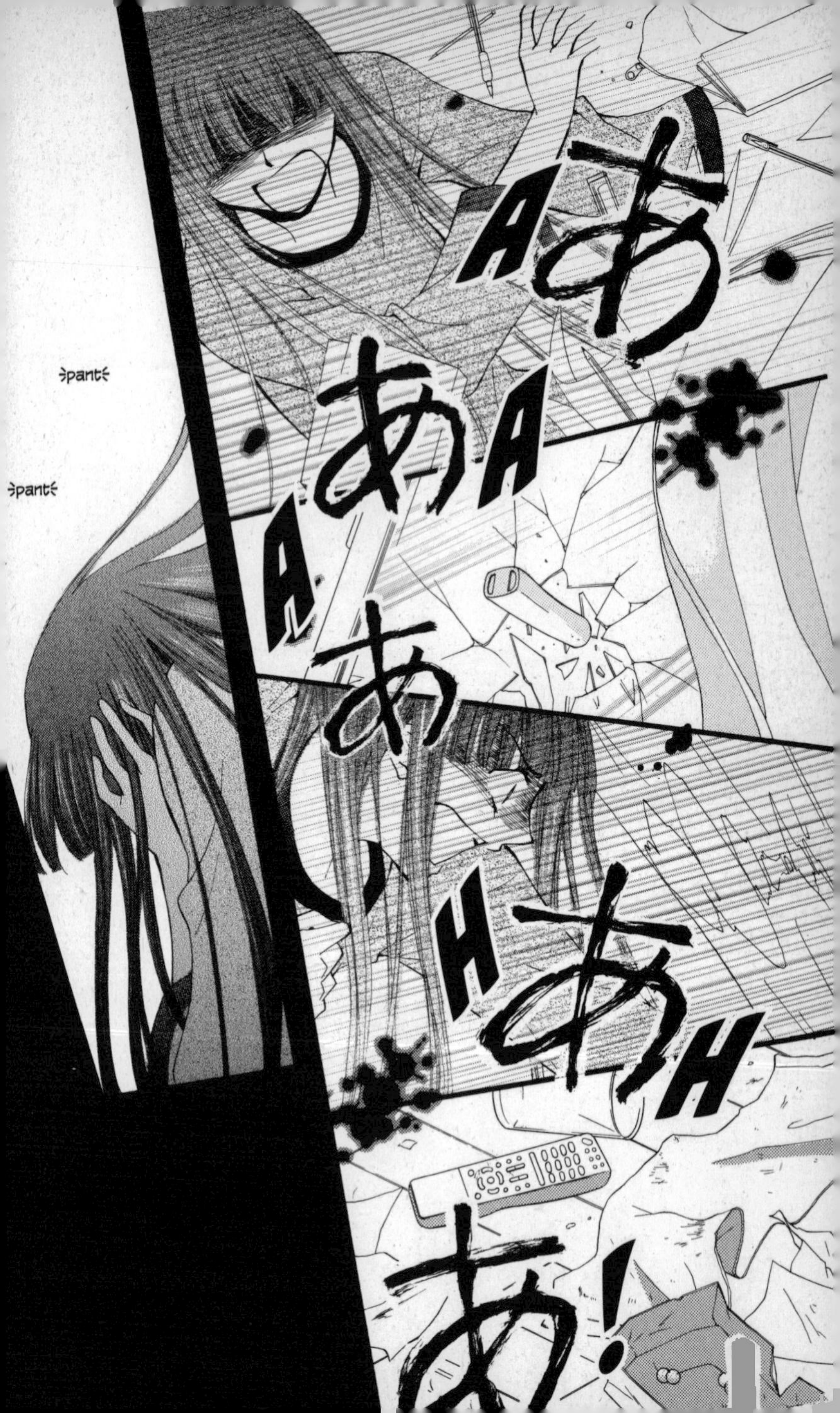

あAあAAあ
HあH
あ!
pant
pant

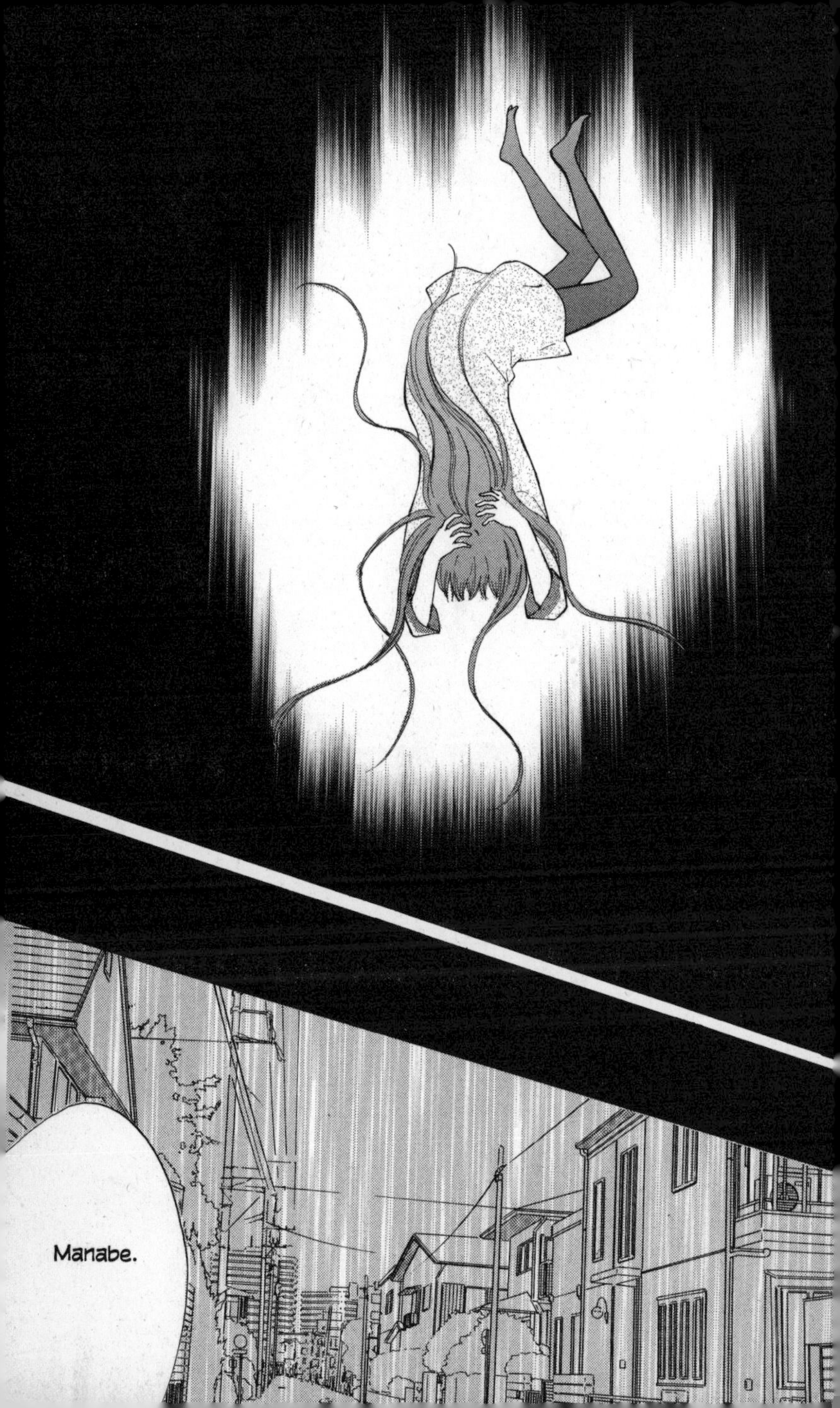
Manabe.

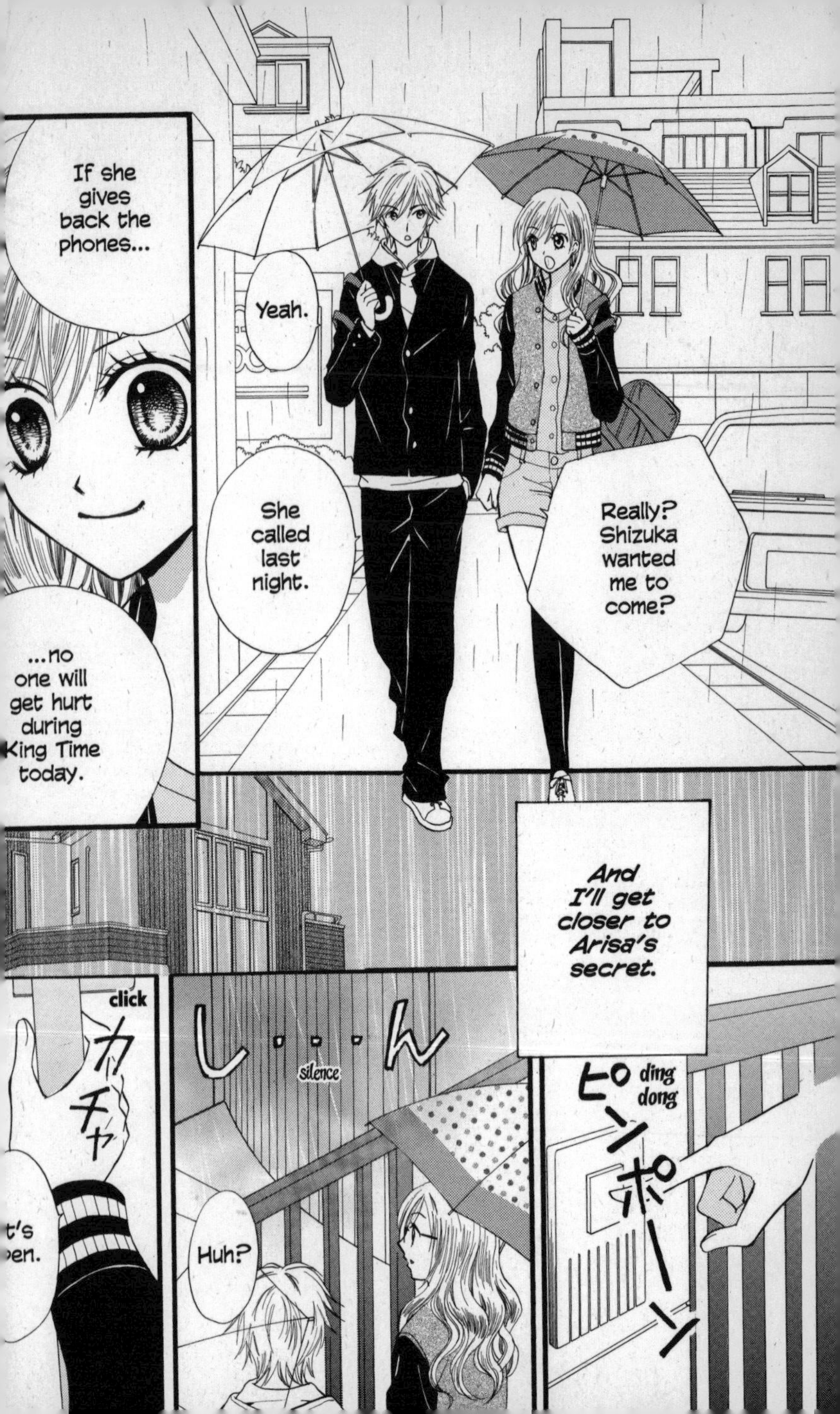
Really? Shizuka wanted me to come?
Yeah.
She called last night.
If she gives back the phones...
...no one will get hurt during King Time today.
And I'll get closer to Arisa's secret.
ピンポーン
ding dong
しーん
silence
Huh?
カチャ
click
t's pen.

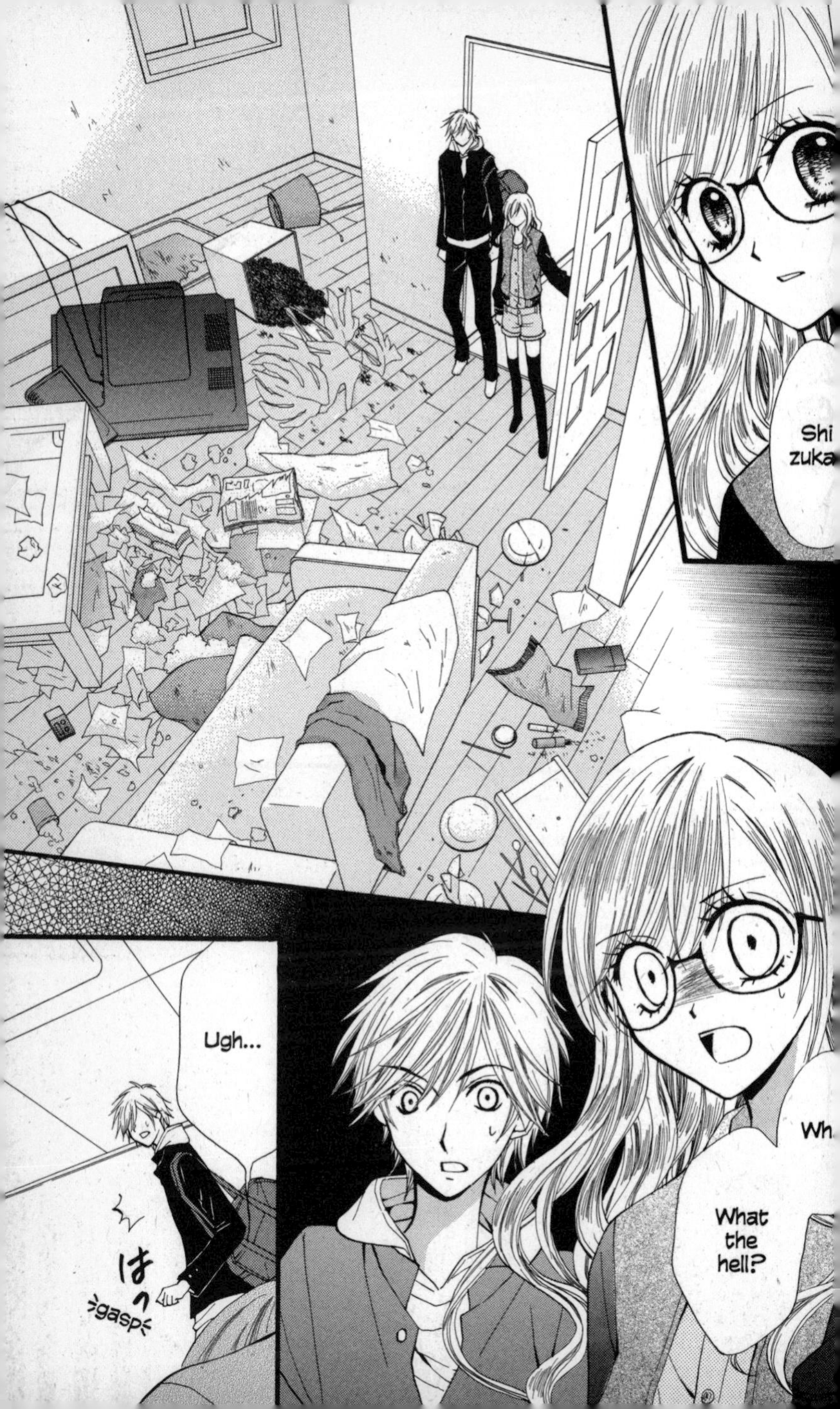

Shi zuka
Wh
What the hell?
Ugh...
はっ
gasp

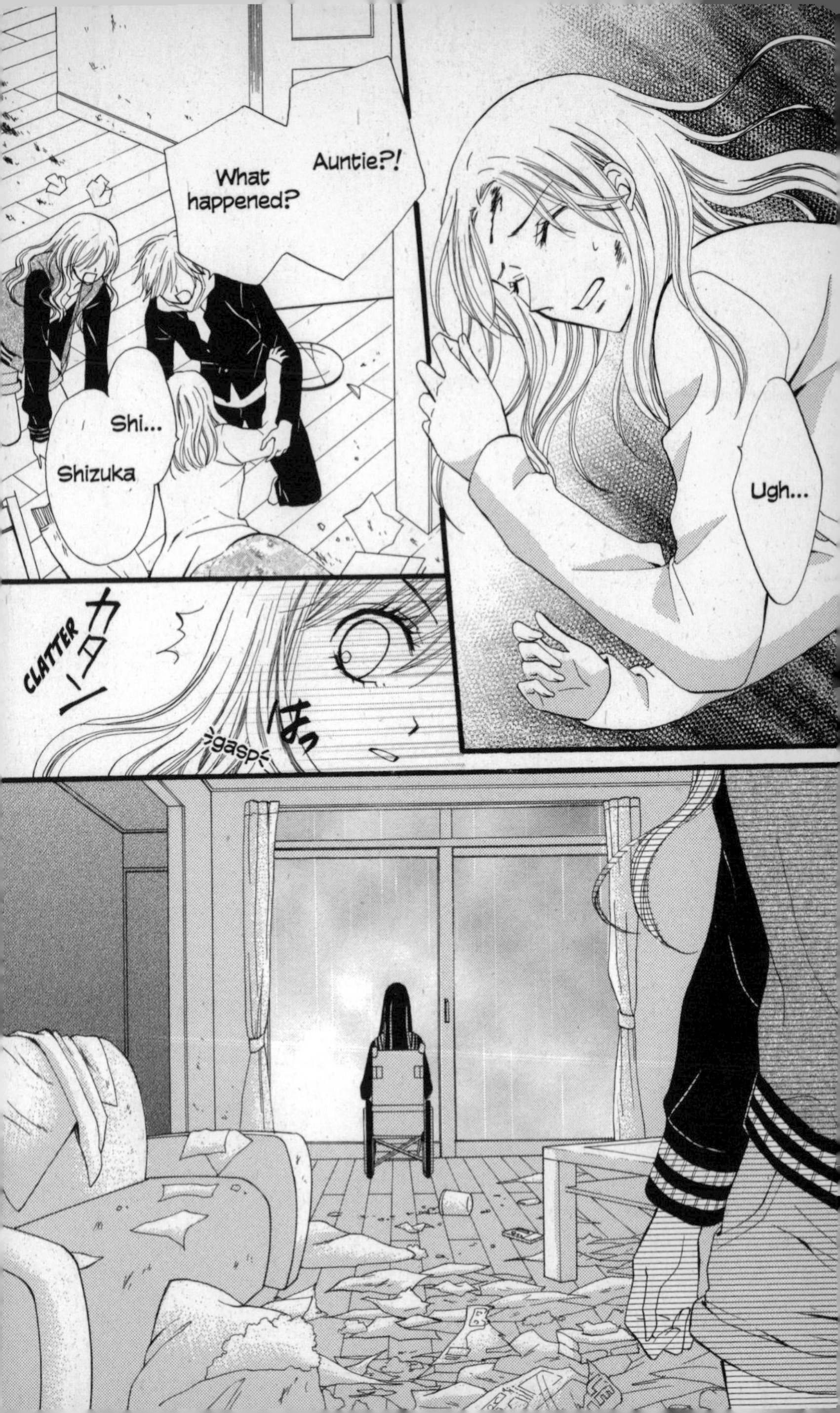
Ugh...
Auntie?!
What happened?
Shi...
Shizuka
カタン
CLATTER
はっ
gasp

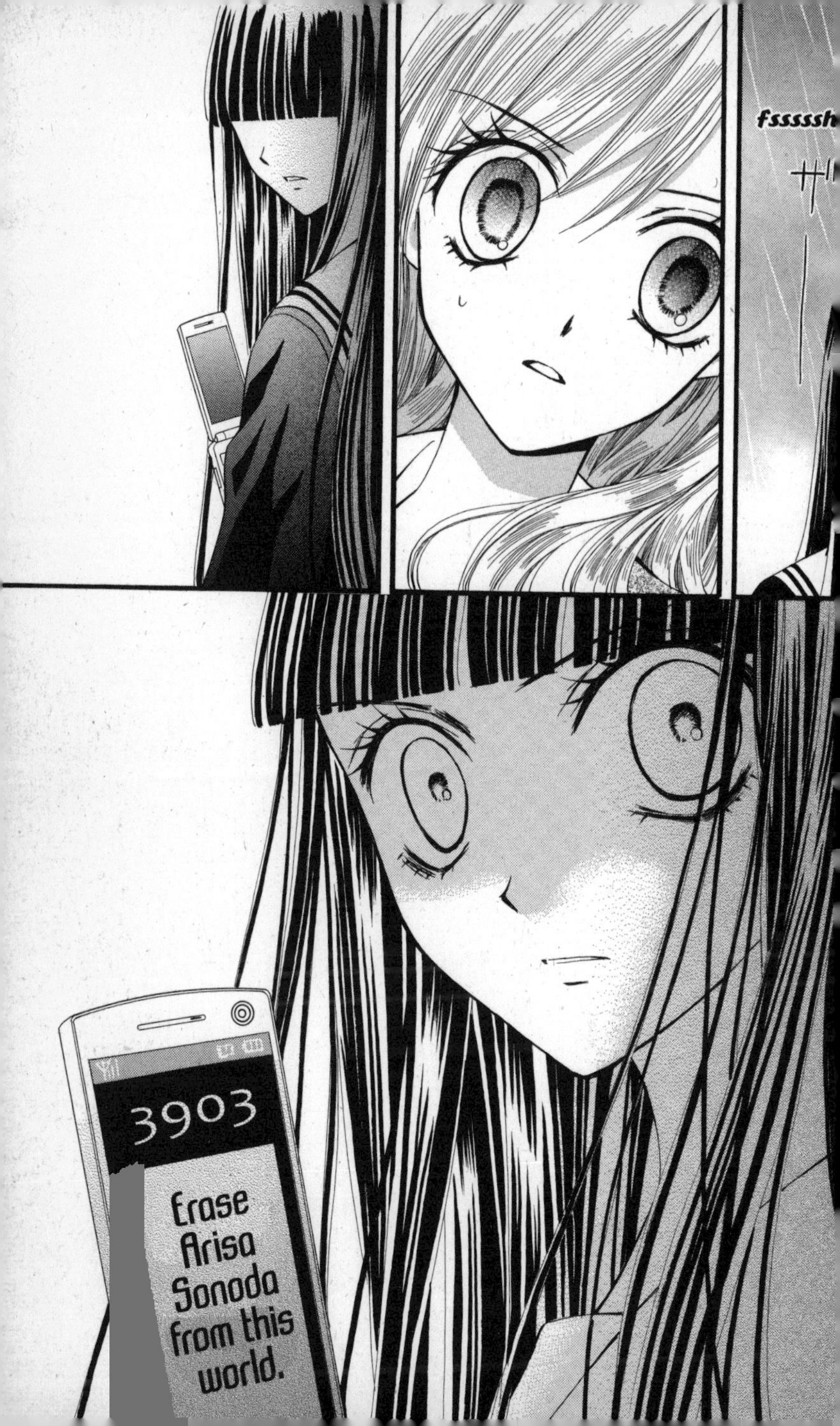
fssssh
ザー
3903
Erase Arisa Sonoda from this world.

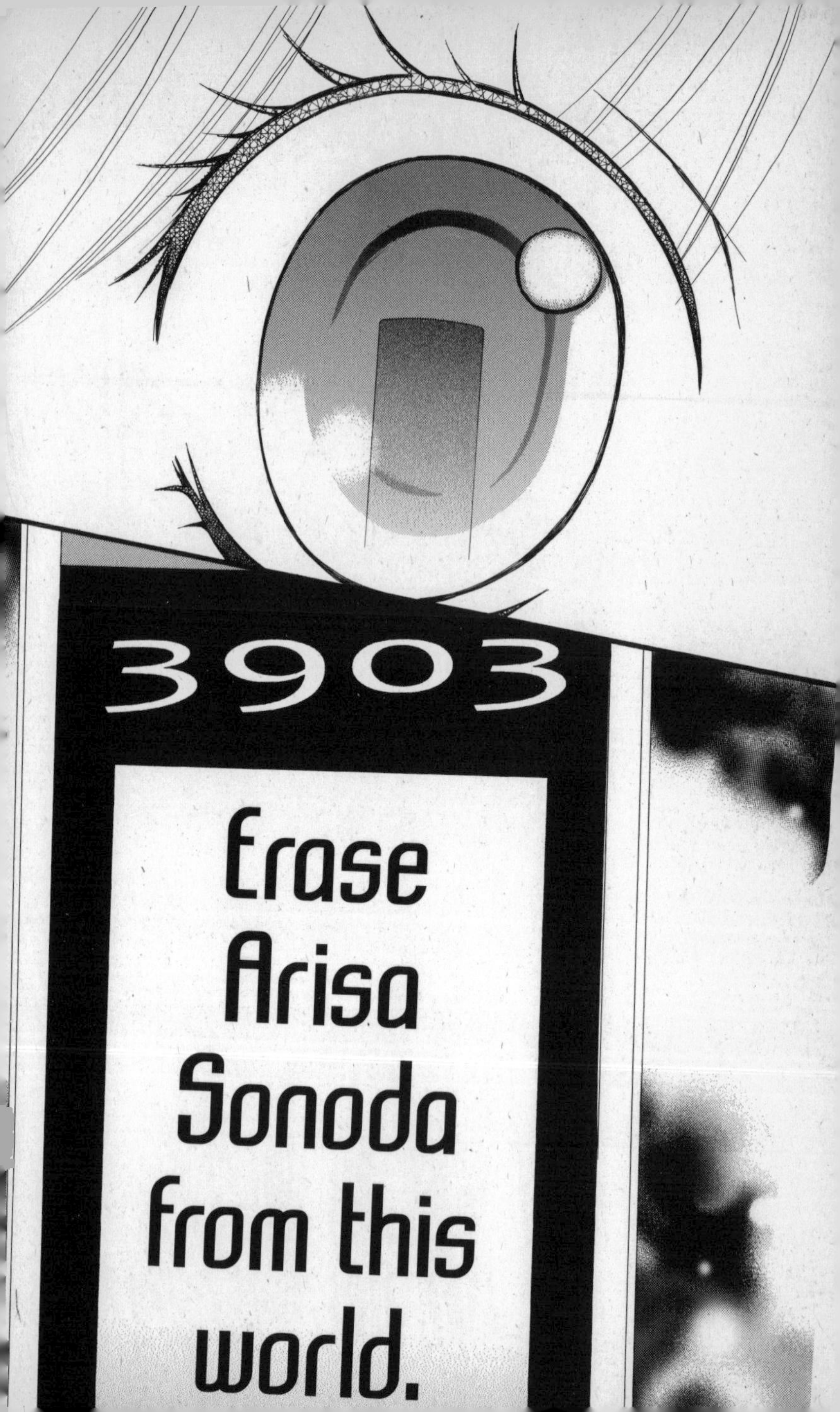
3903
Erase Arisa Sonoda from this world.

Chapter 22: The Path of a Wish

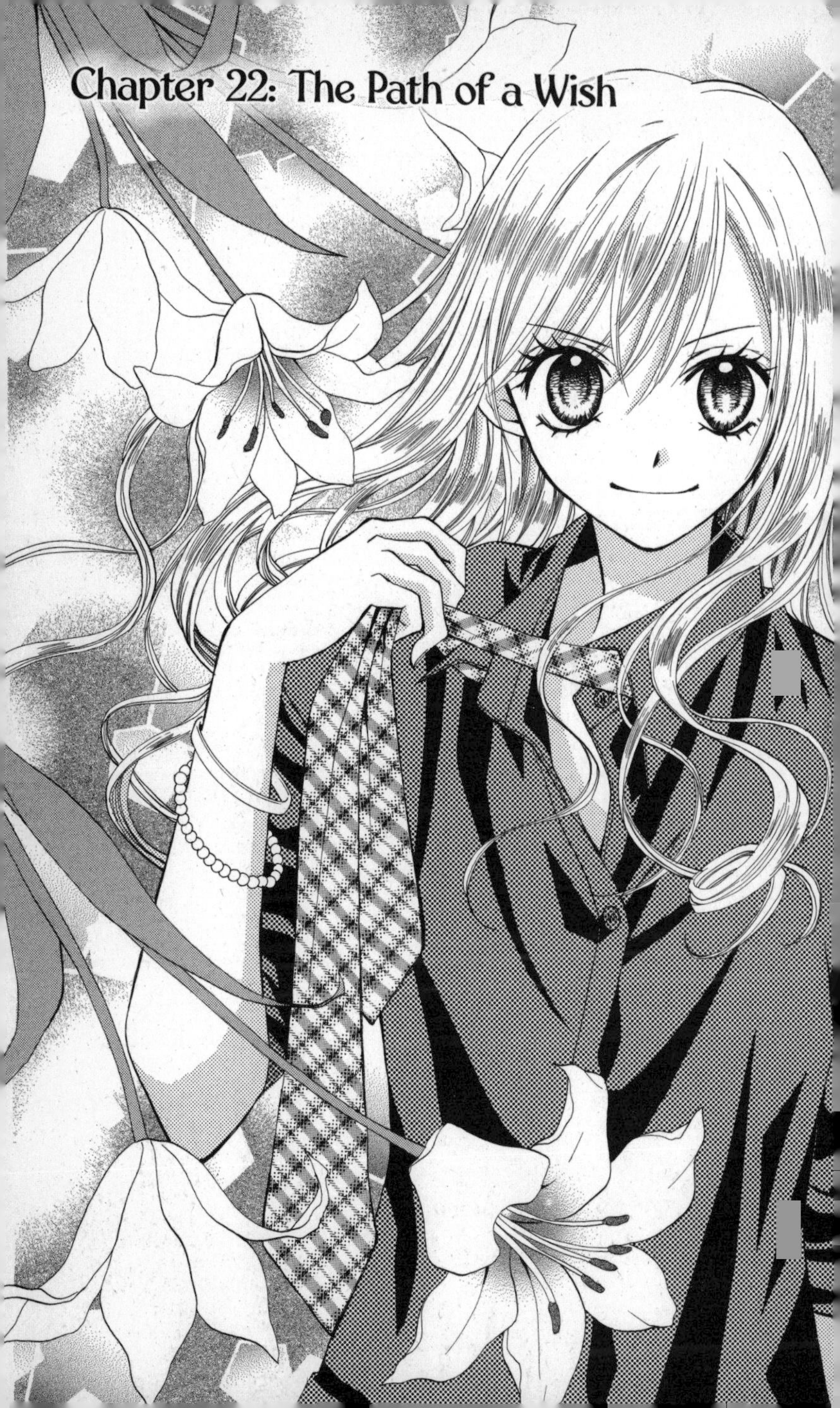

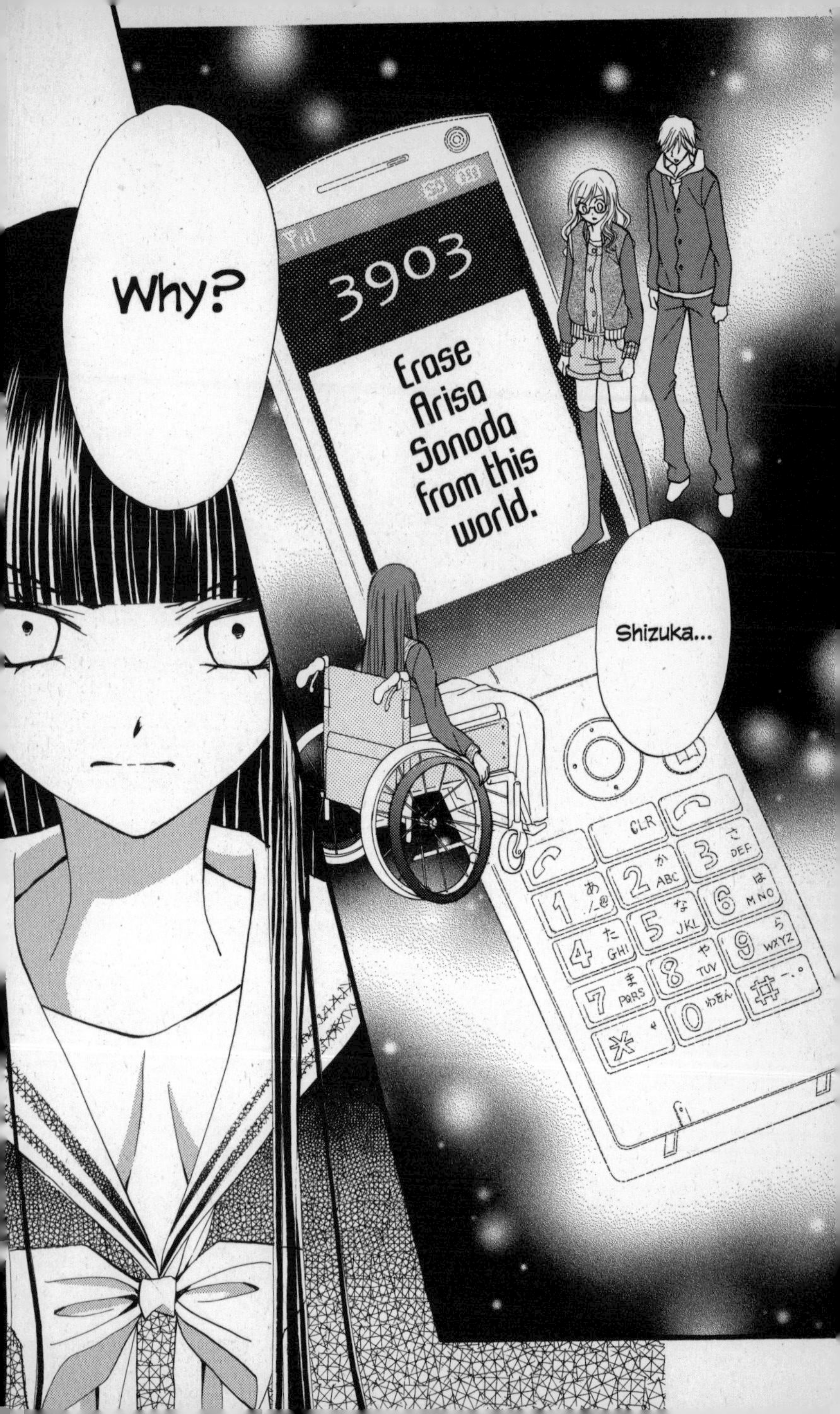
3903
Erase Arisa Sonoda from this world.
Shizuka...
Why?

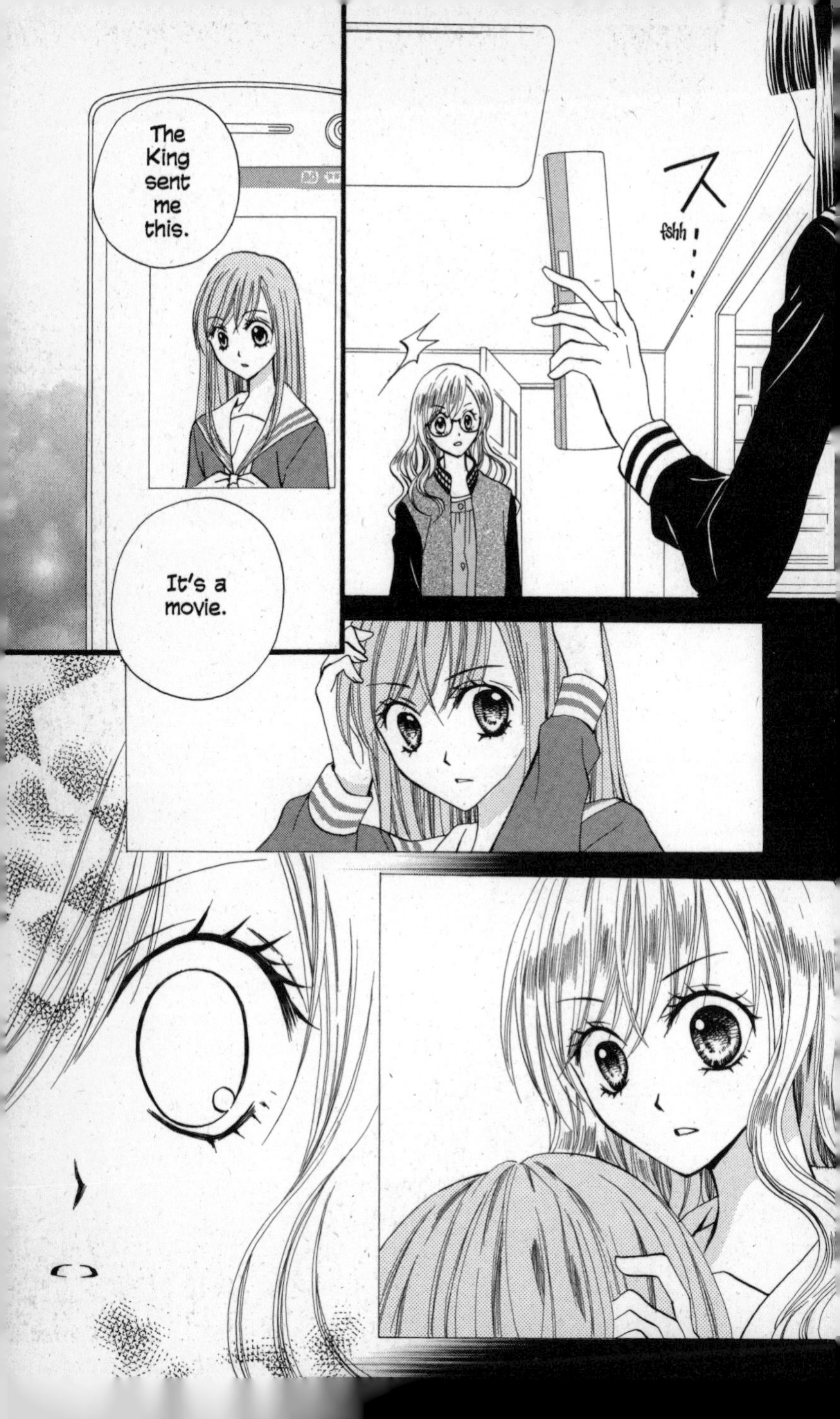
ス
fshh
The King sent me this.
It's a movie.

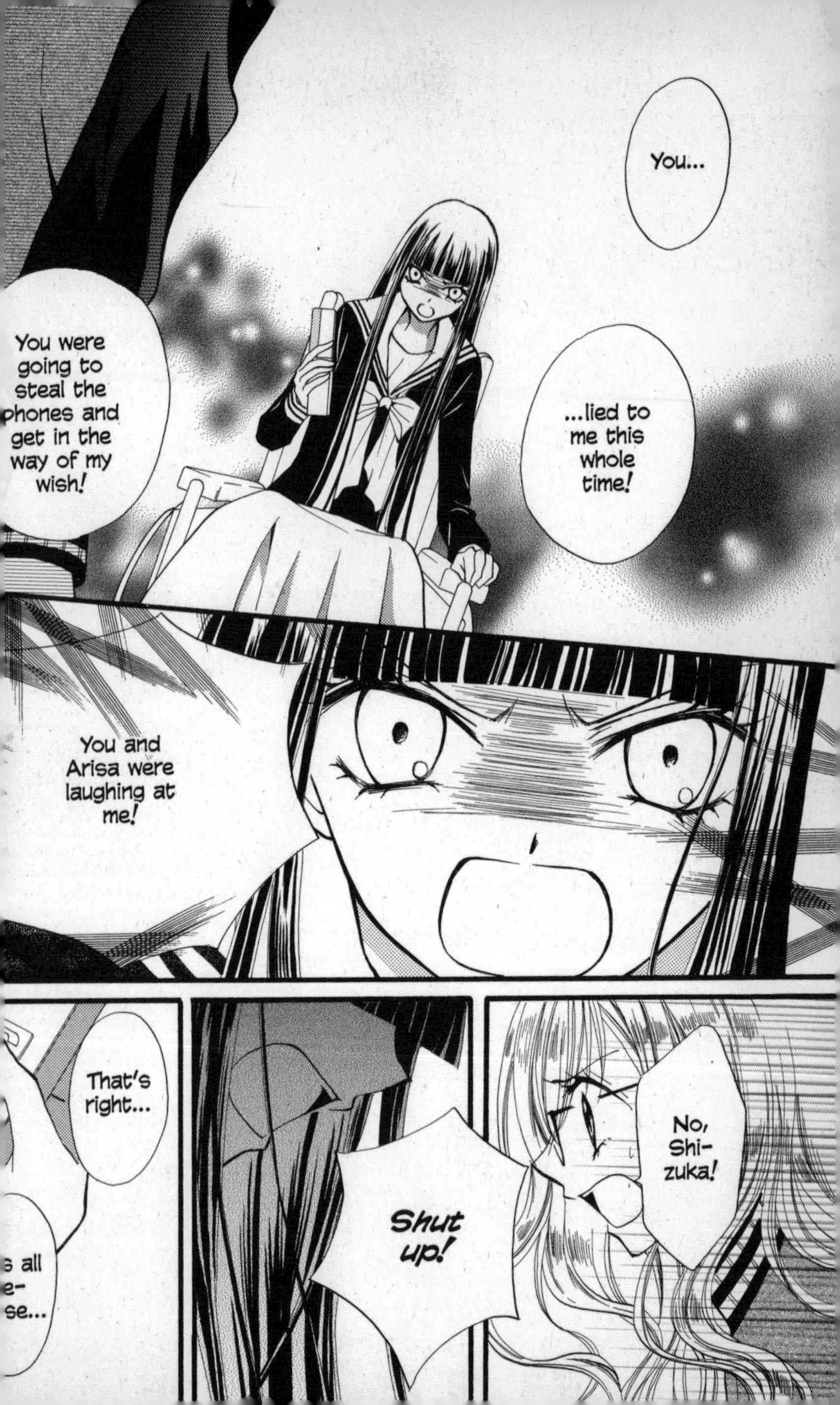
You...
...lied to me this whole time!
You were going to steal the phones and get in the way of my wish!
You and Arisa were laughing at me!
No, Shi-zuka!
Shut up!
That's right...
s all e- se...

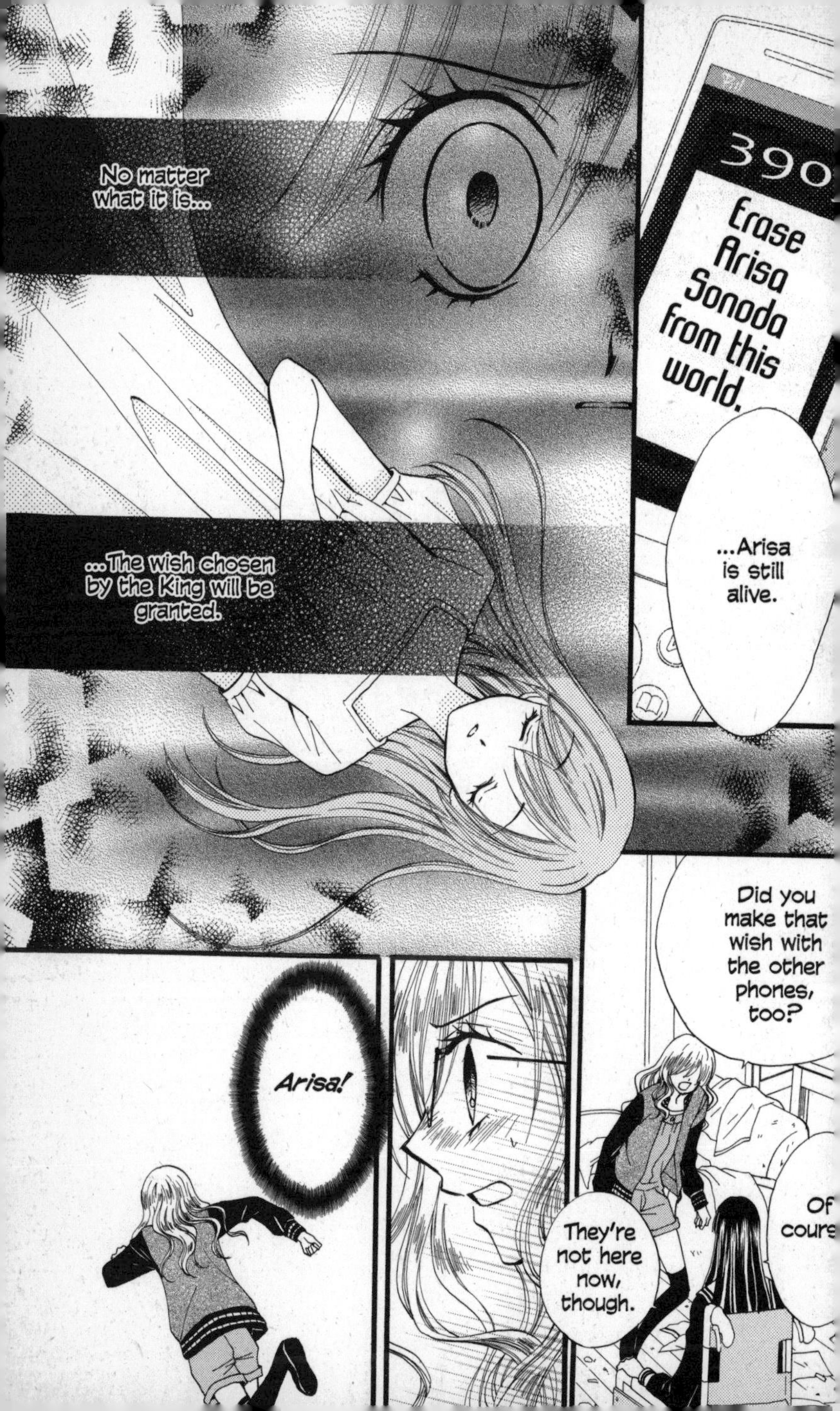
390
Erase Arisa Sonoda from this world.
...Arisa is still alive.
No matter what it is...
...The wish chosen by the King will be granted.
Did you make that wish with the other phones, too?
Of cours
They're not here now, though.
Arisa!

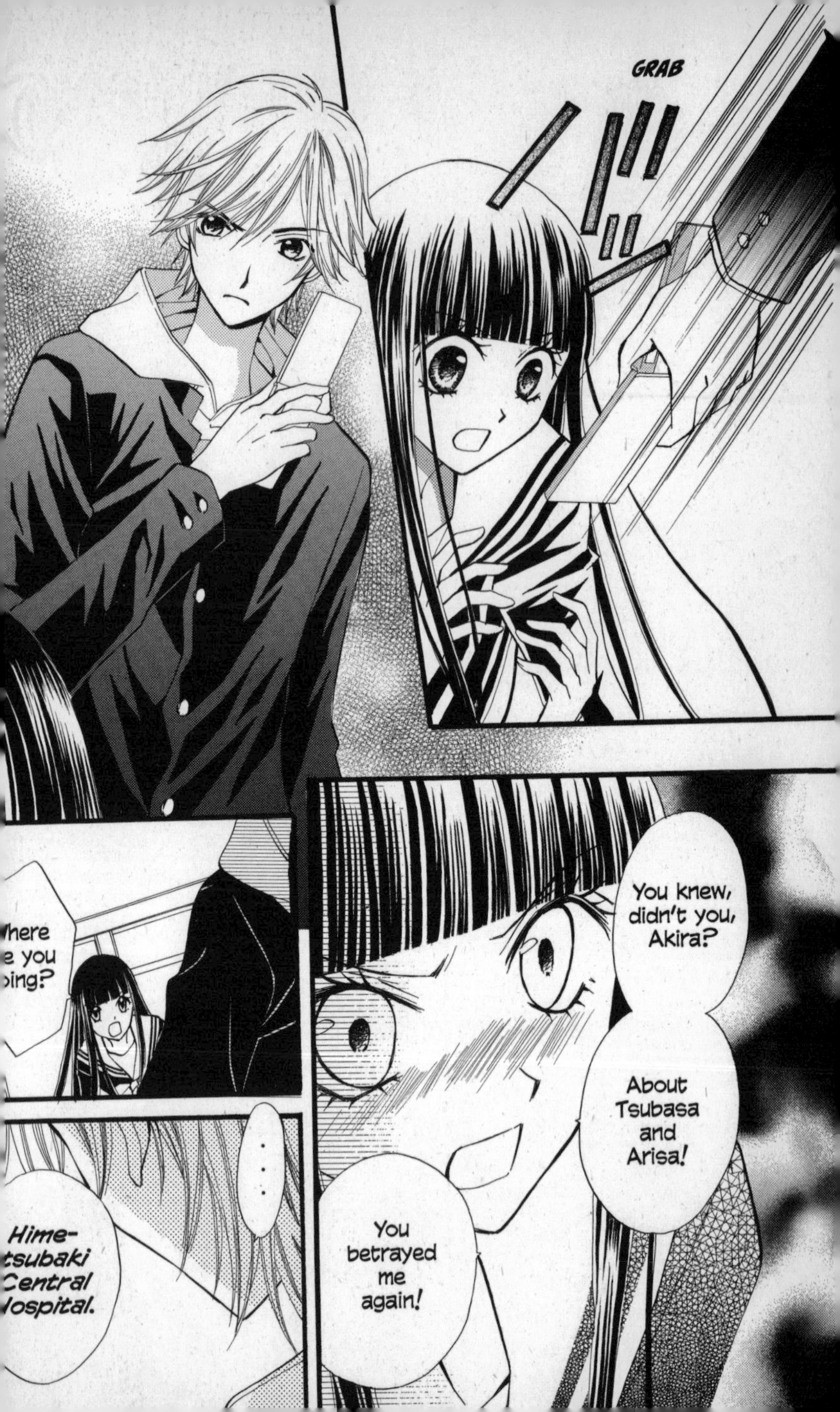
GRAB
You knew, didn't you, Akira?
About Tsubasa and Arisa!
You betrayed me again!
here e you oing?
...
Hime-tsubaki Central ospital.

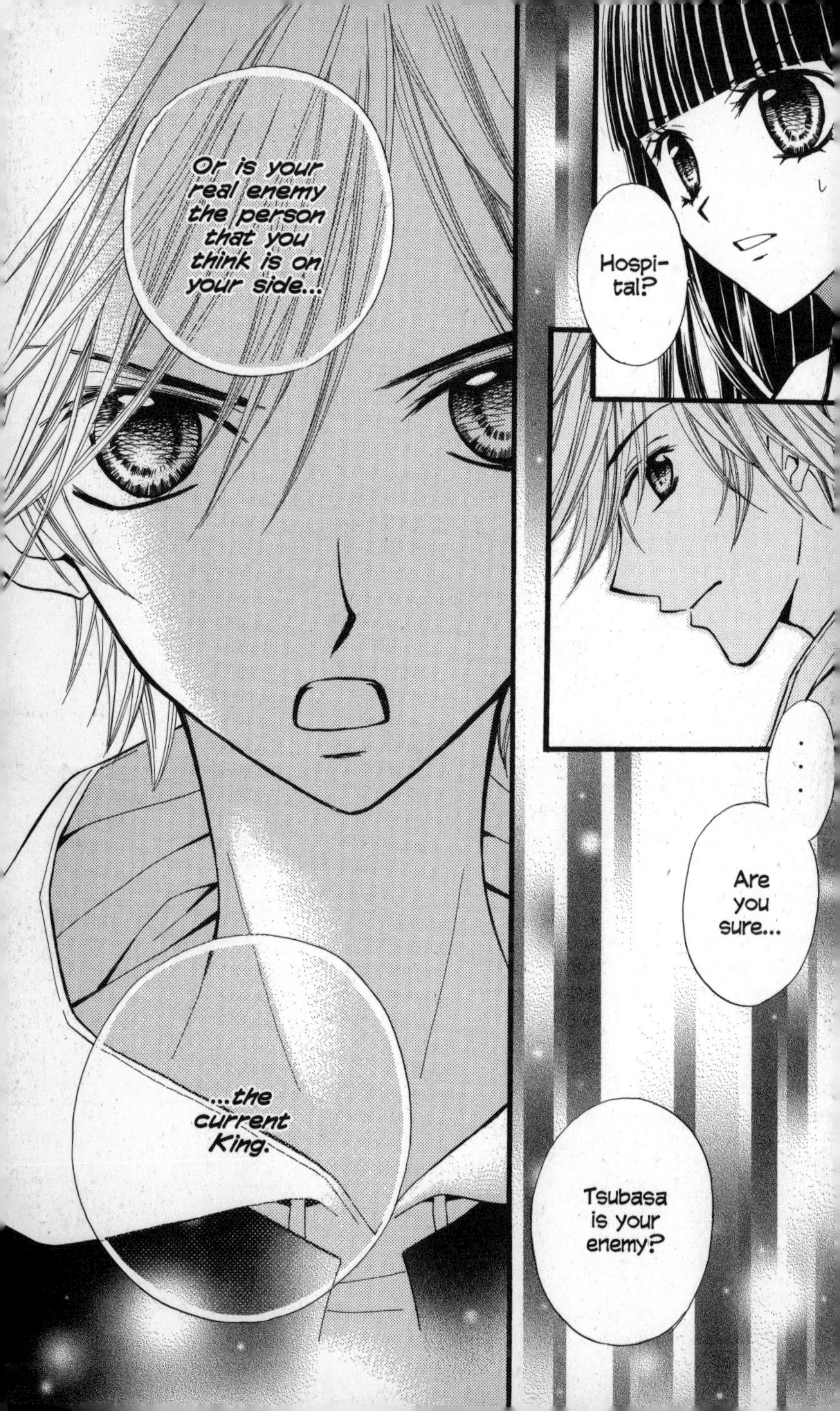
Hospi-tal?
...
Are you sure...
Tsubasa is your enemy?
Or is your real enemy the person that you think is on your side...
...the current King.

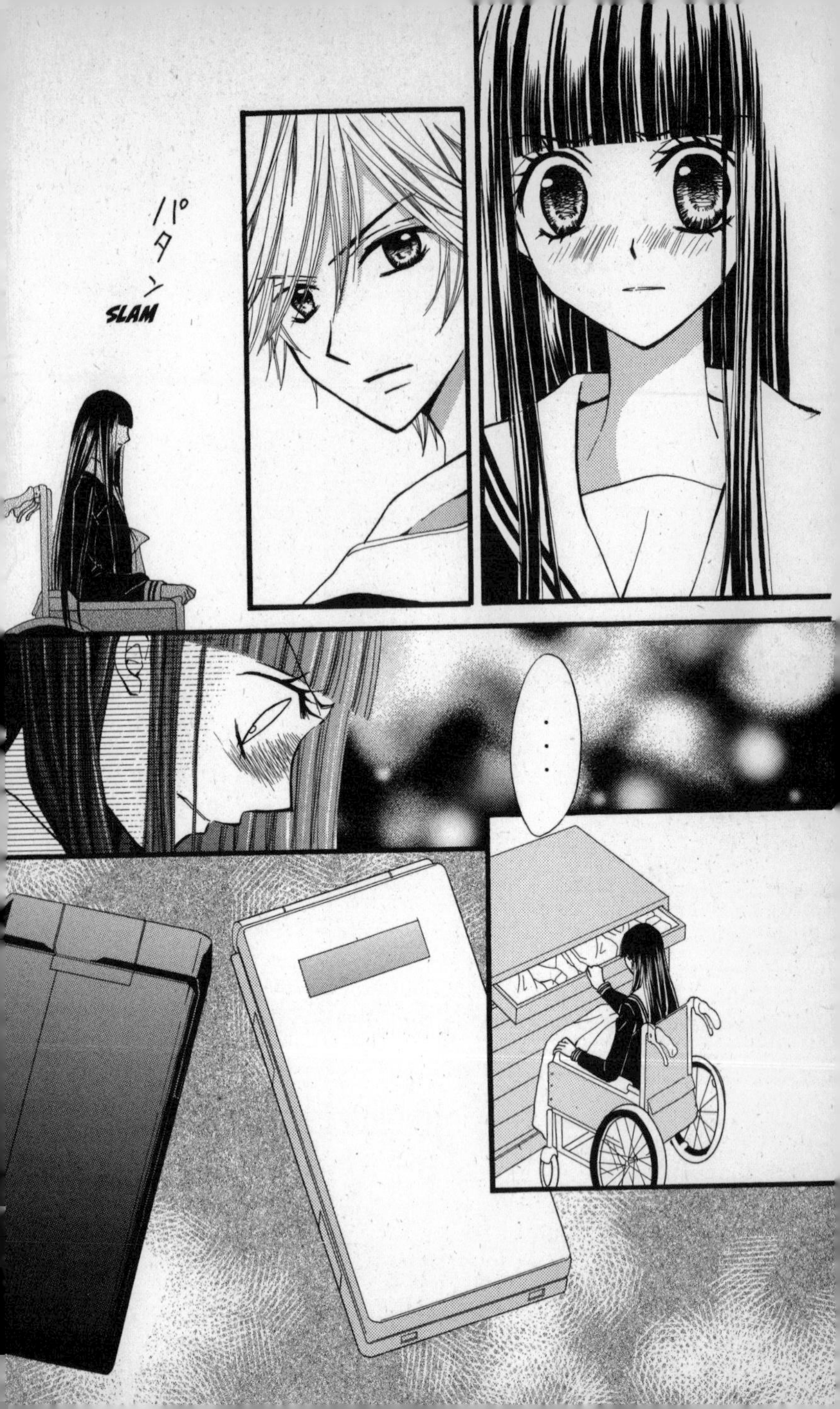
パタン
SLAM
…

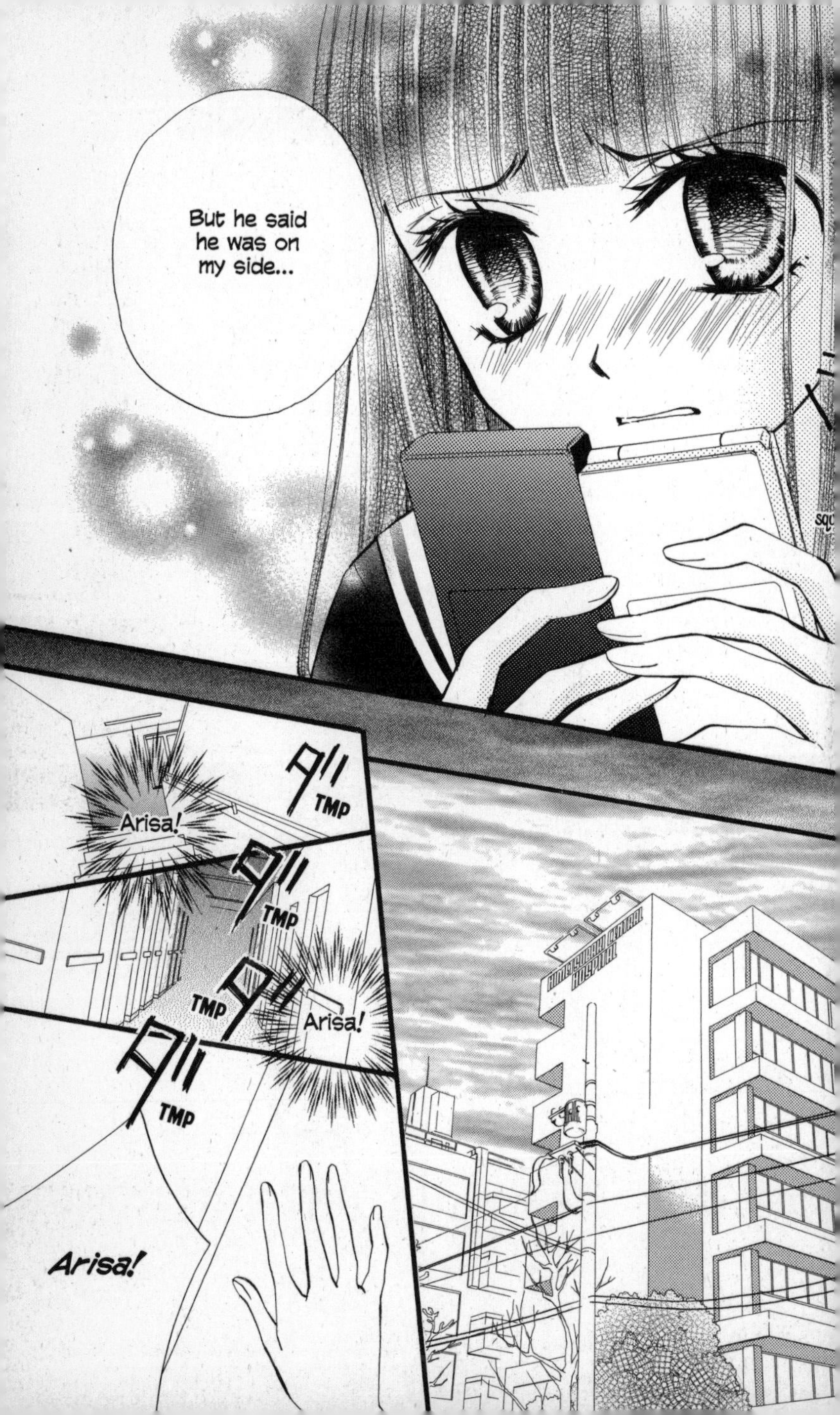

squ
But he said he was on my side...
TMP
Arisa!
TMP
Arisa!
TMP
TMP
Arisa!

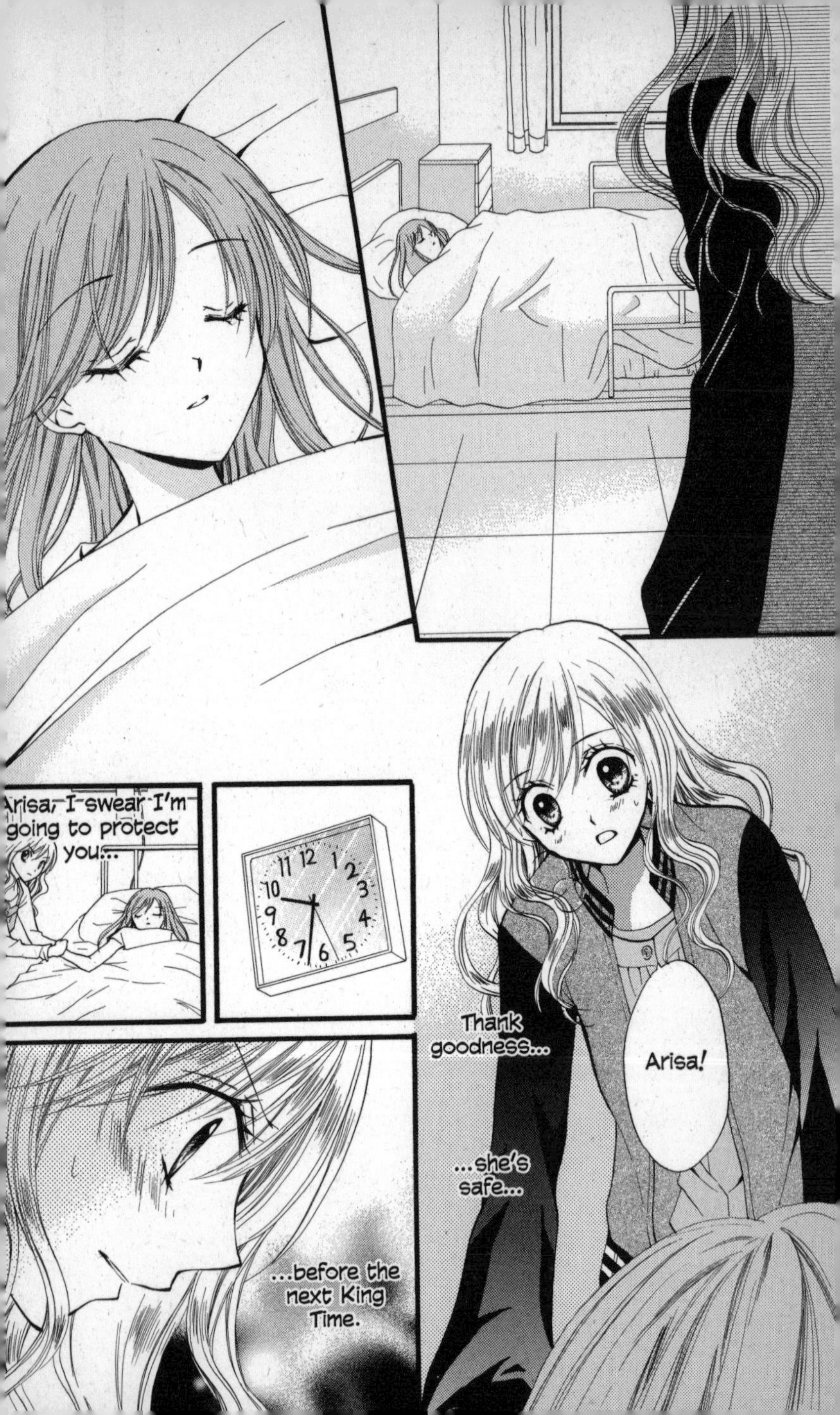
Arisa!
Thank goodness...
...she's safe...
Arisa, I swear I'm going to protect you...
...before the next King Time.

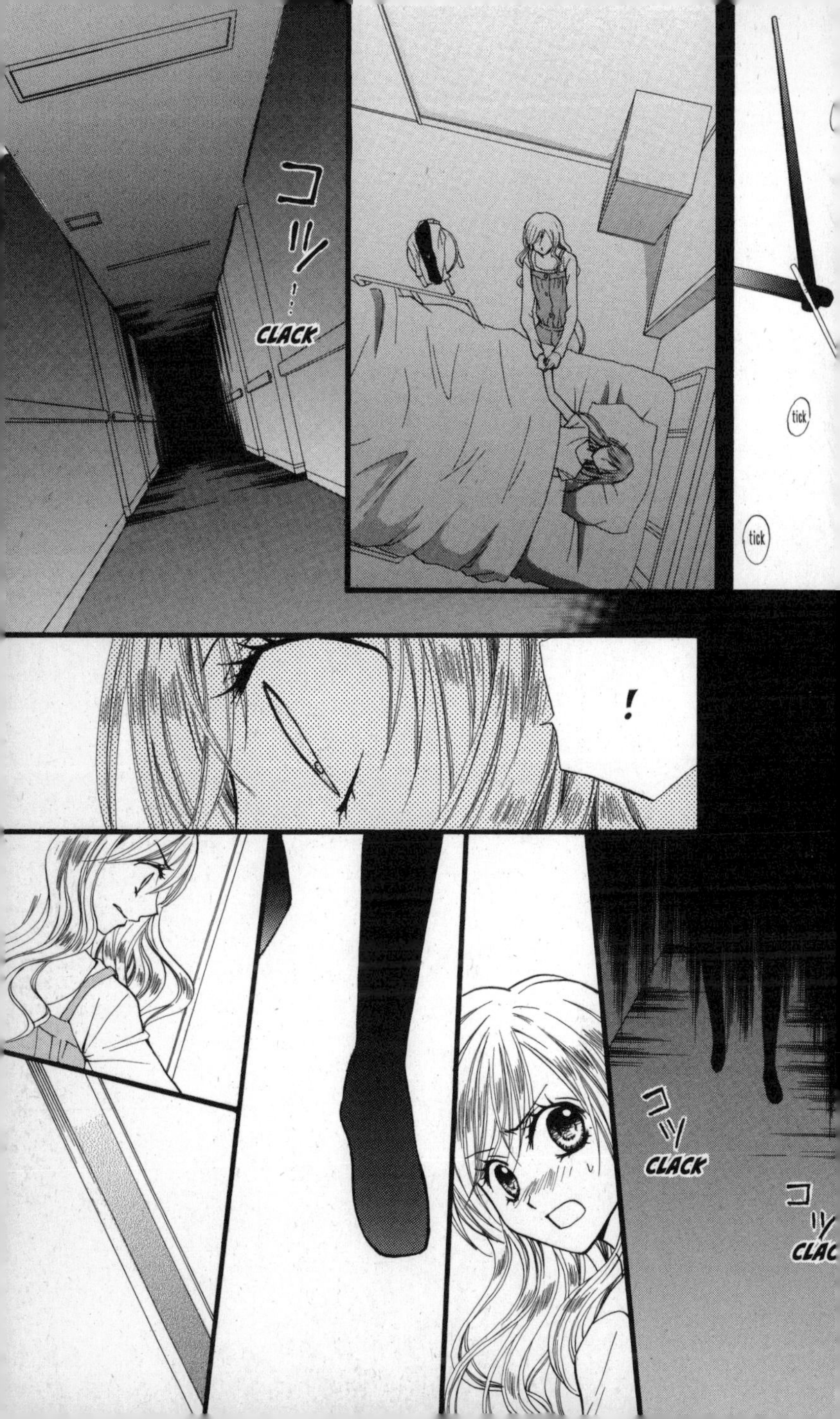
tick
tick
コツ…
CLACK
!
コツ
CLACK
コツ
CLAC

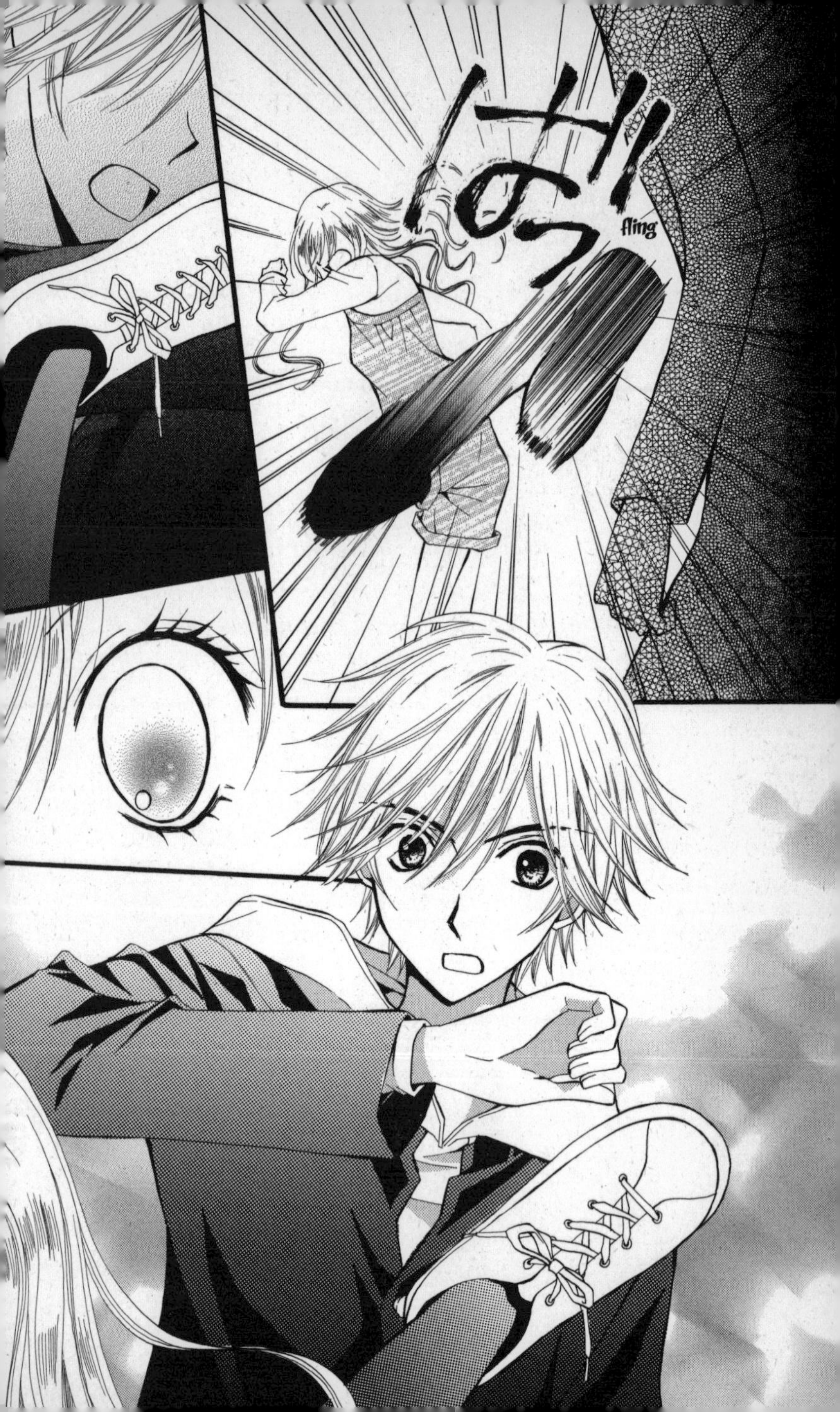
fling

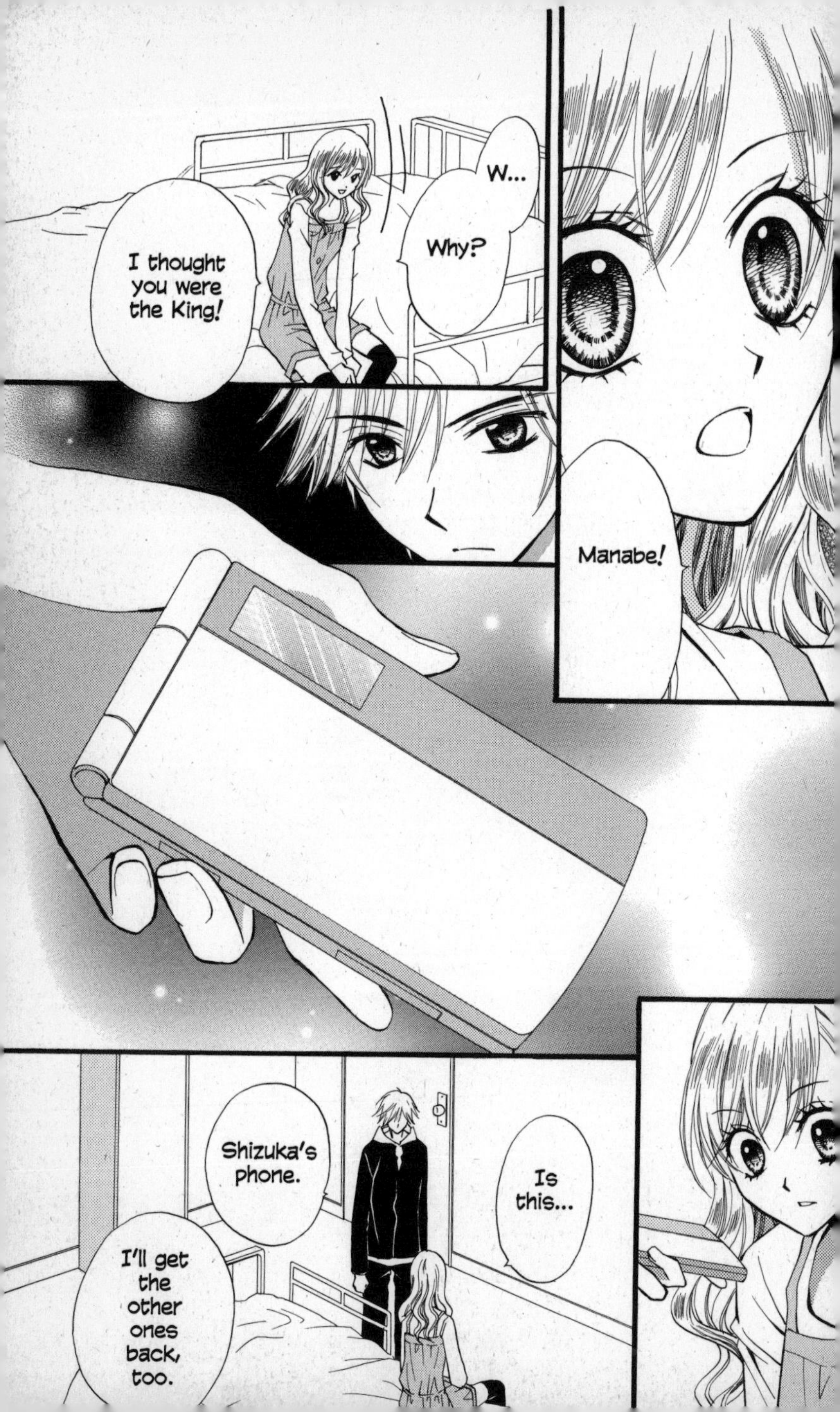

Manabe!
W...
Why?
I thought you were the King!
Is this...
Shizuka's phone.
I'll get the other ones back, too.

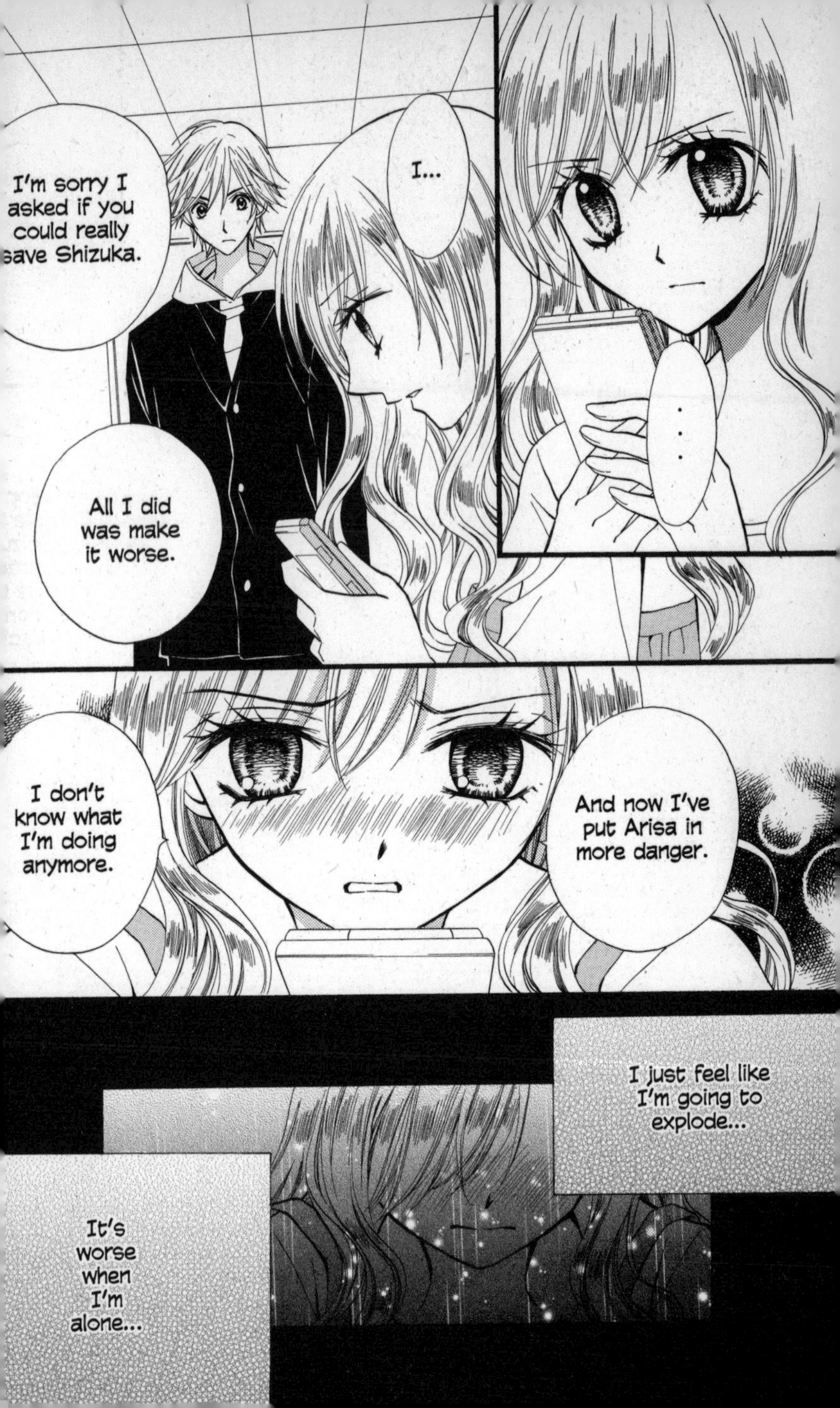
...
I...
I'm sorry I asked if you could really save Shizuka.
All I did was make it worse.
And now I've put Arisa in more danger.
I don't know what I'm doing anymore.
I just feel like I'm going to explode...
It's worse when I'm alone...

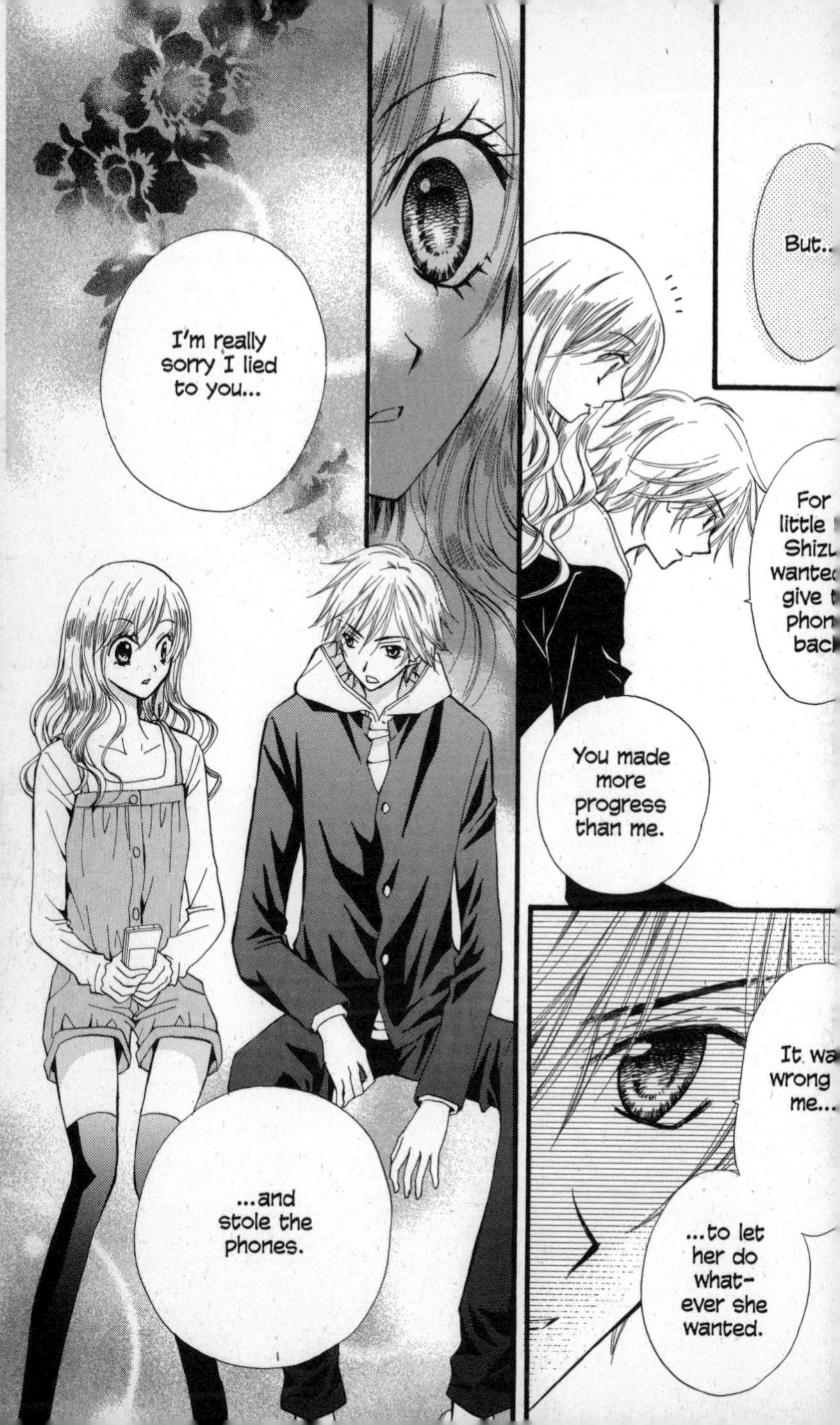
But..
For little Shizu wante give phon bac
You made more progress than me.
It wa wrong me...
...to let her do what-ever she wanted.
I'm really sorry I lied to you...
...and stole the phones.

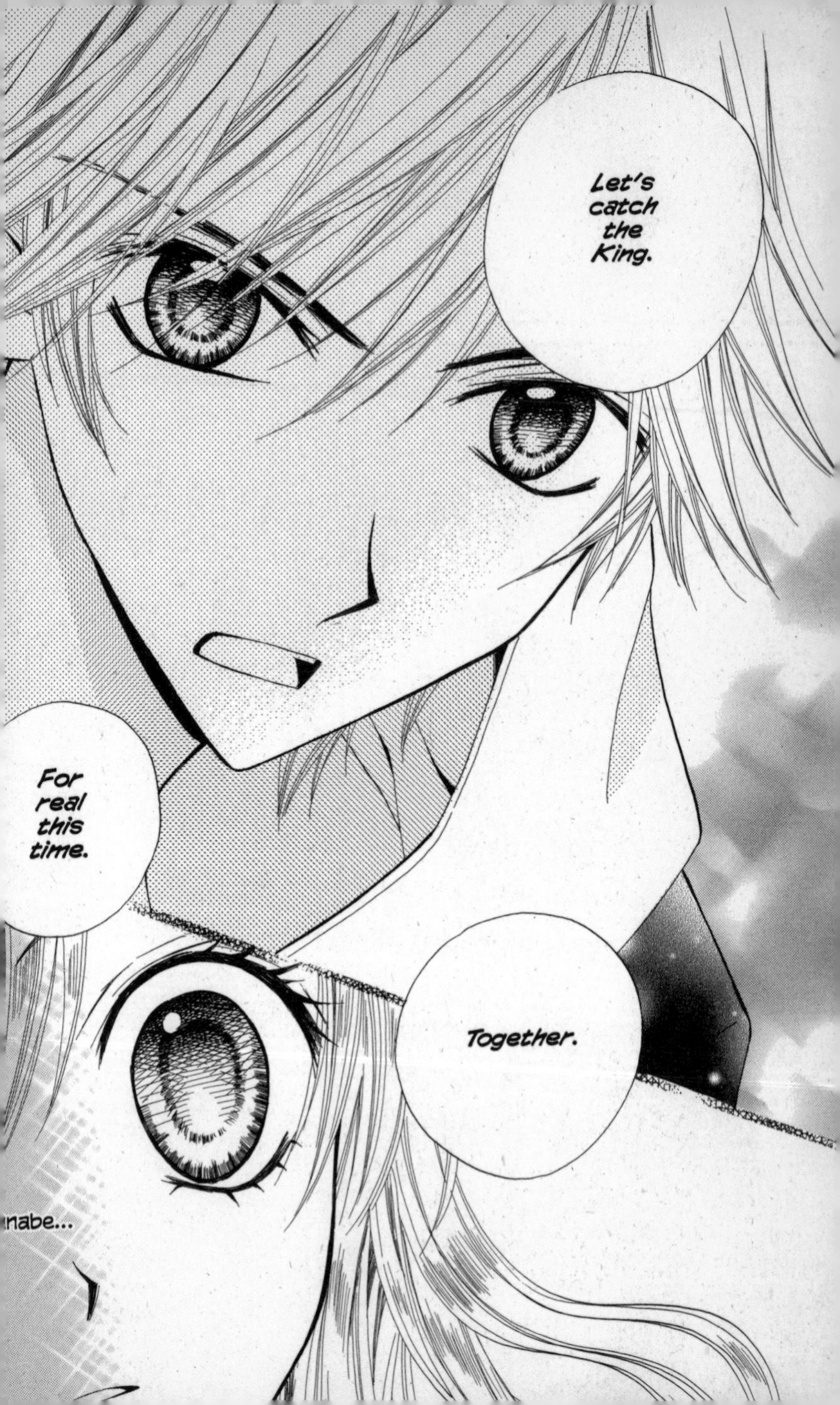
Let's catch the King.
For real this time.
Together.
nabe...

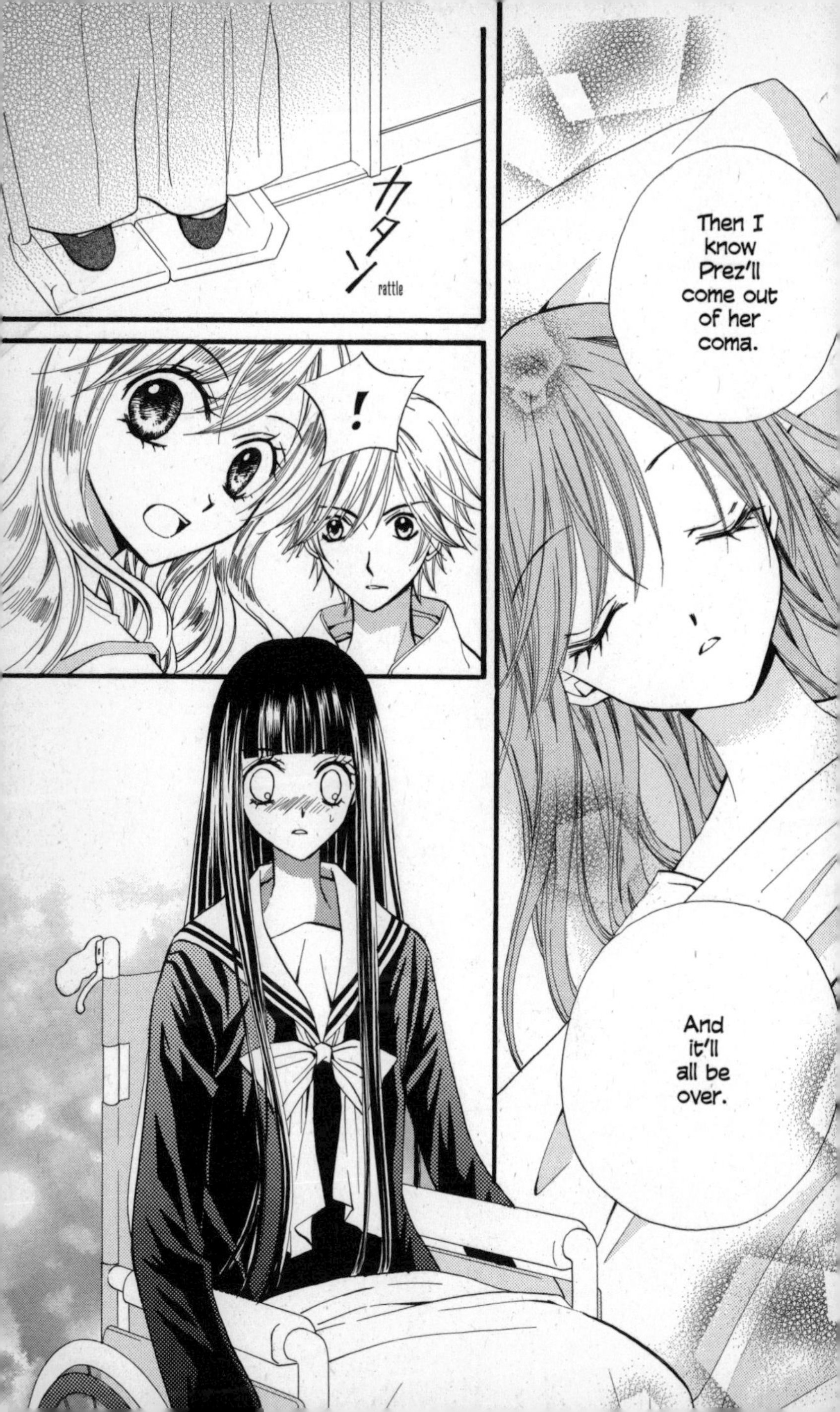
Then I know Prez'll come out of her coma.
And it'll all be over.
カタン
rattle
!

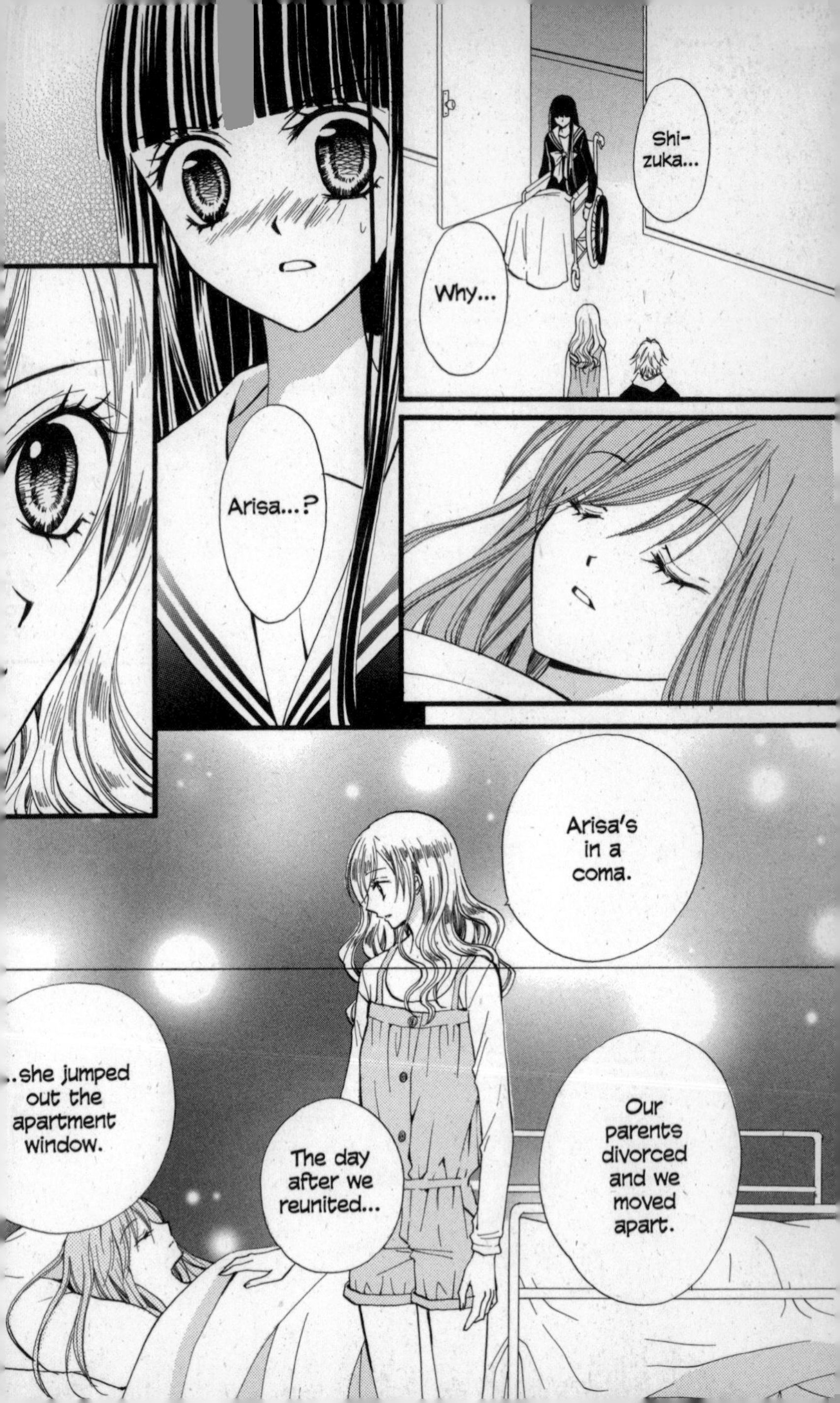

Shi-zuka...
Why...
Arisa...?
Arisa's in a coma.
Our parents divorced and we moved apart.
The day after we reunited...
..she jumped out the apartment window.

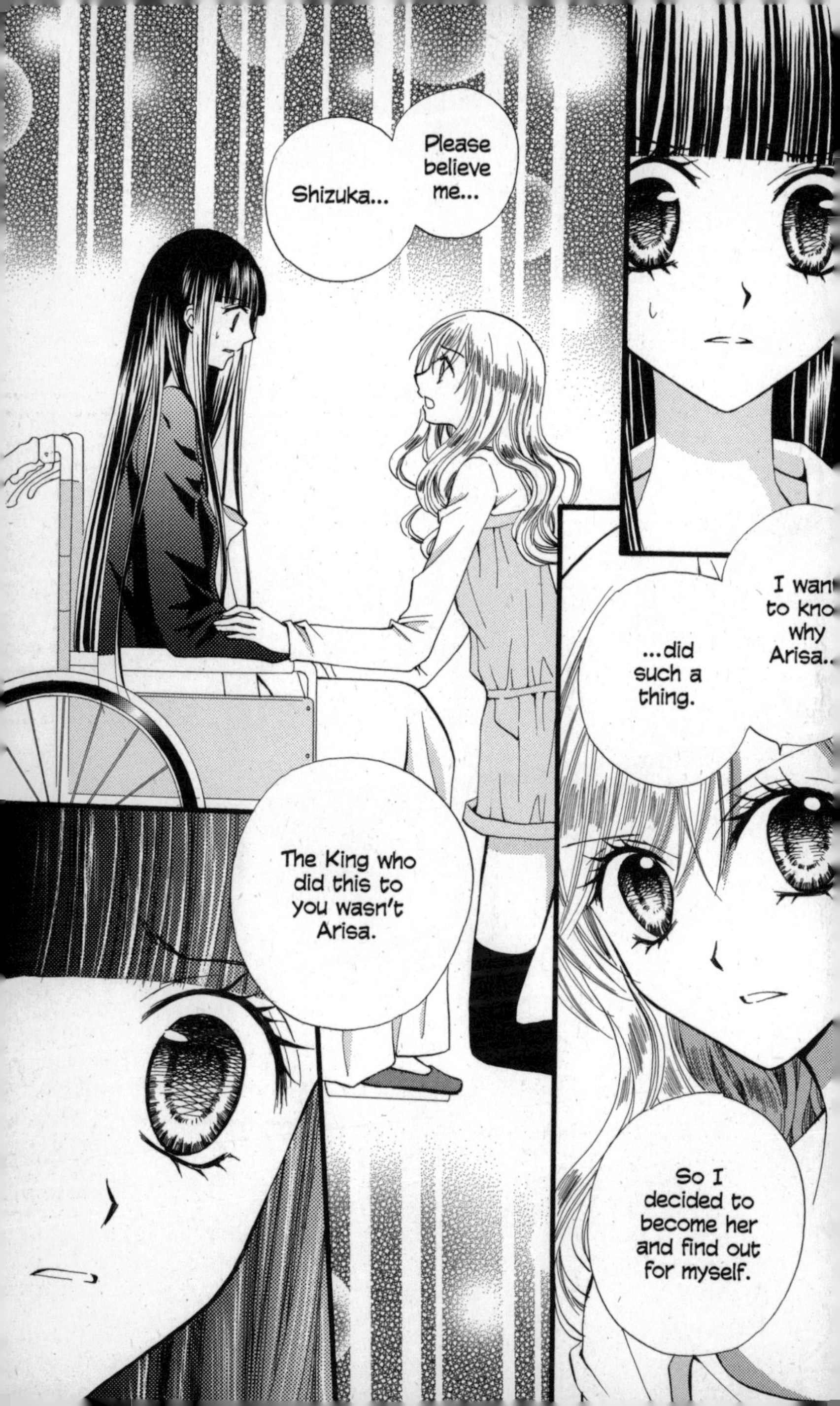
Please believe me...
Shizuka...
The King who did this to you wasn't Arisa.
I wan to kno why Arisa..
...did such a thing.
So I decided to become her and find out for myself.

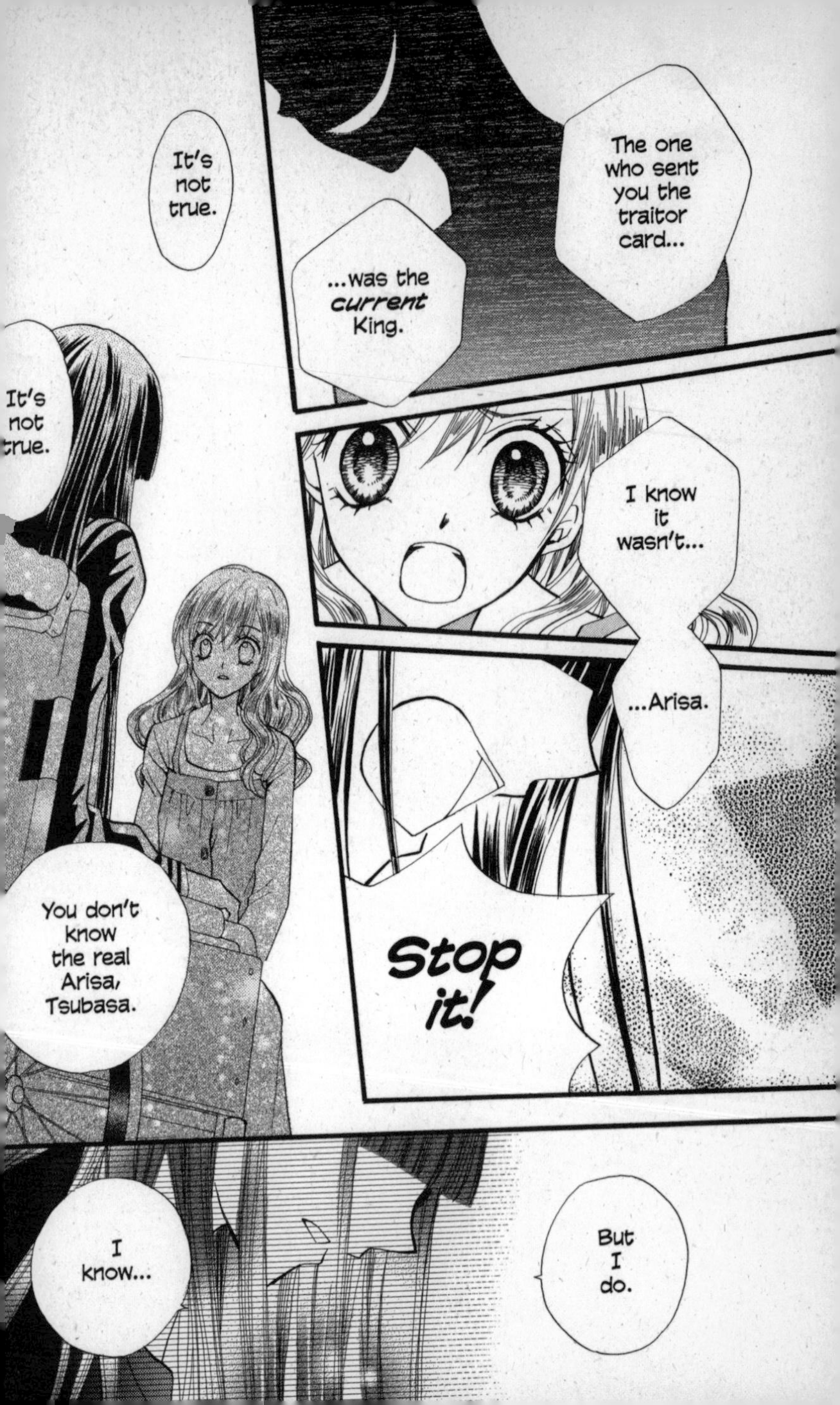

The one who sent you the traitor card...
...was the *current* King.
I know it wasn't...
...Arisa.
Stop it!
It's not true.
It's not true.
You don't know the real Arisa, Tsubasa.
But I do.
I know...

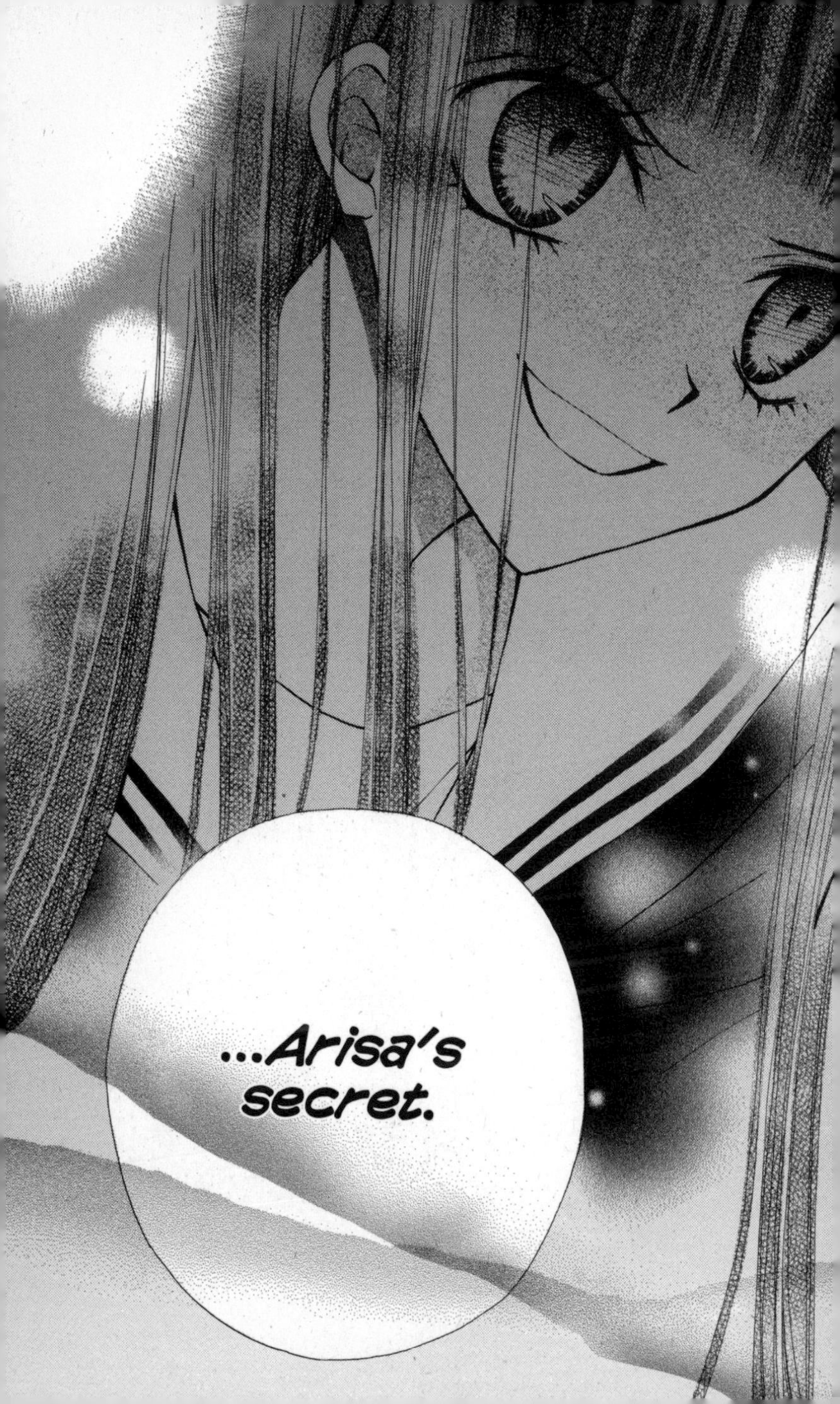
...Arisa's secret.

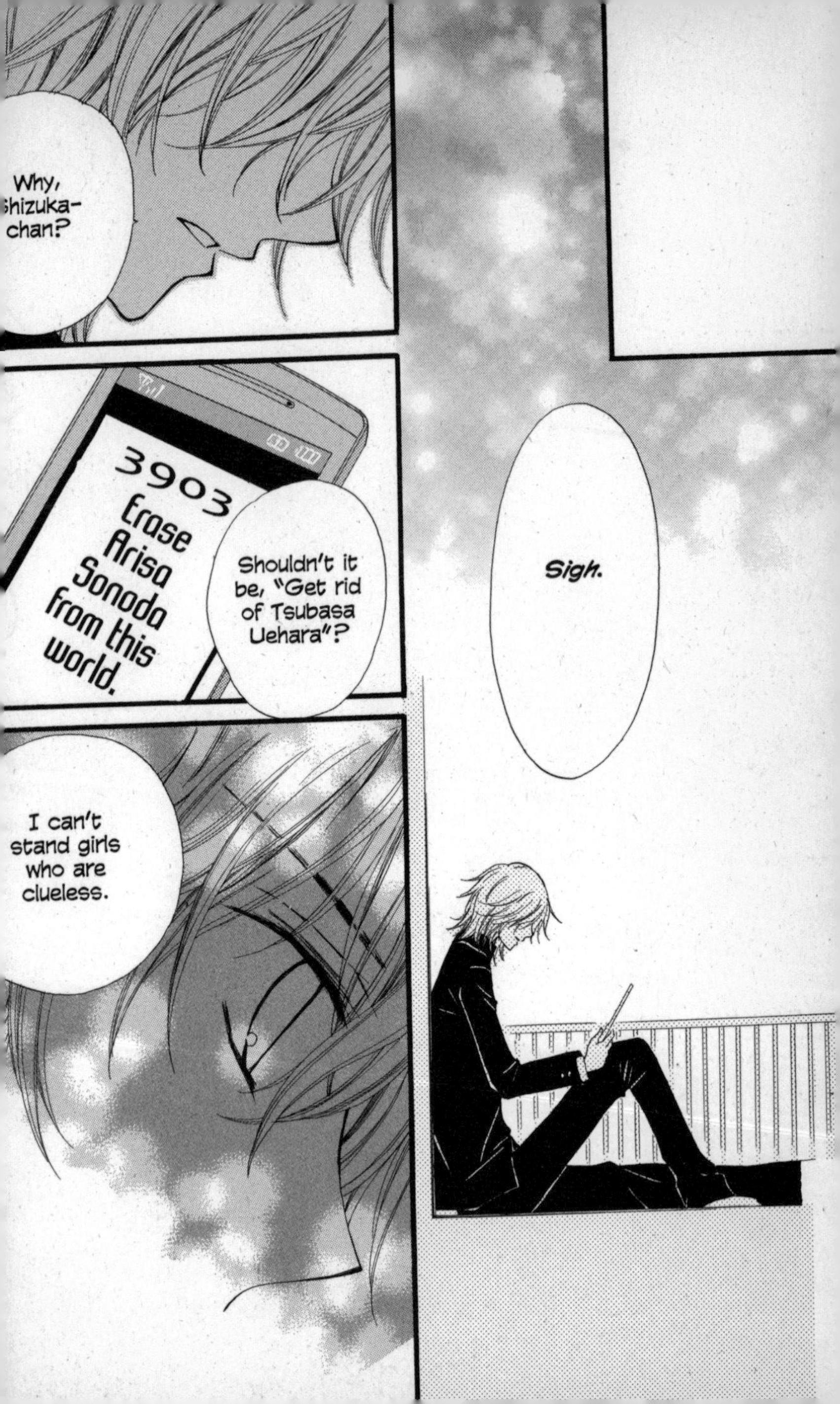
Sigh.
Why, Shizuka-chan?
3903 Erase Arisa Sonoda from this world.
Shouldn't it be, "Get rid of Tsubasa Uehara"?
I can't stand girls who are clueless.

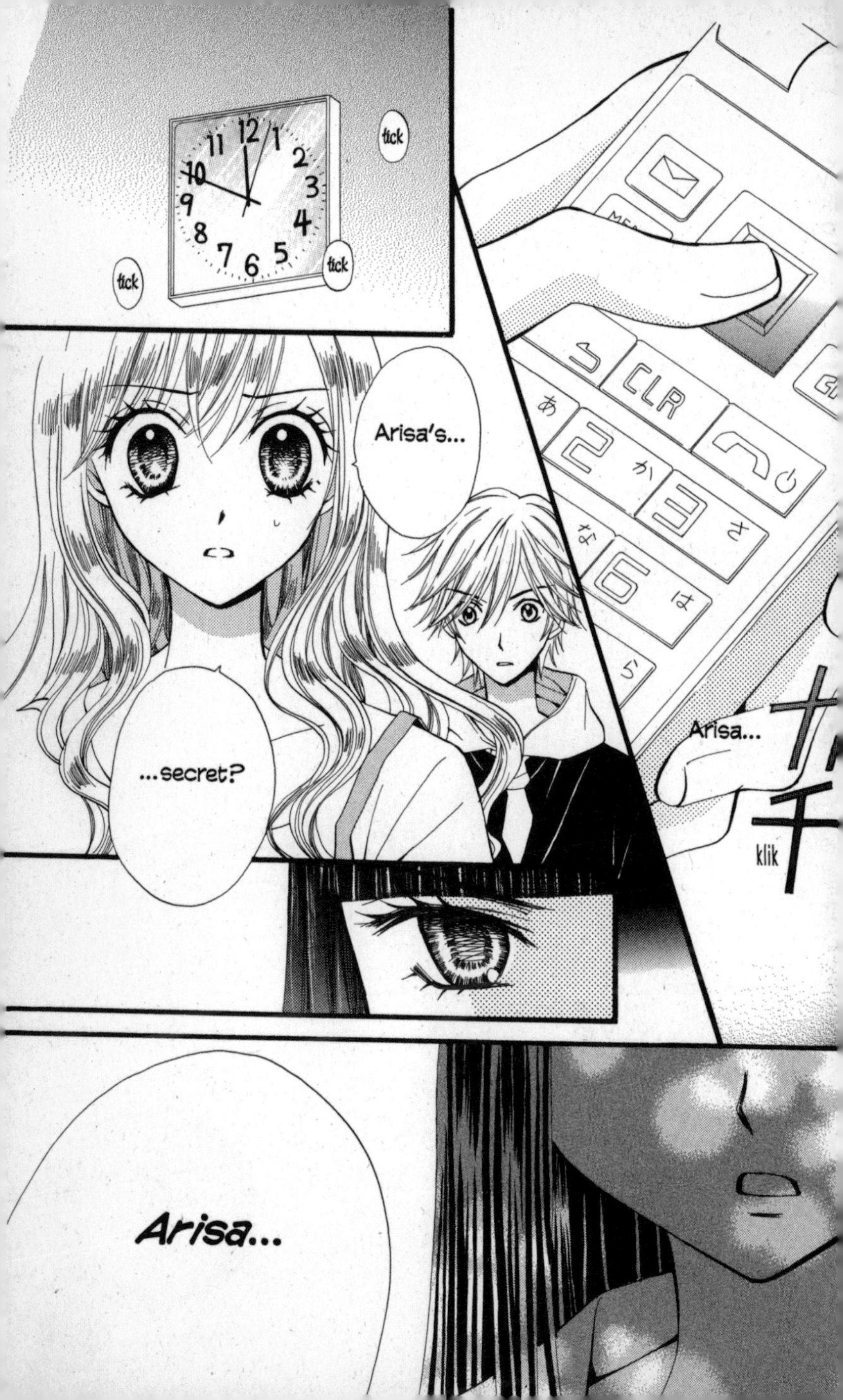
Arisa...
klik
tick
tick
tick
Arisa's...
...secret?
Arisa...

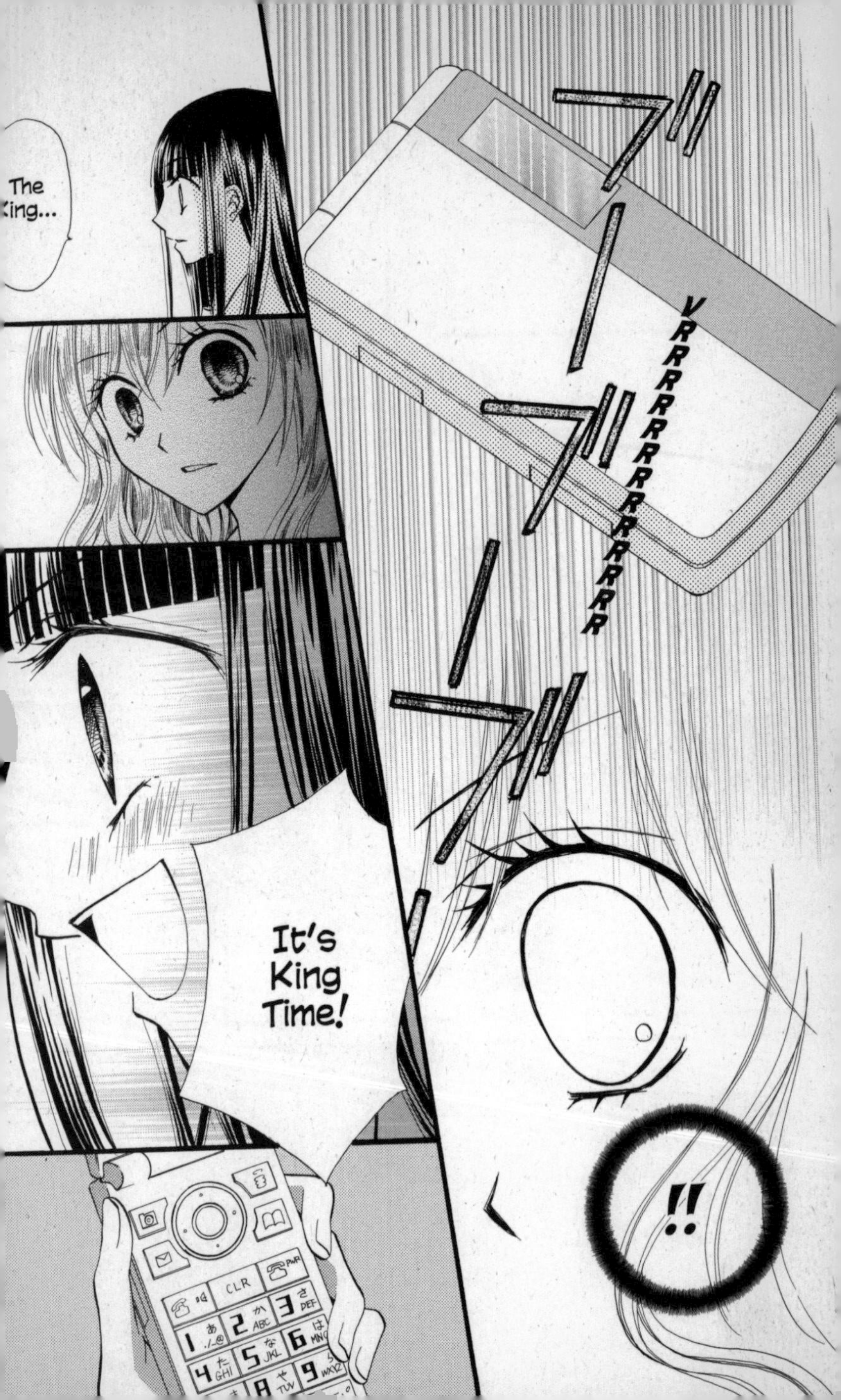
VRRRRRRRRRRRR
!!
The King...
It's King Time!

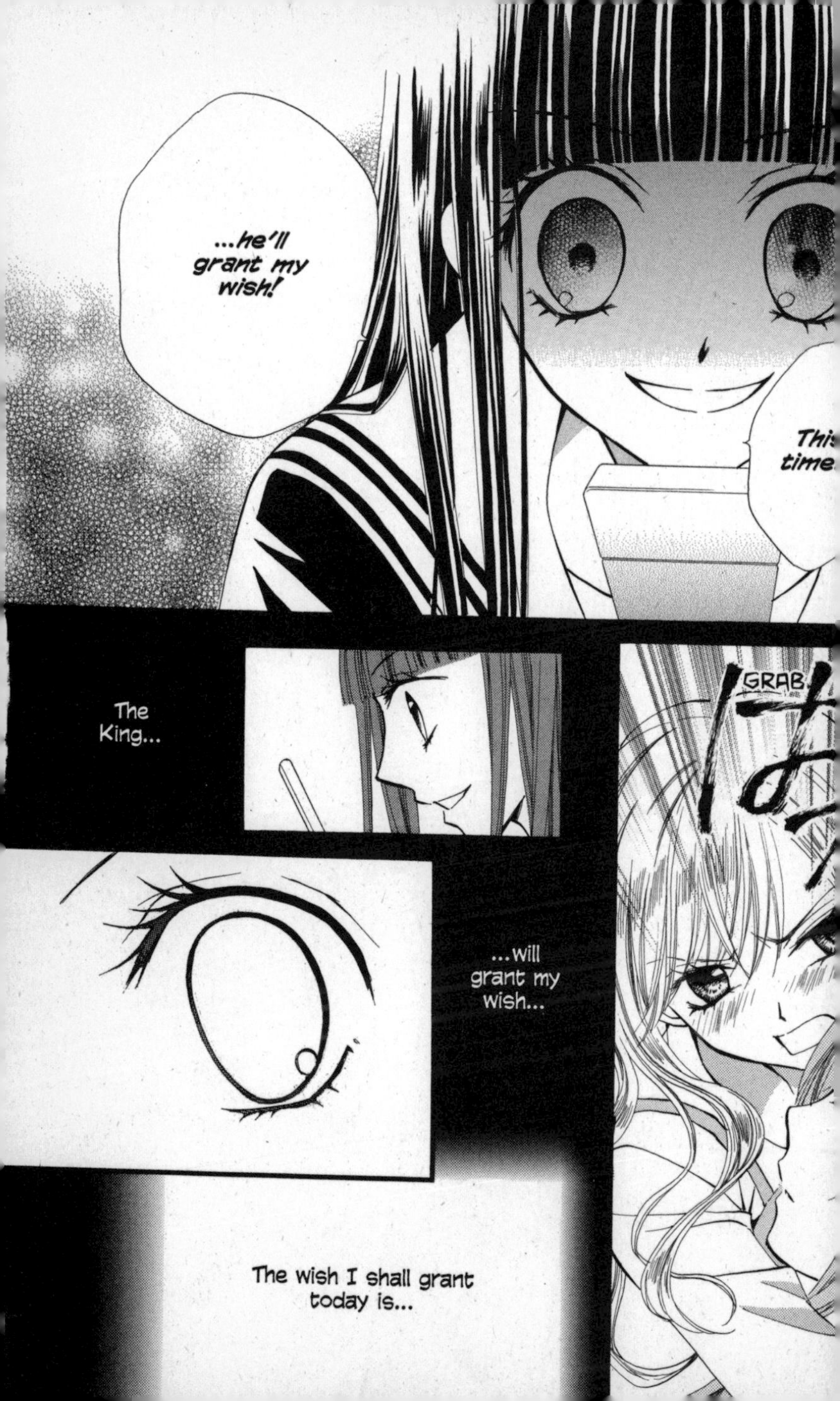

This time
...he'll grant my wish!
GRAB
The King...
...will grant my wish...
The wish I shall grant today is...

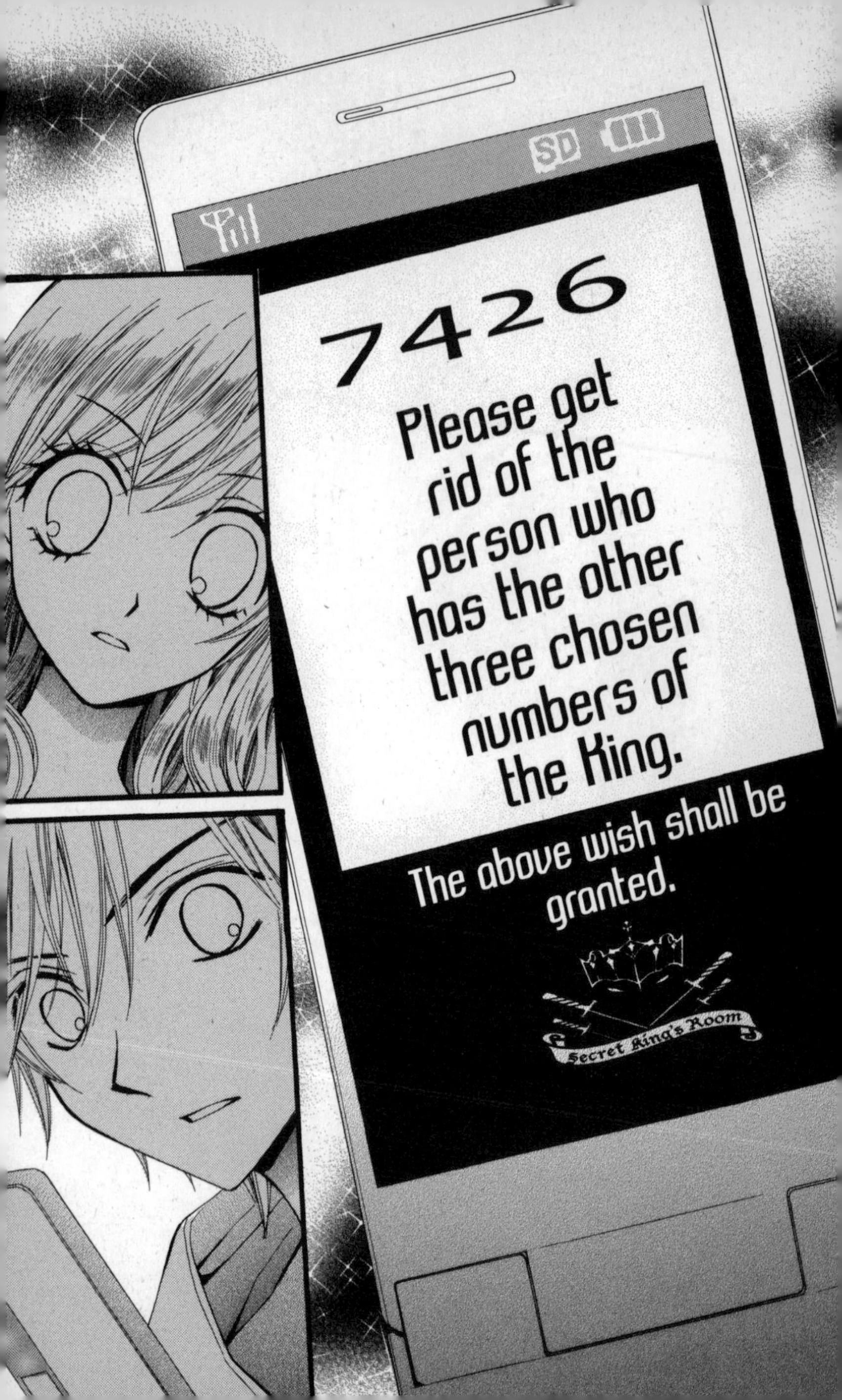

7426
Please get rid of the person who has the other three chosen numbers of the King.
The above wish shall be granted.
Secret King's Room

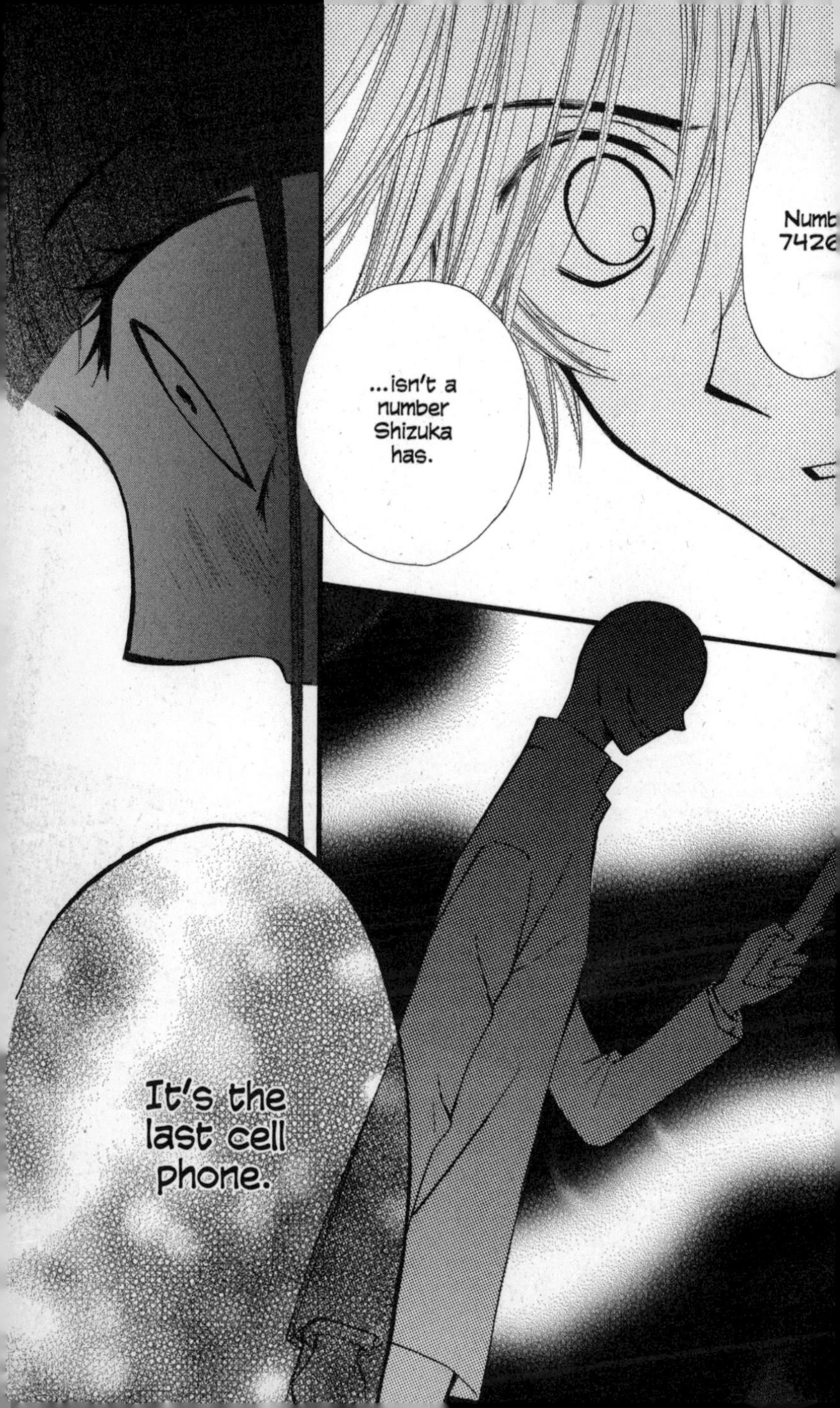
Numb
7426
...isn't a number Shizuka has.
It's the last cell phone.

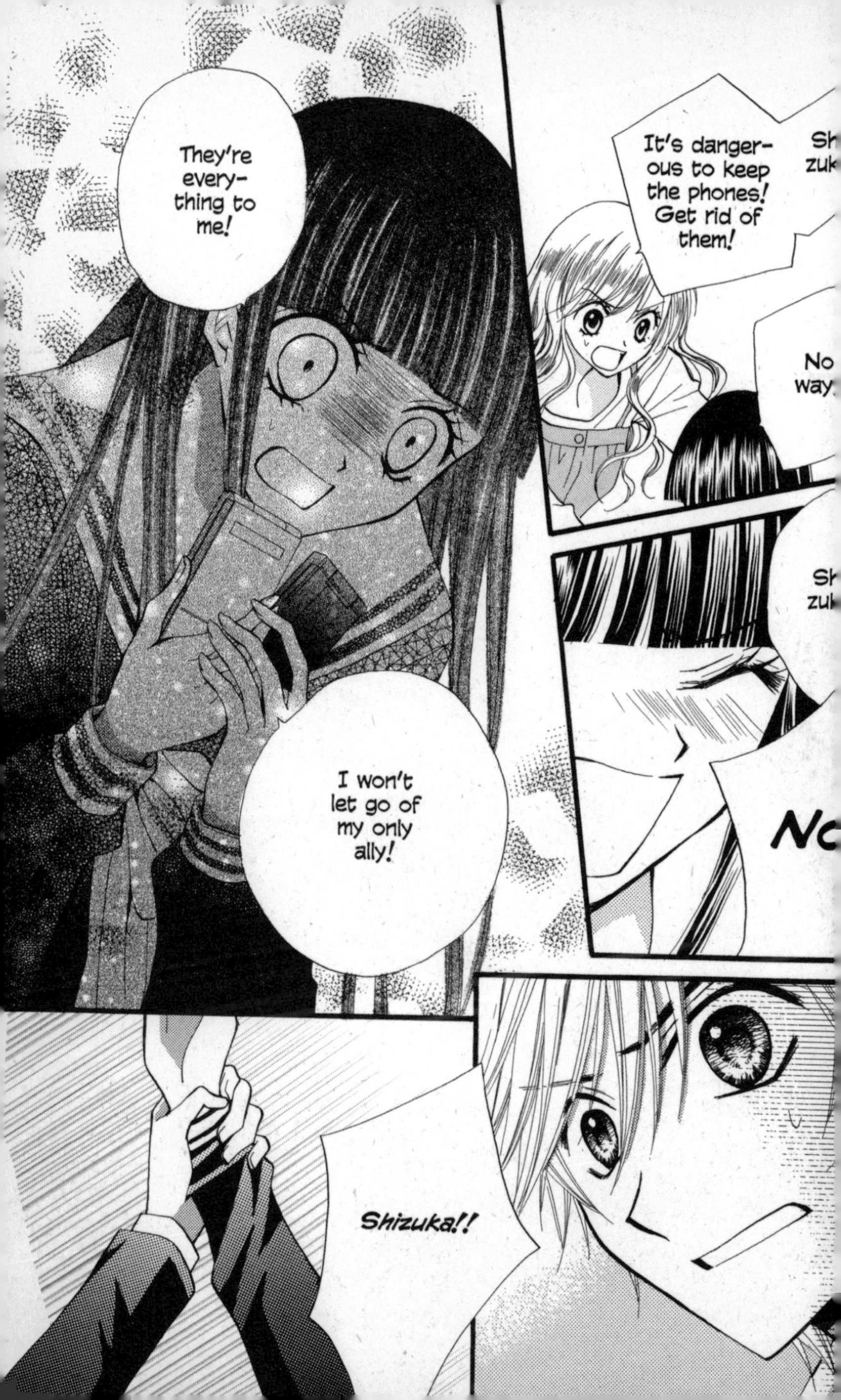
Sh zuk
It's danger-ous to keep the phones! Get rid of them!
No way.
Sh zu
No
They're every-thing to me!
I won't let go of my only ally!
Shizuka!!

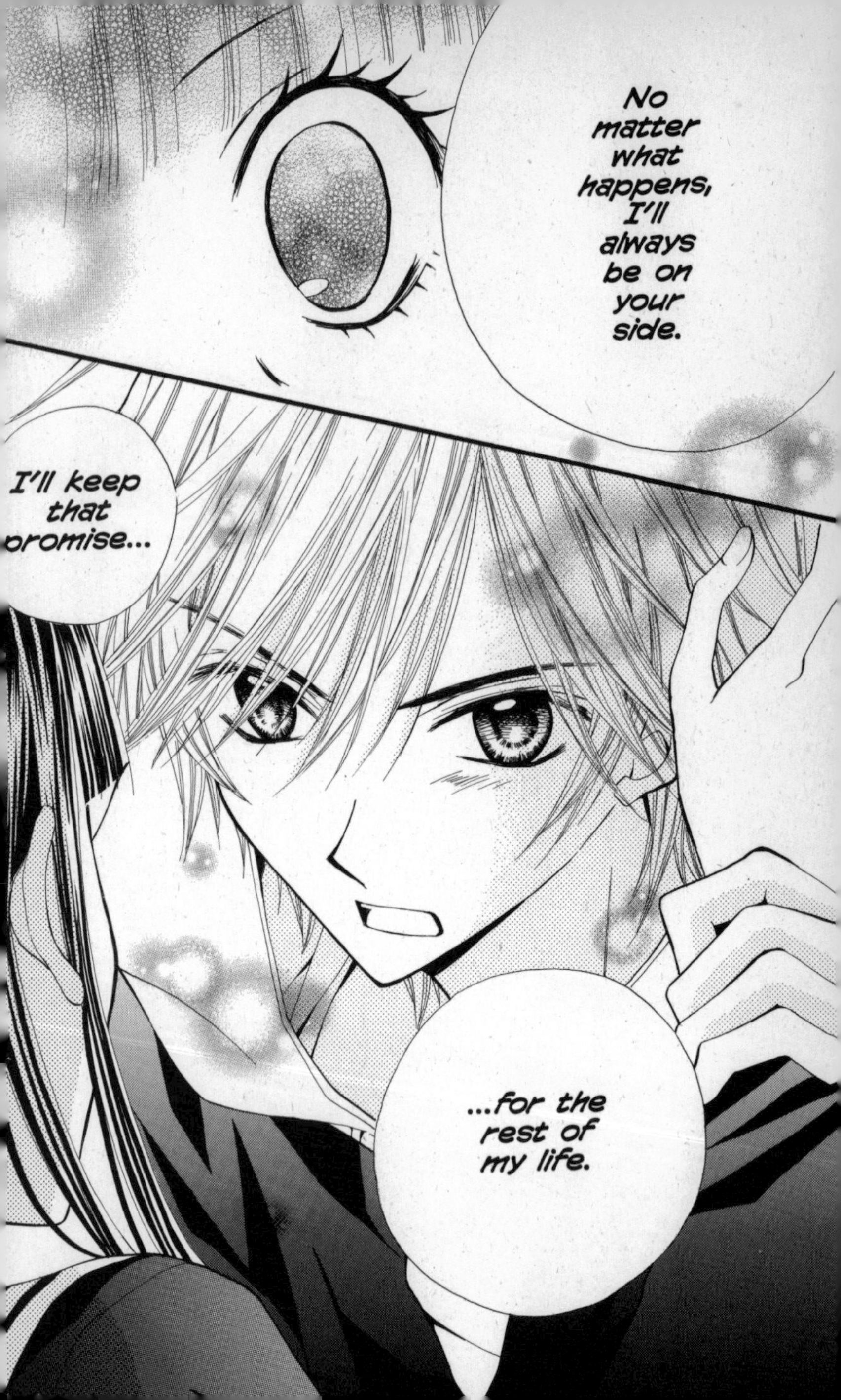
No matter what happens, I'll always be on your side.
I'll keep that promise...
...for the rest of my life.

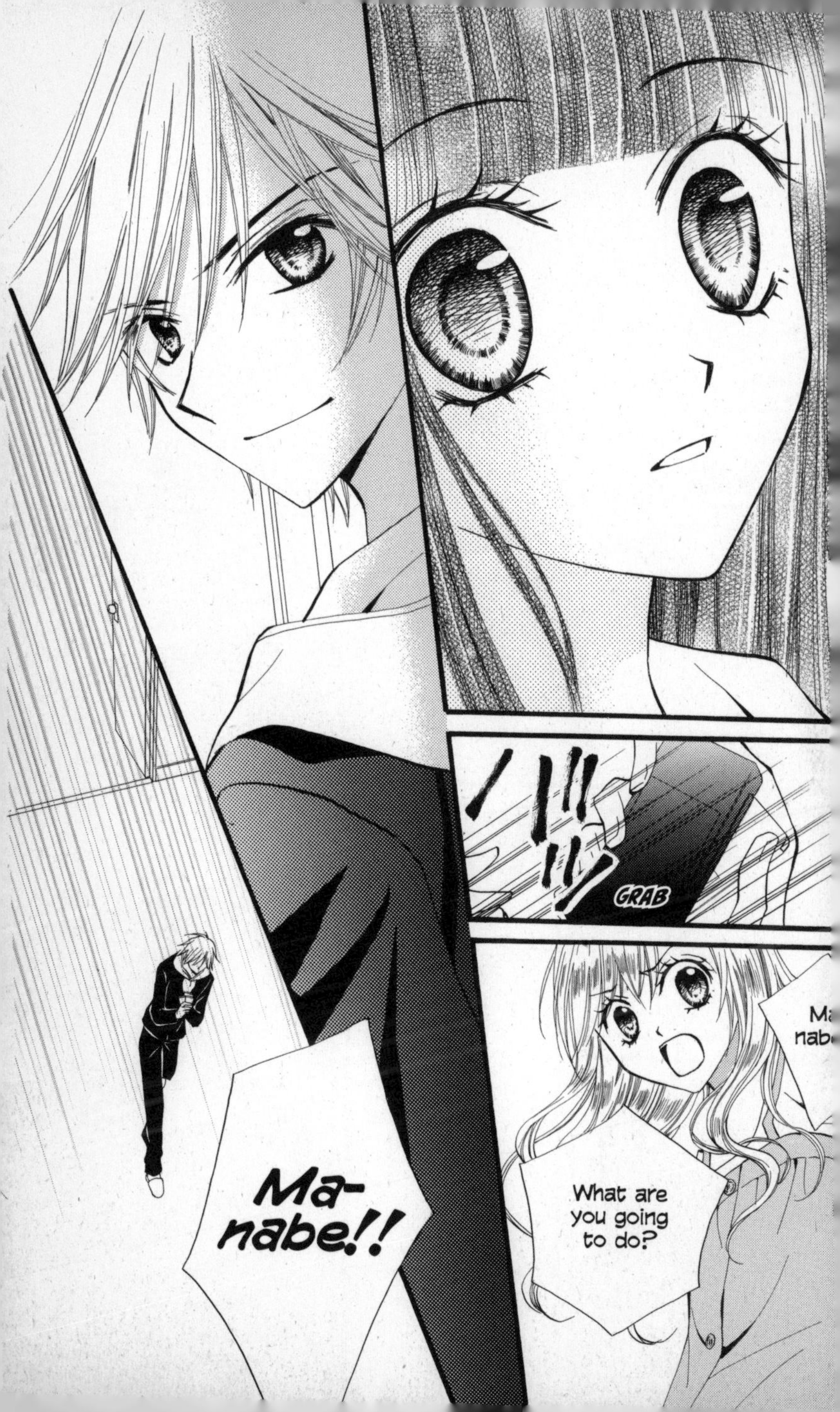
GRAB
Ma nabe
What are you going to do?
Ma-nabe!!

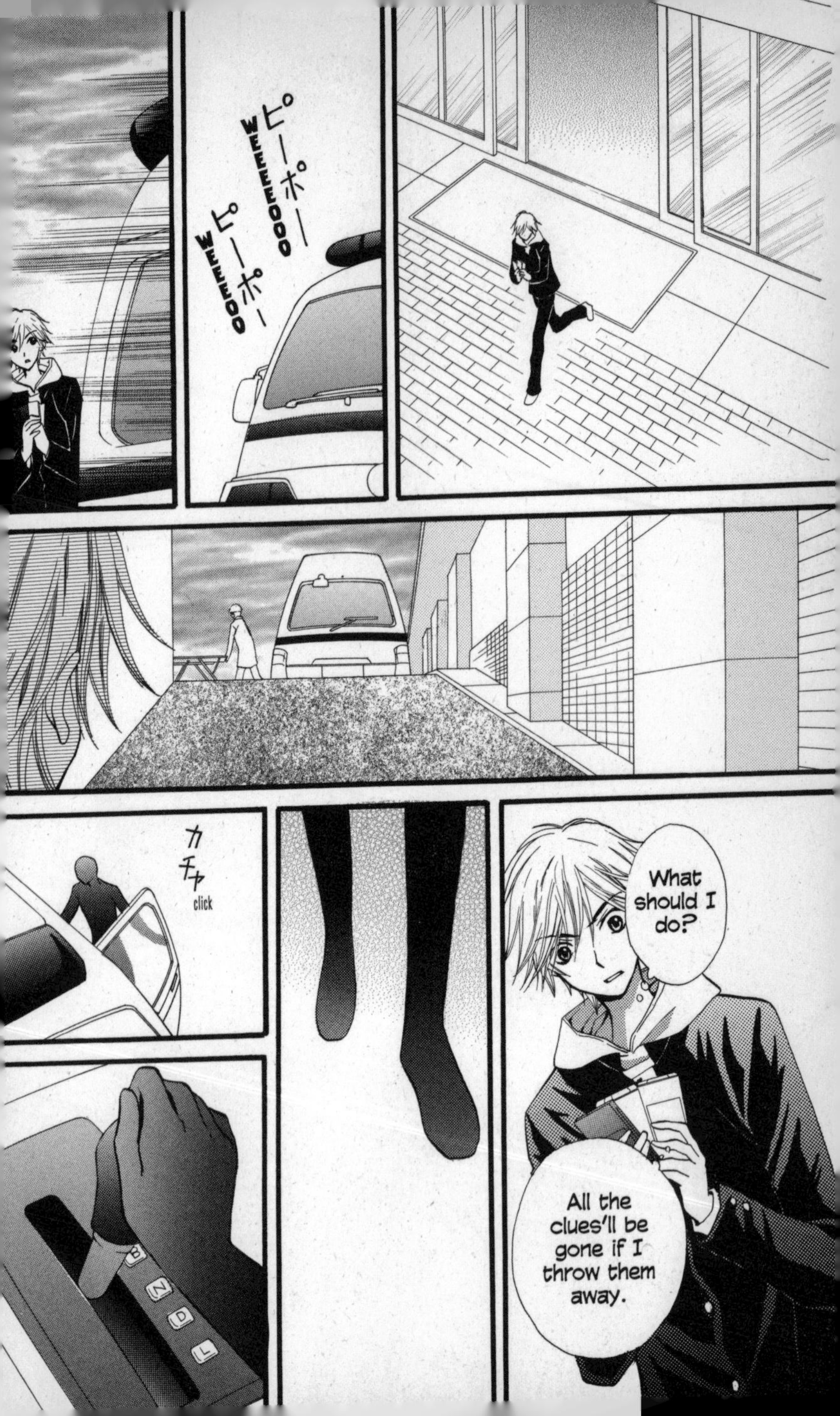

ピーポー WEEEEEOOO
ピーポー WEEEEOO
What should I do?
All the clues'll be gone if I throw them away.
カチャ click

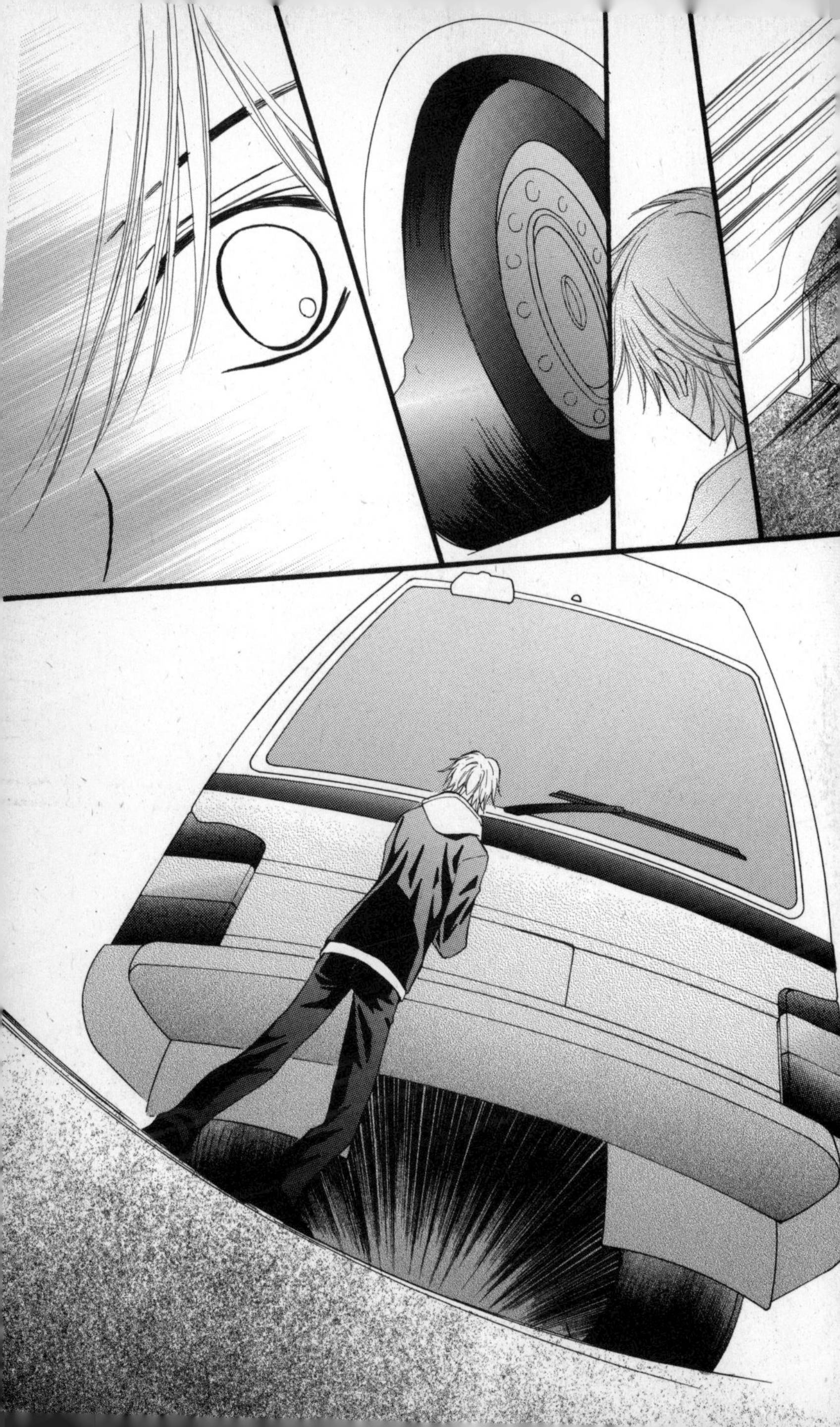

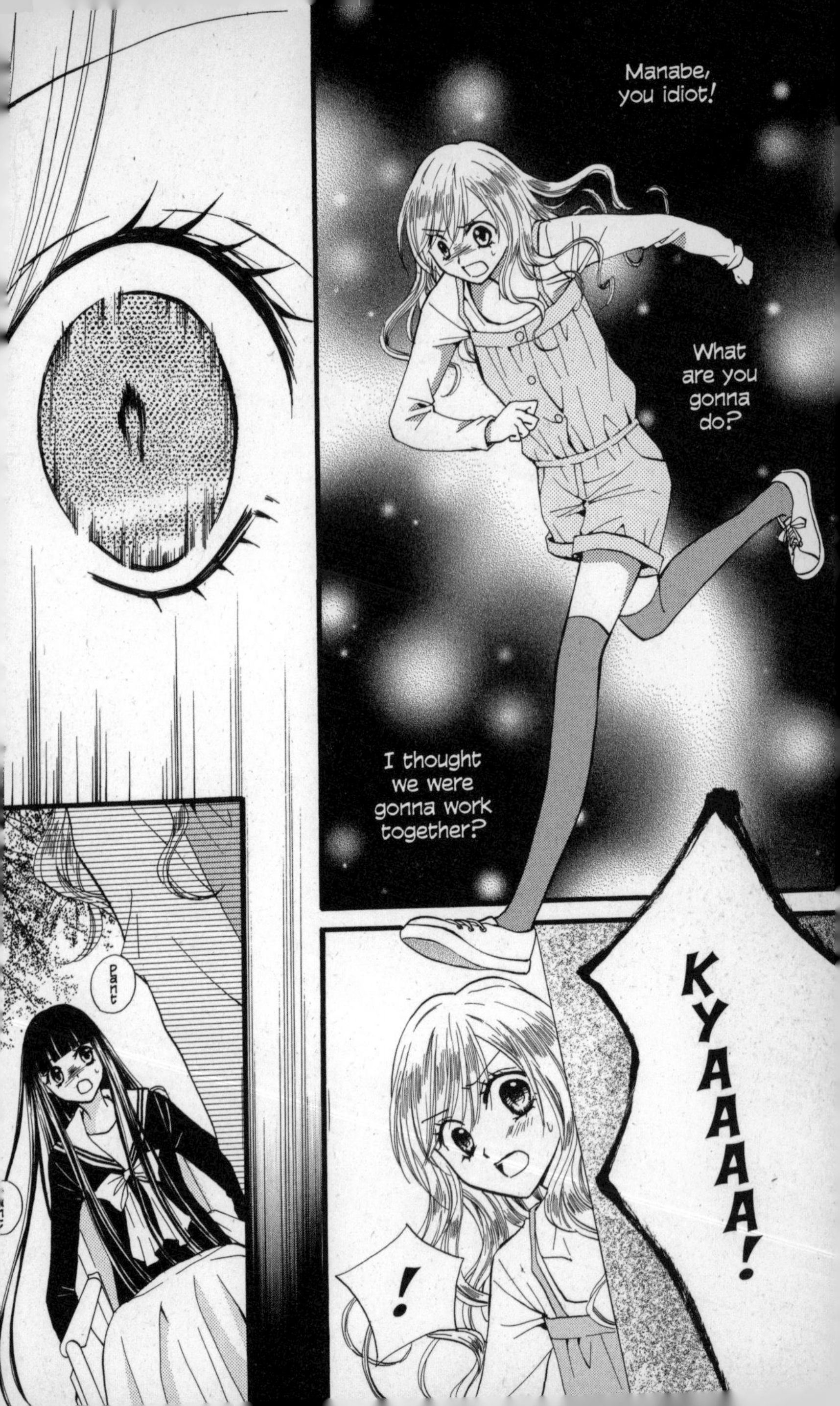

Manabe, you idiot!
What are you gonna do?
I thought we were gonna work together?
KYAAAA!
!
pant

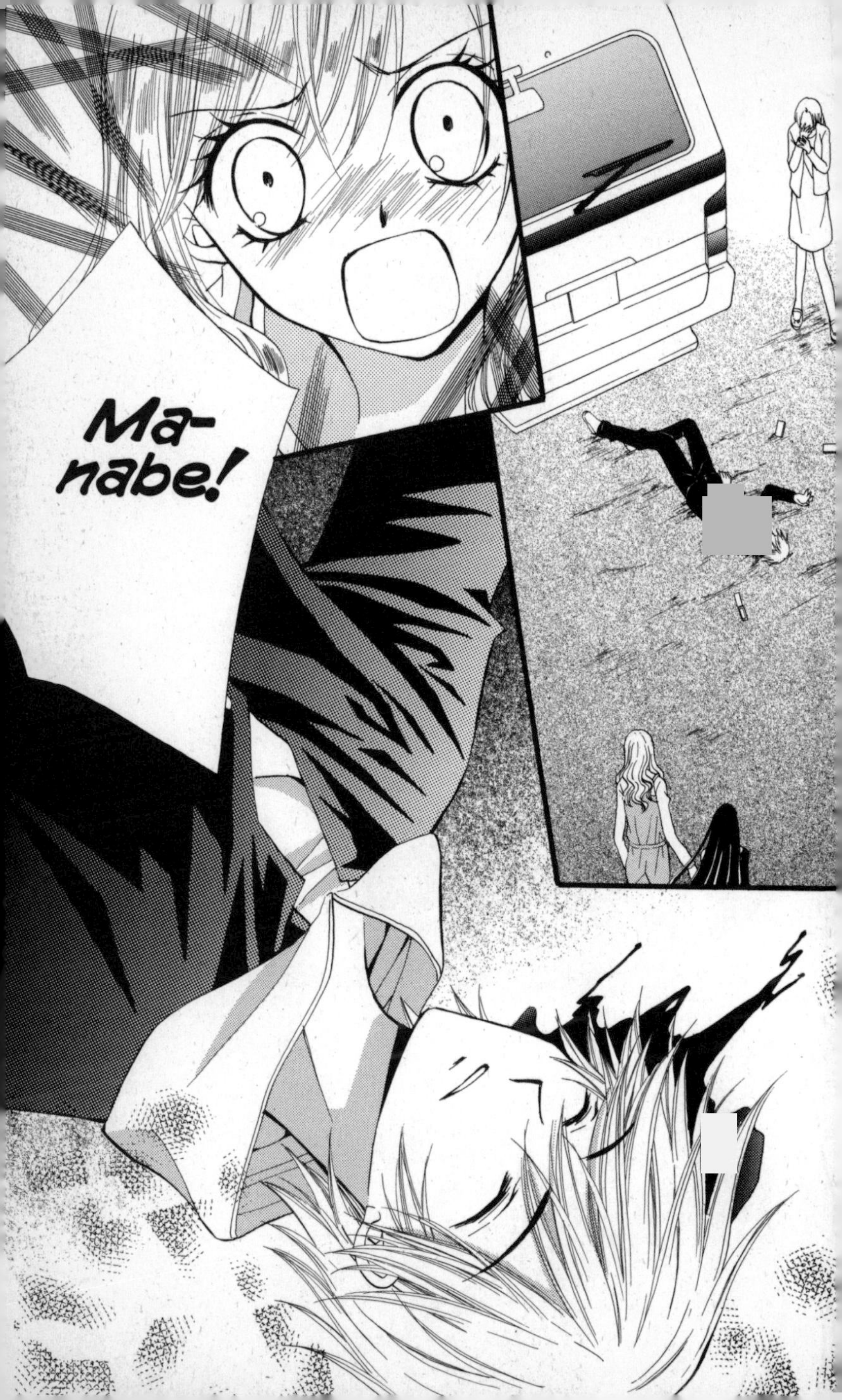
Ma-nabe!

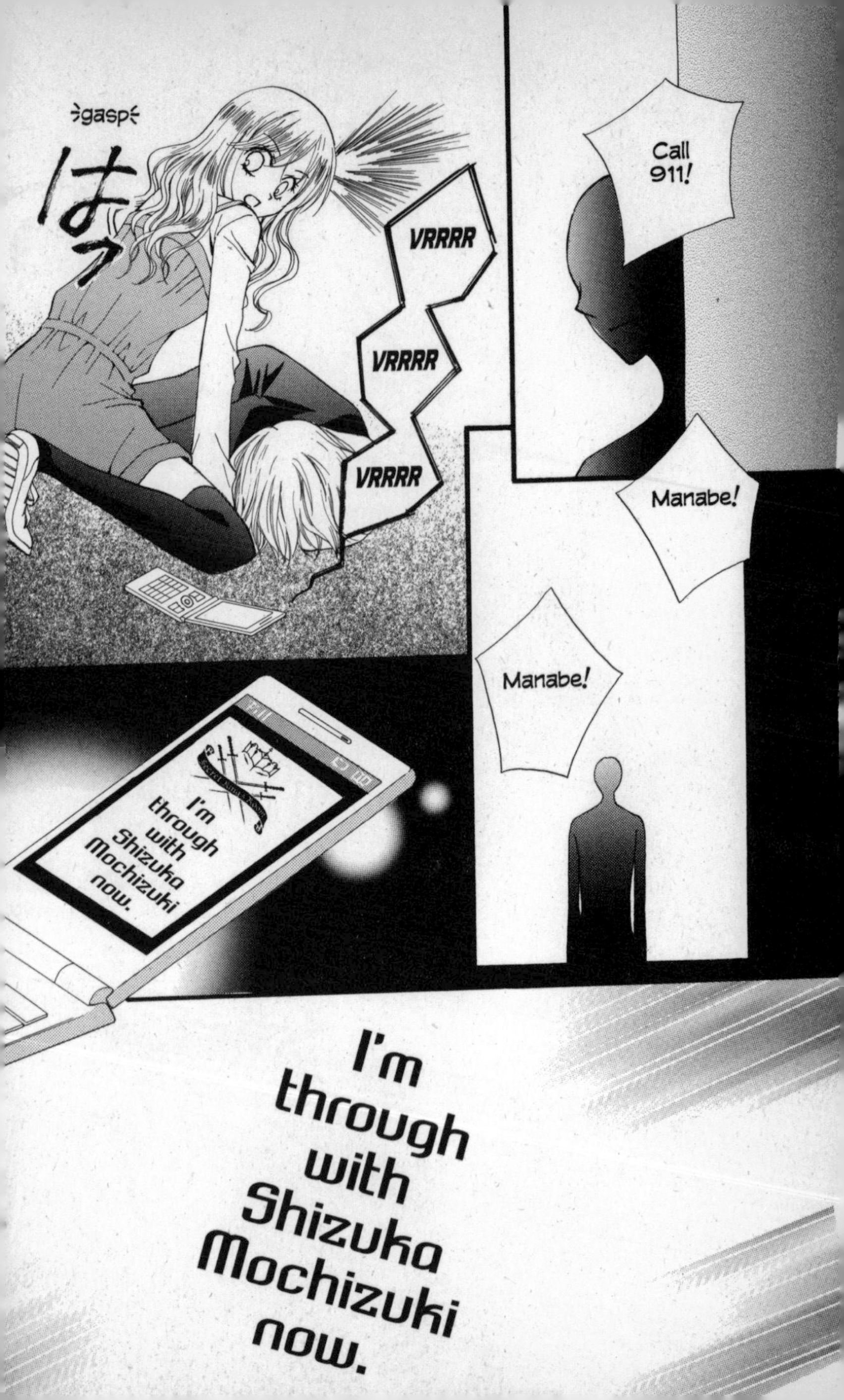
Call 911!
gasp
はっ
VRRRR
VRRRR
VRRRR
Manabe!
Manabe!
I'm through with Shizuka Mochizuki now.
I'm through with Shizuka Mochizuki now.

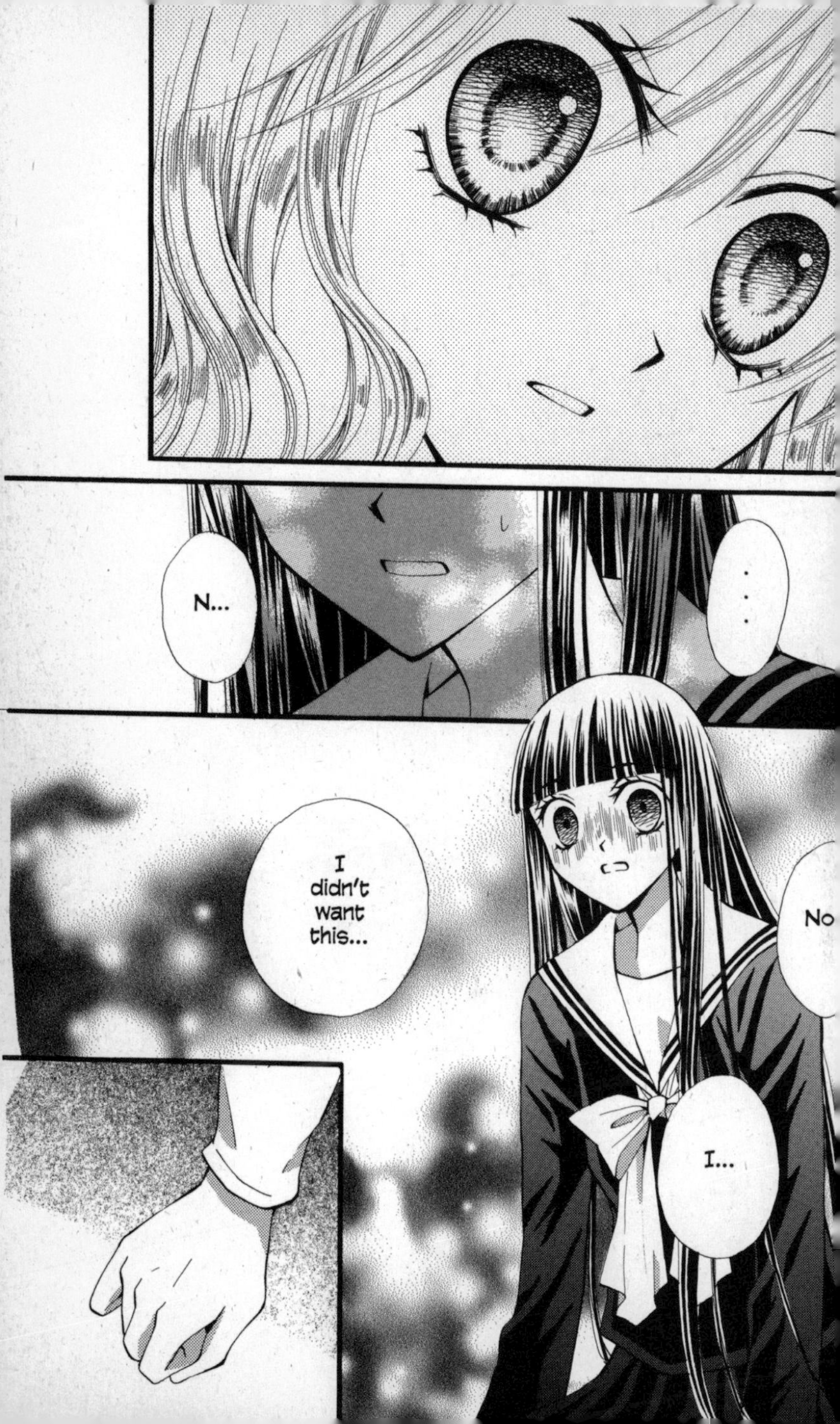

...
N...
No
I didn't want this...
I...

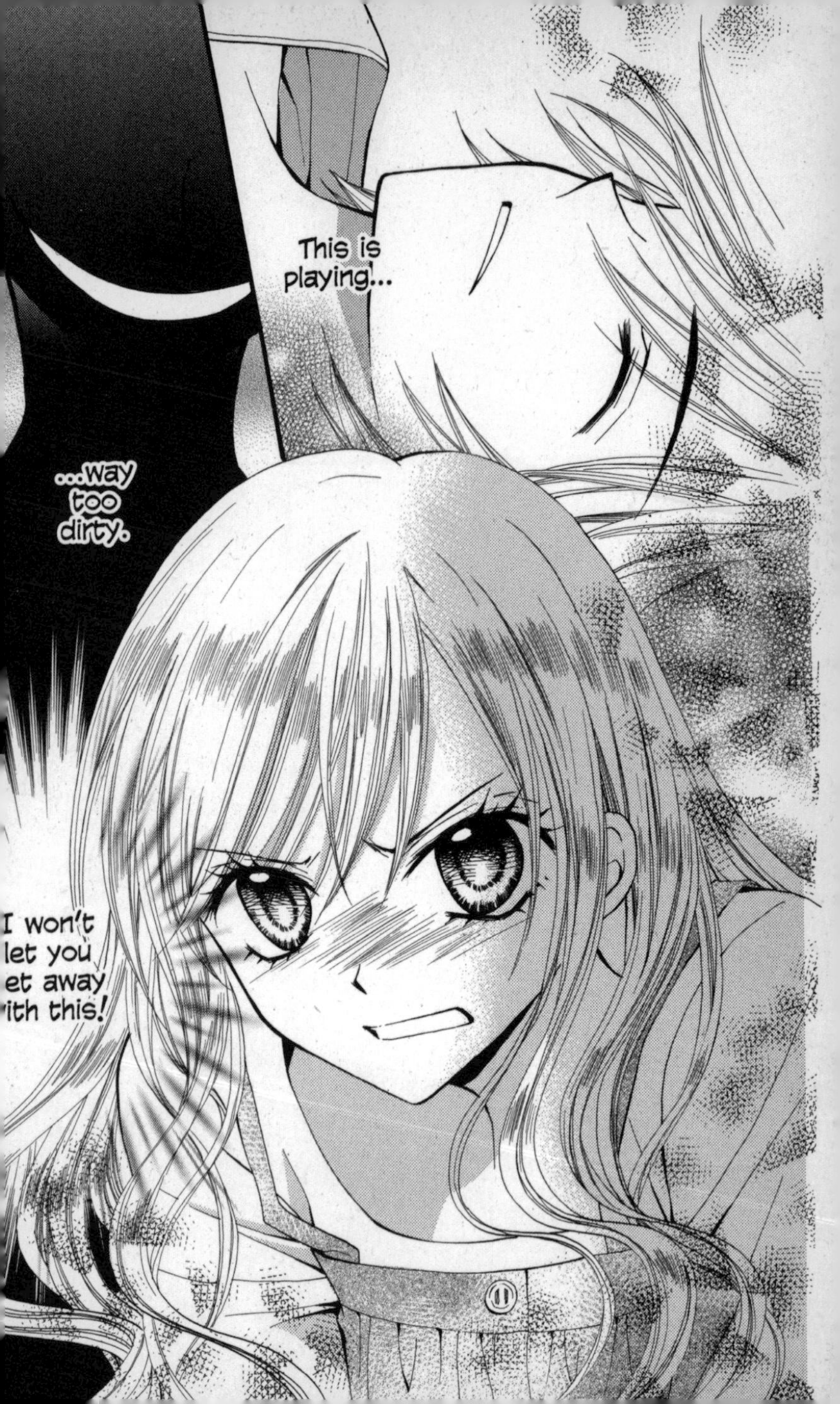
This is playing...
...way too dirty.
I won't let you et away ith this!

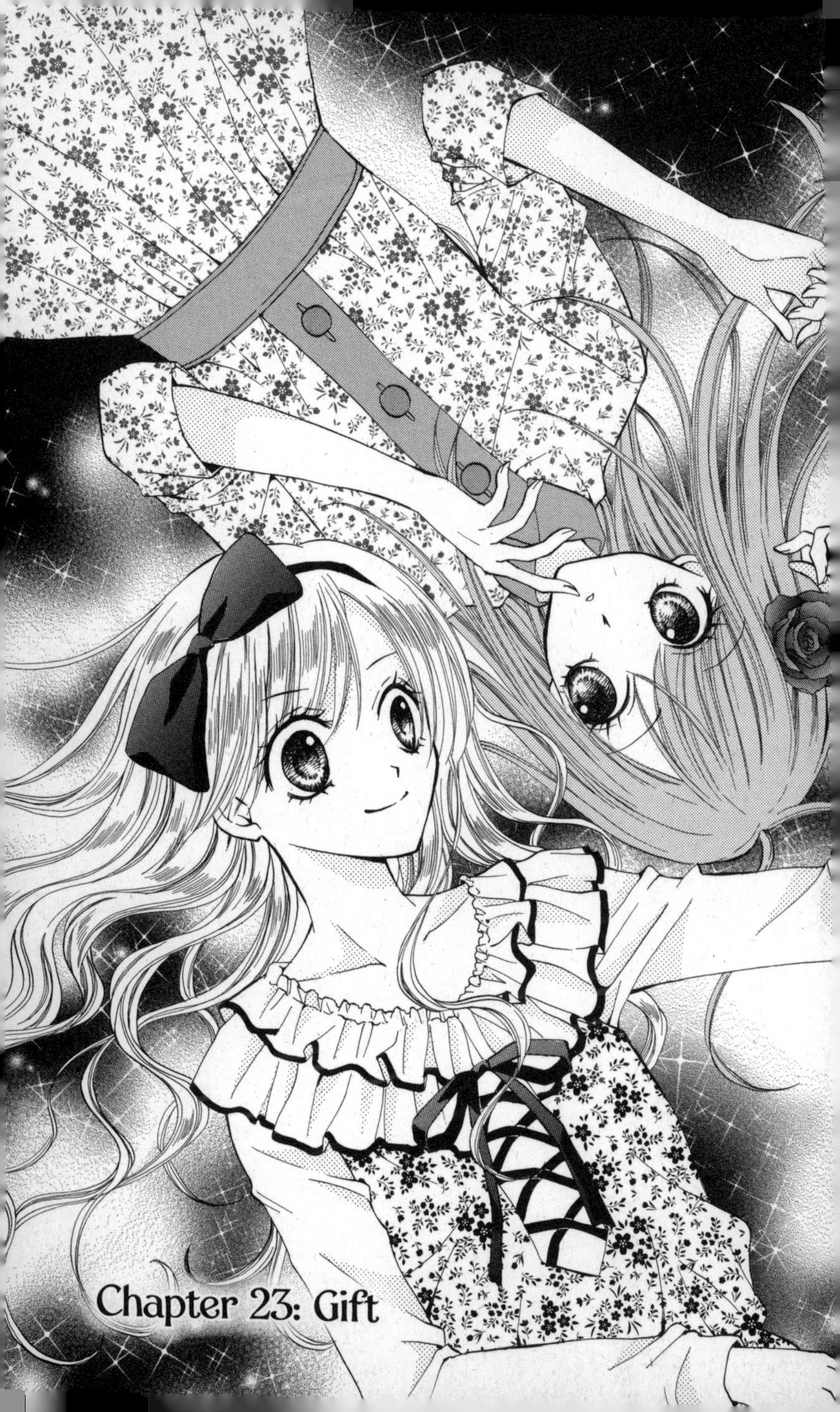
Chapter 23: Gift

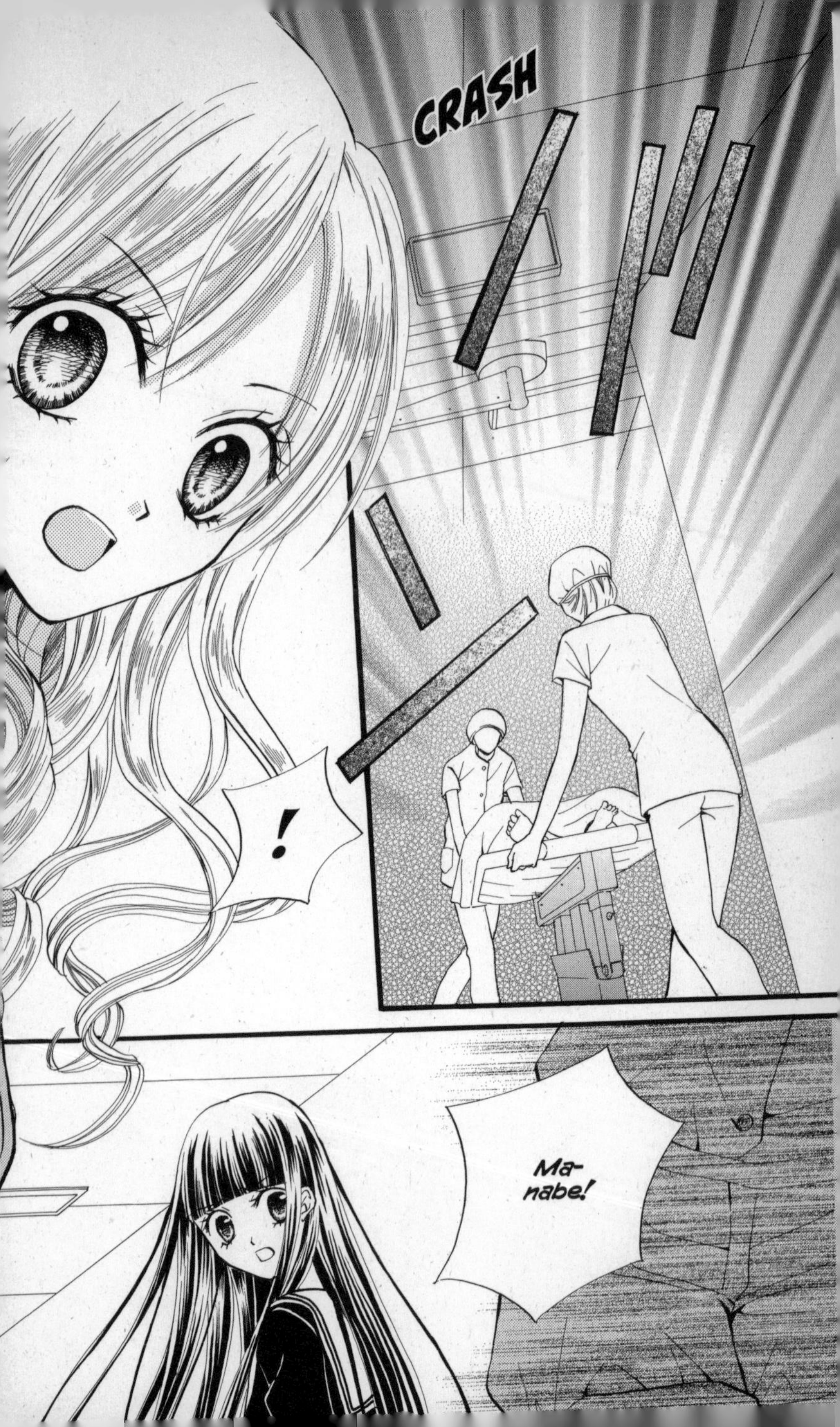
CRASH
!
Ma-nabe!

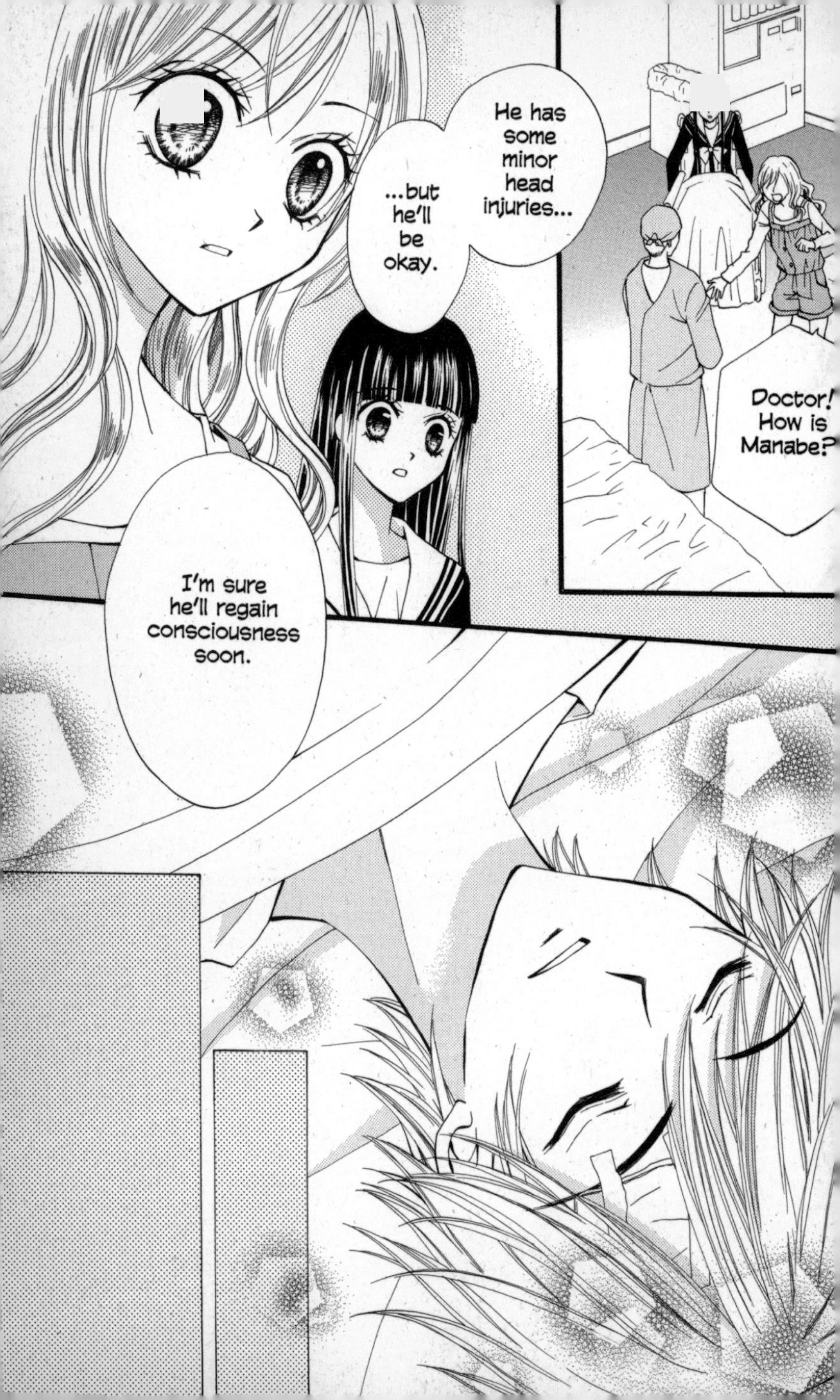

Doctor! How is Manabe?
He has some minor head injuries...
...but he'll be okay.
I'm sure he'll regain consciousness soon.

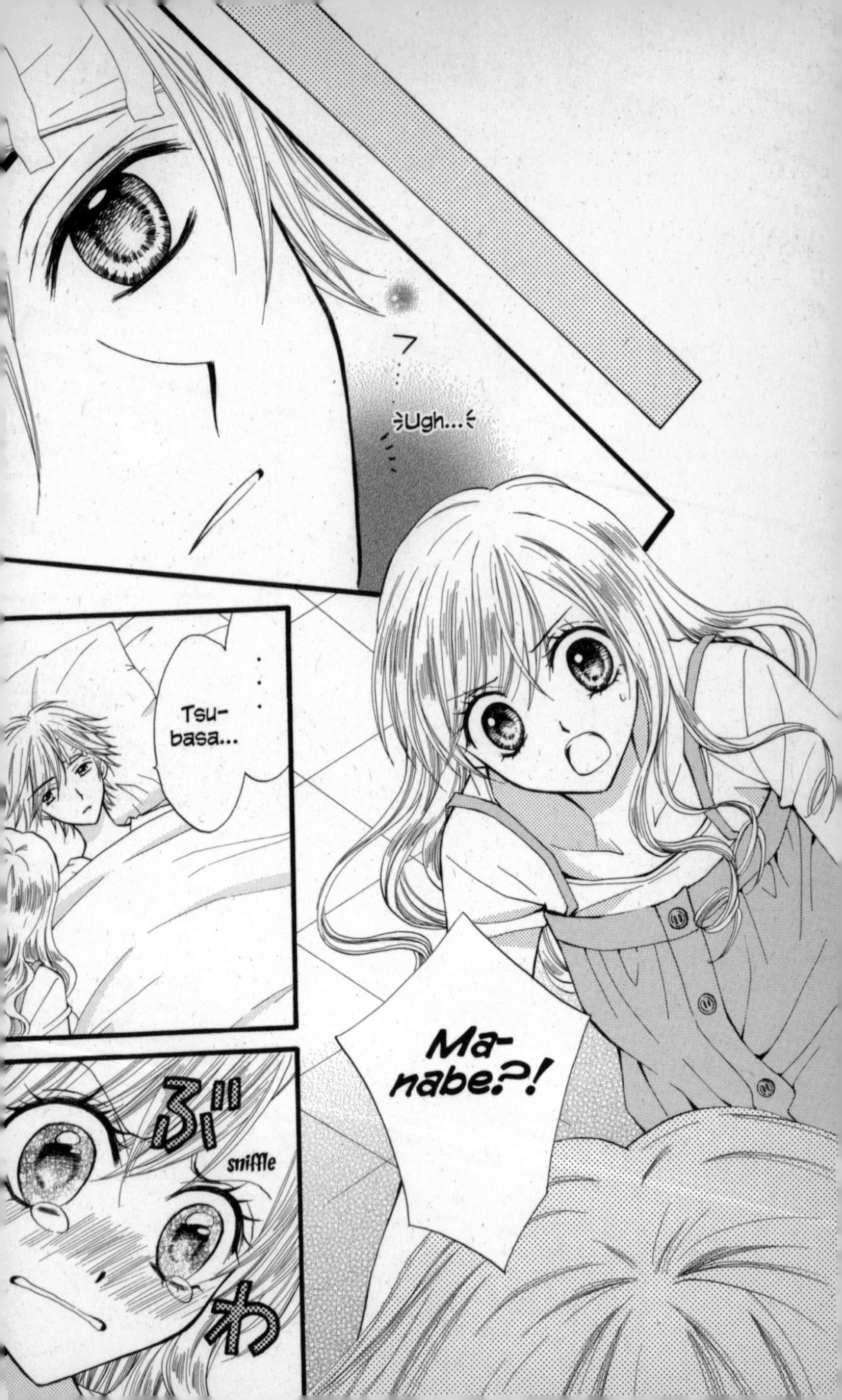

Ugh...
Ma-nabe?!
...
Tsu-basa...
ぶわ
sniffle

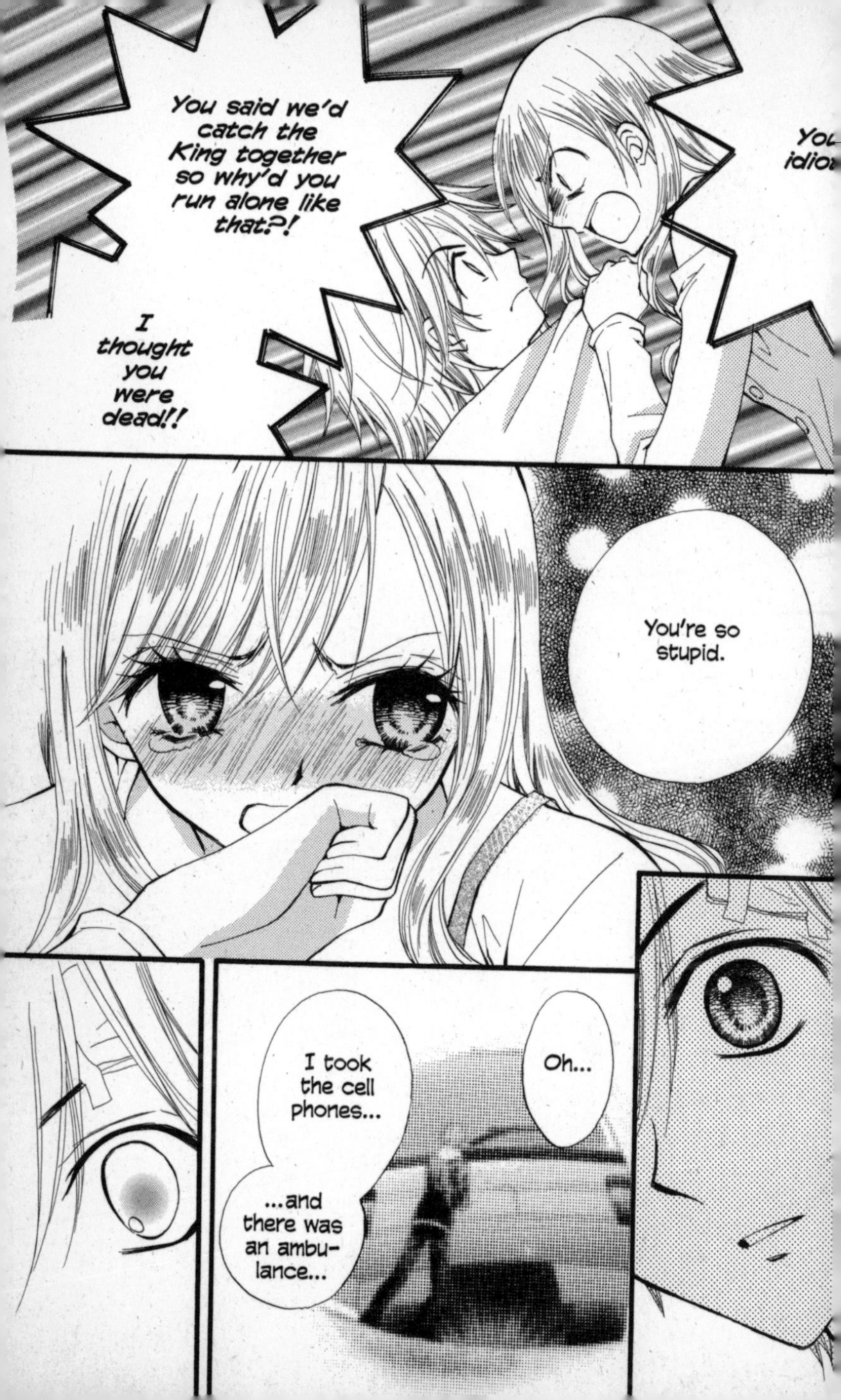
You idio
You said we'd catch the King together so why'd you run alone like that?!
I thought you were dead!!
You're so stupid.
Oh...
I took the cell phones...
...and there was an ambulance...

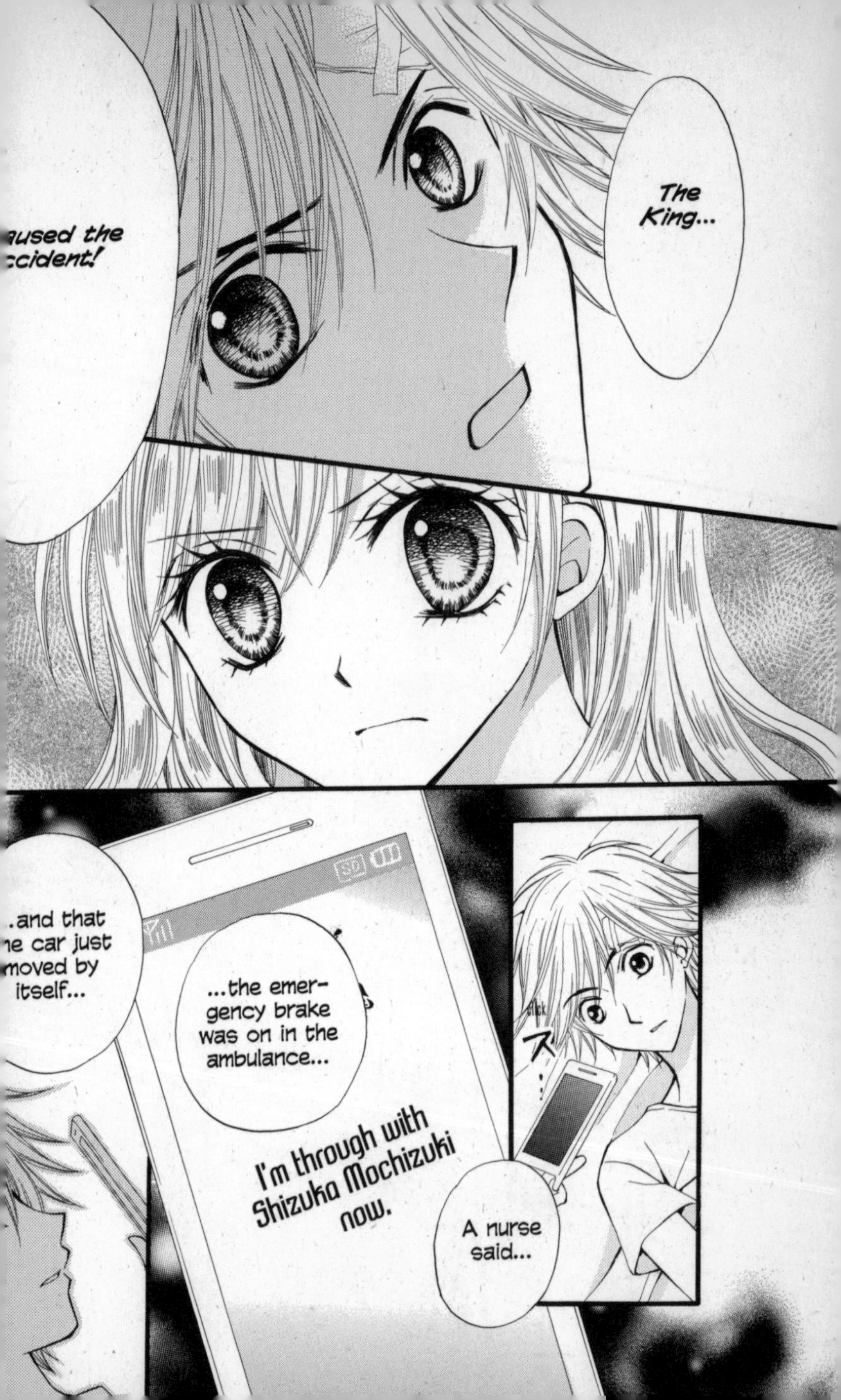

The King...
aused the ccident!
click
A nurse said...
...the emer-gency brake was on in the ambulance...
.and that ne car just moved by itself...
I'm through with Shizuka Mochizuki now.

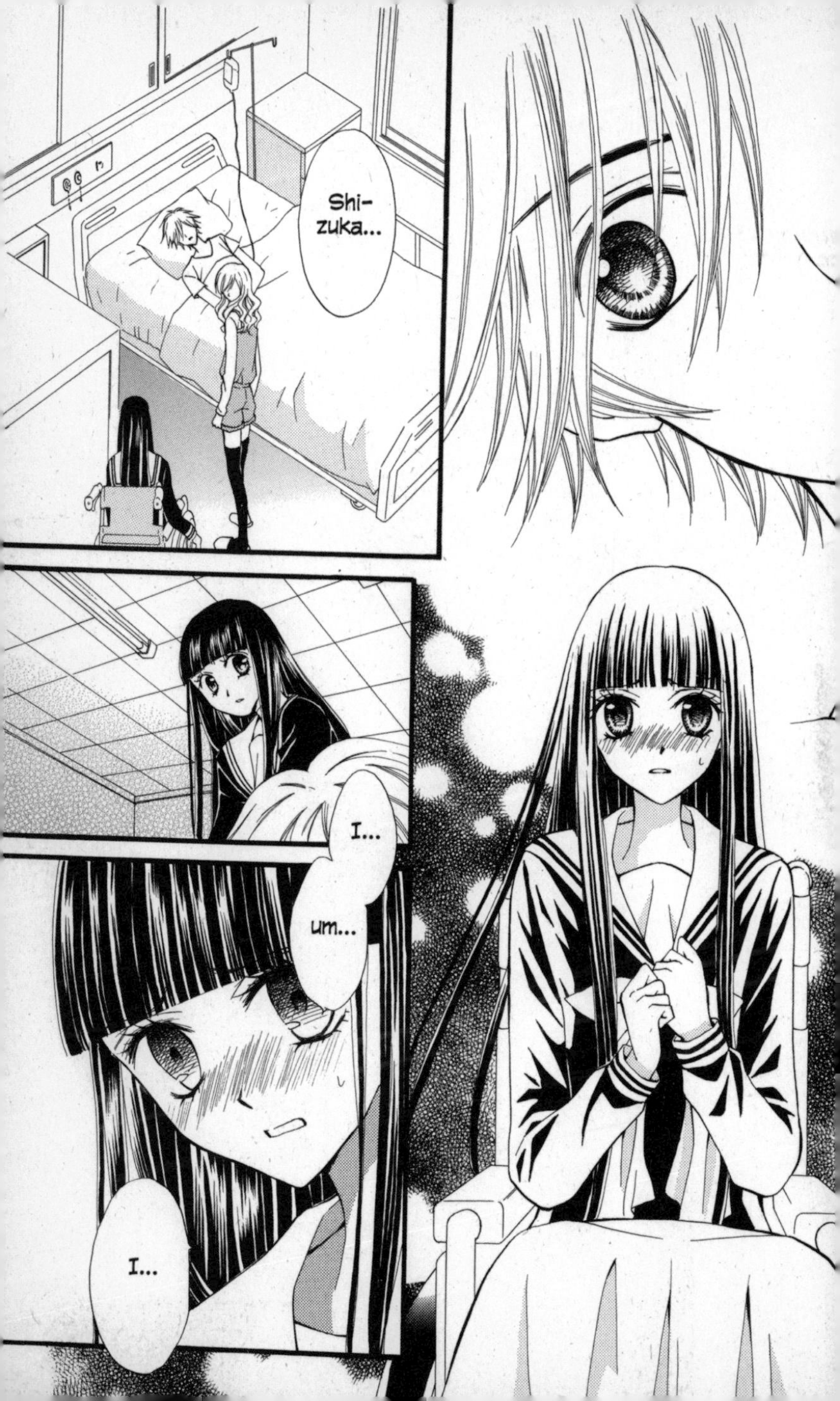
Shi-zuka...
I...
um...
I...

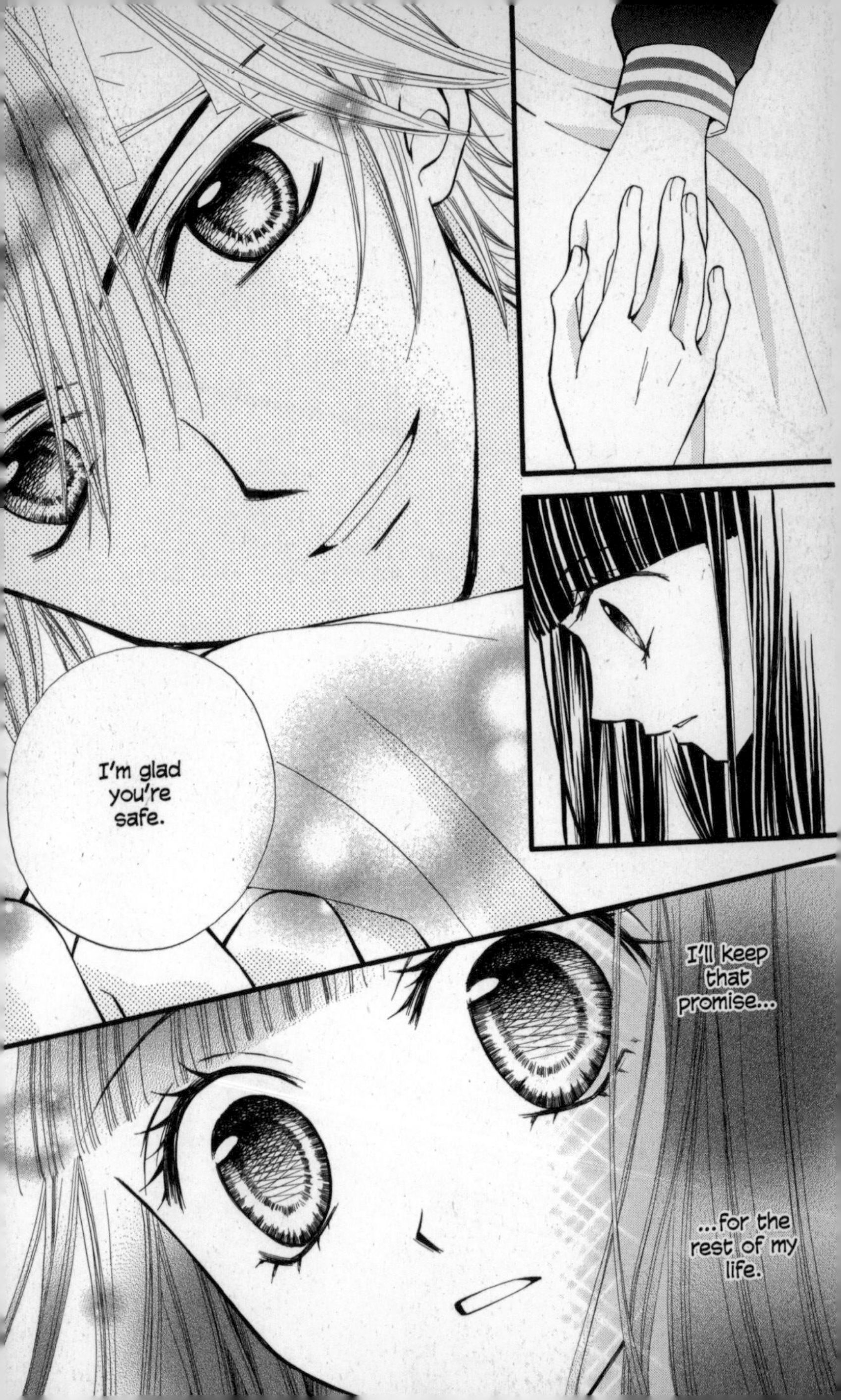
I'm glad you're safe.
I'll keep that promise...
...for the rest of my life.

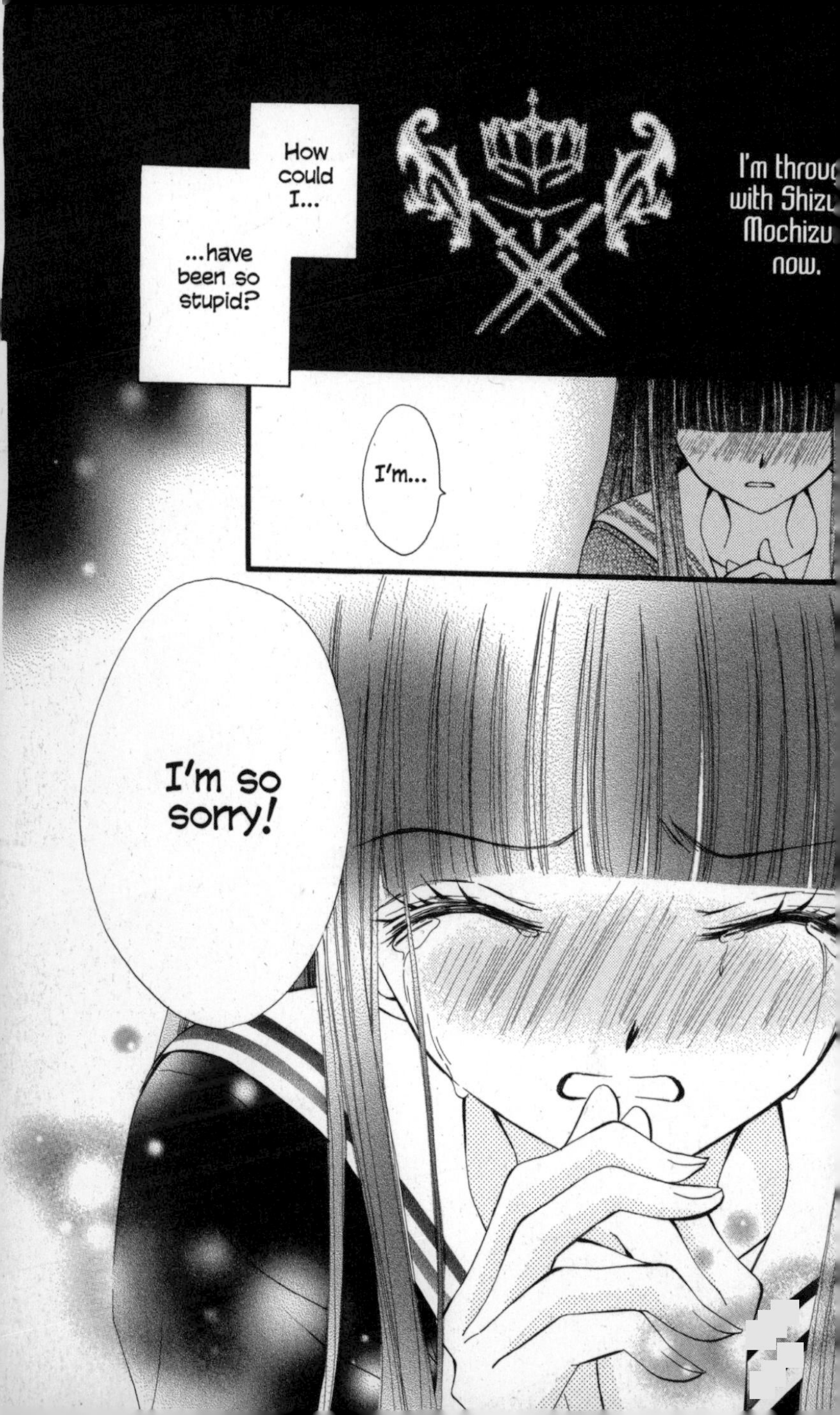
I'm throu
with Shizu
Mochizu
now.
How could I...
...have been so stupid?
I'm...
I'm so sorry!

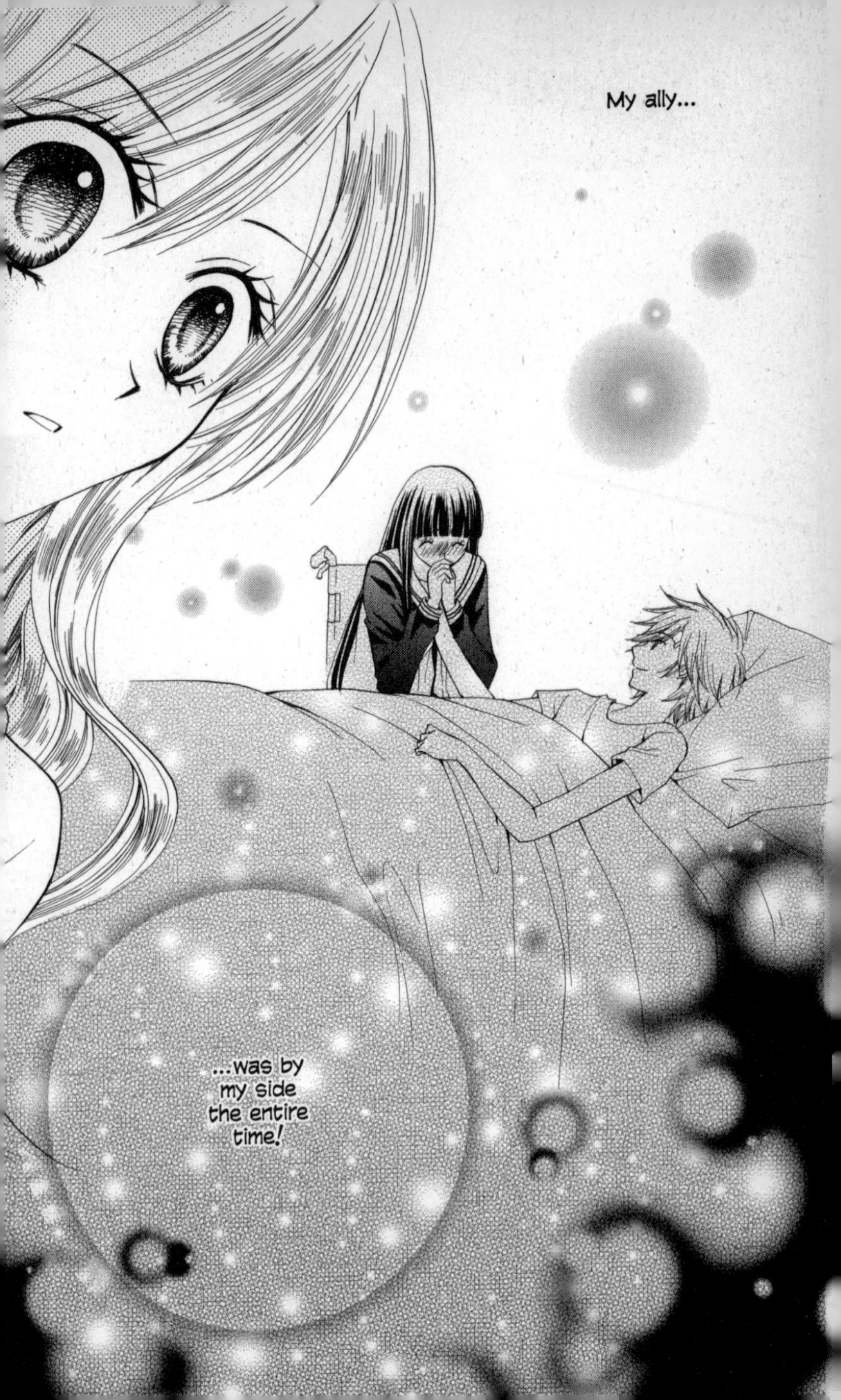
My ally...
...was by my side the entire time!

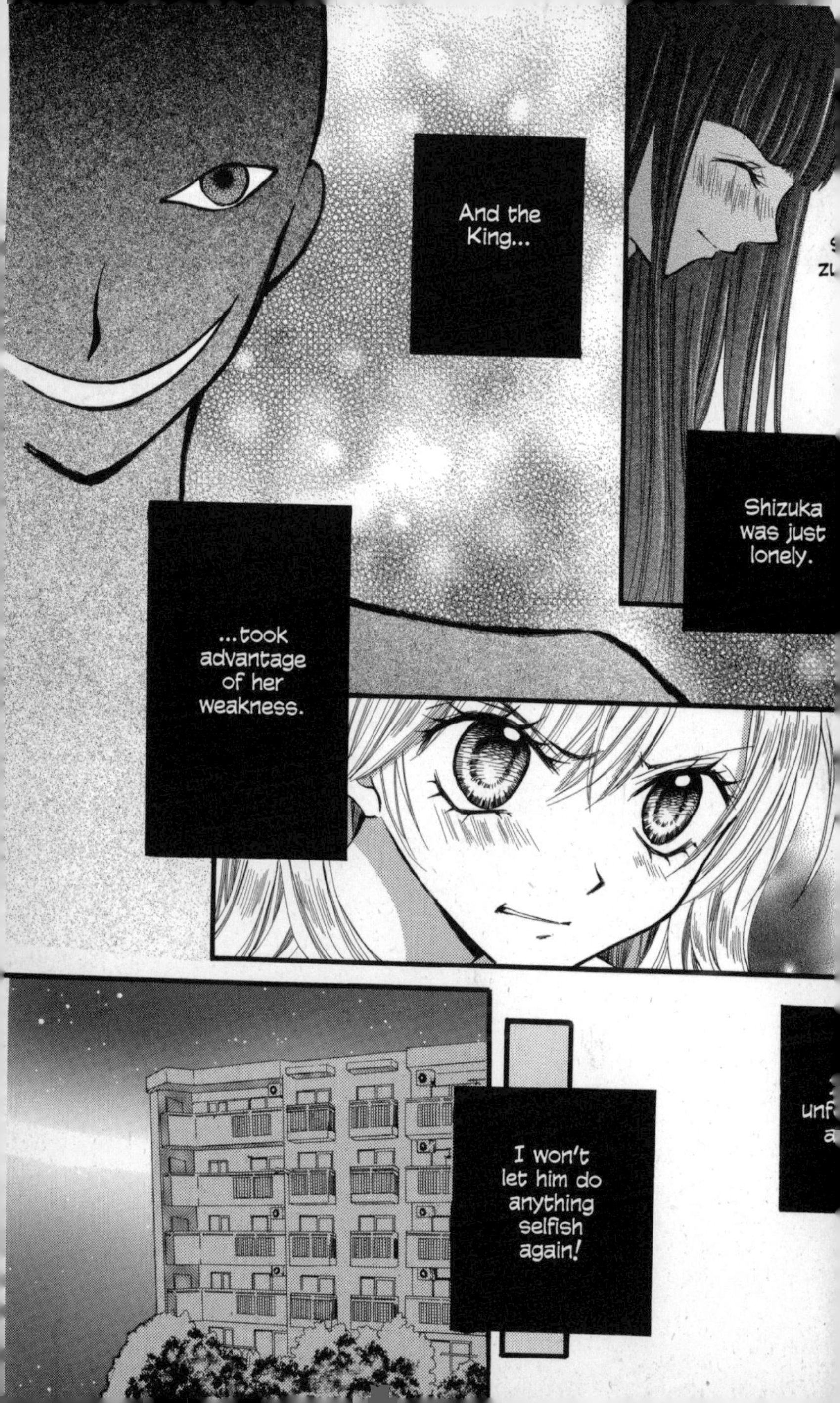
Shizuka was just lonely.
And the King...
...took advantage of her weakness.
I won't let him do anything selfish again!

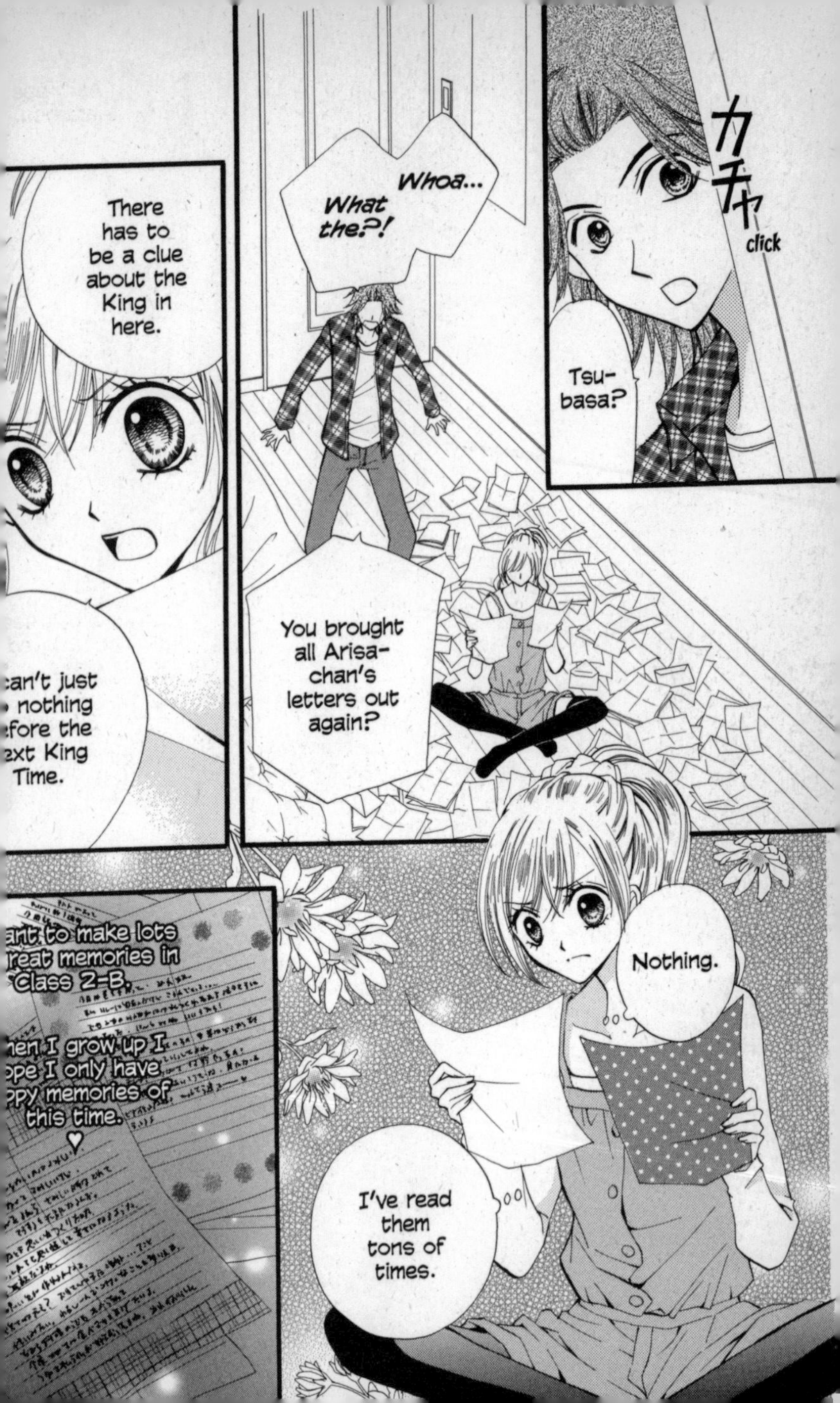
カチャ
click
Tsu-basa?
Whoa...
What the?!
You brought all Arisa-chan's letters out again?
There has to be a clue about the King in here.
can't just
nothing
fore the
ext King
Time.
Nothing.
I've read them tons of times.
ant to make lots
reat memories in
Class 2-B.
hen I grow up I
ope I only have
ppy memories of
this time.
♥

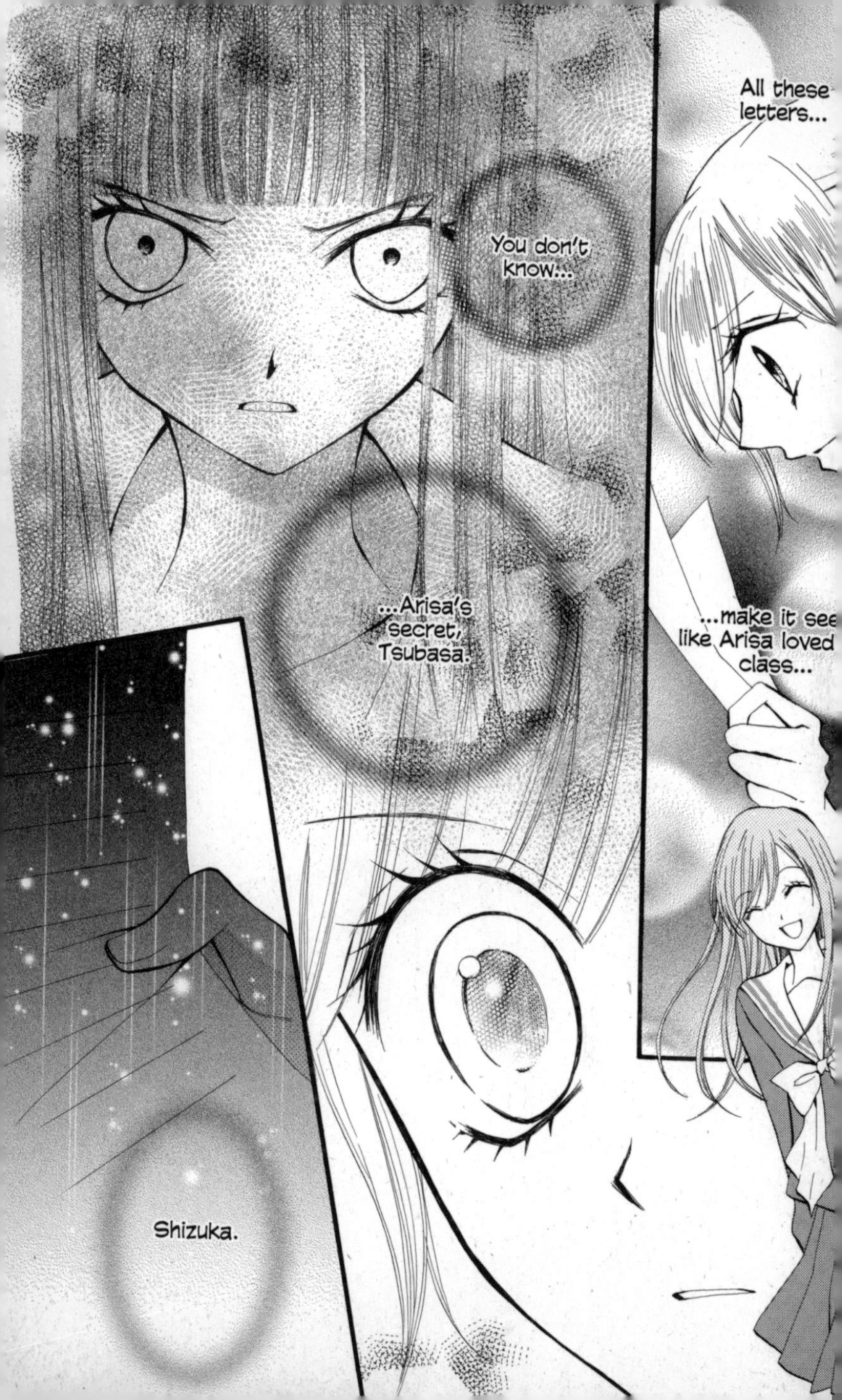
All these letters...
...make it see like Arisa loved class...
You don't know...
...Arisa's secret, Tsubasa.
Shizuka.

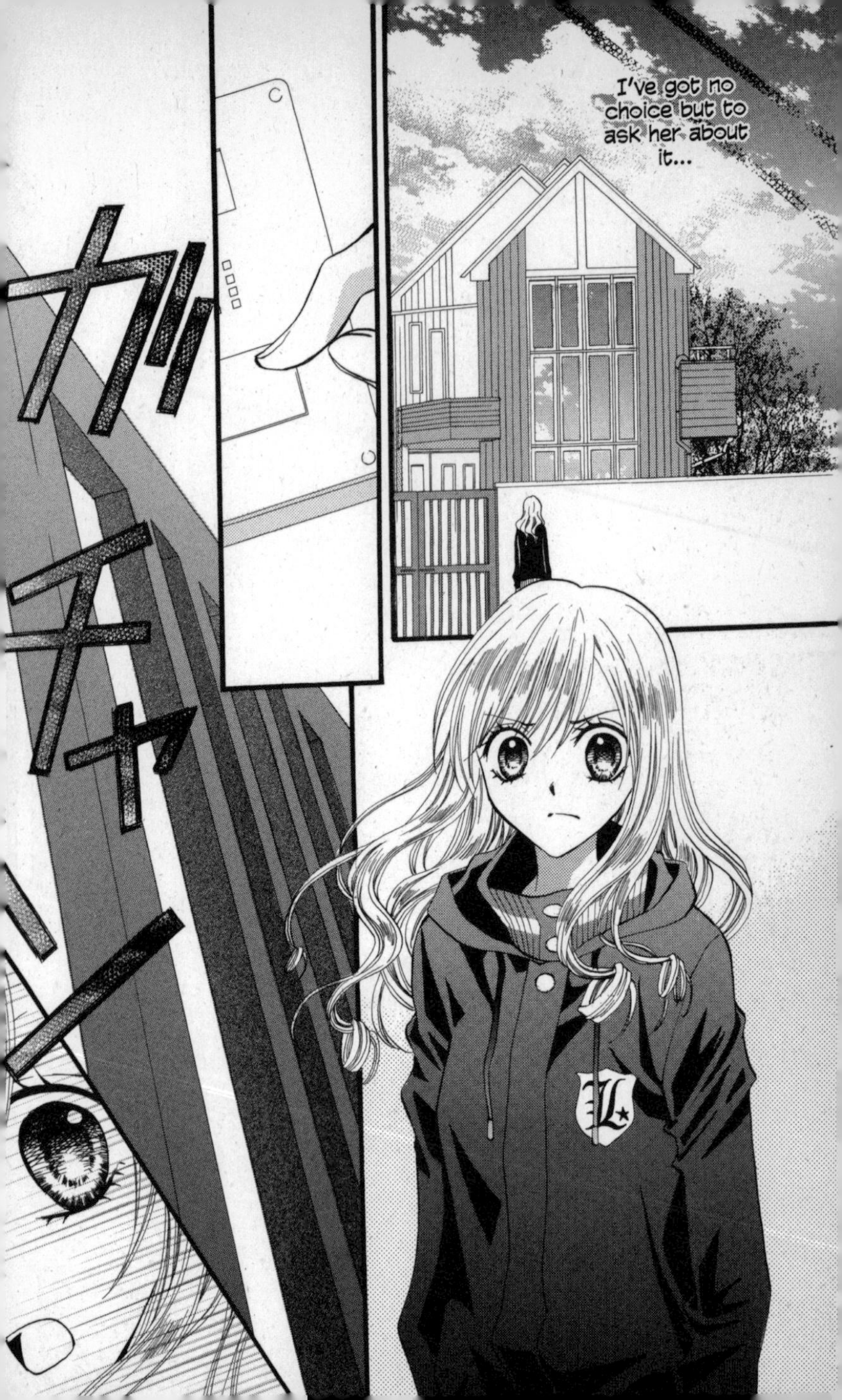
I've got no choice but to ask her about it...
カチャン

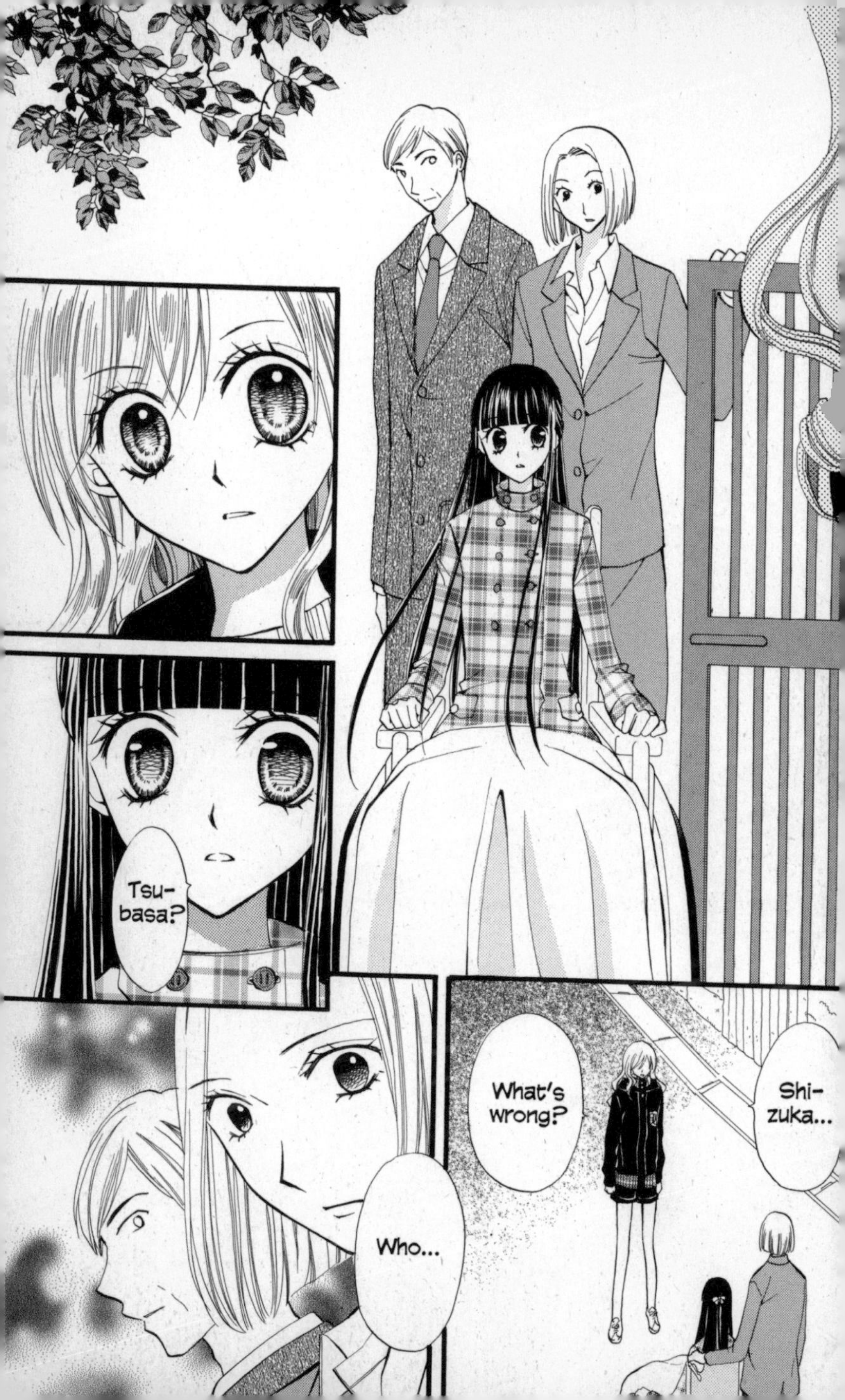
Tsu-basa?
Shi-zuka...
What's wrong?
Who...

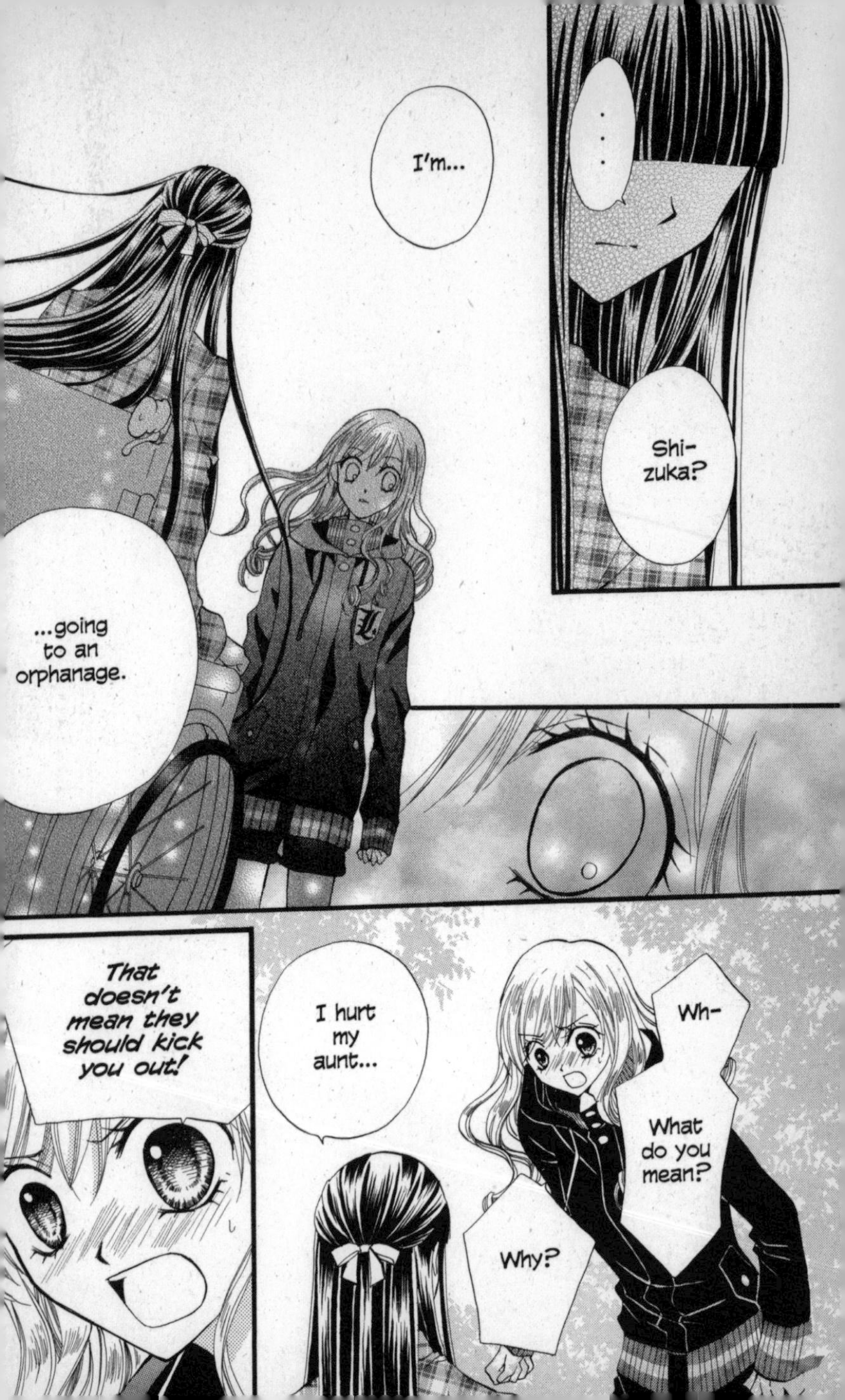
. . .
Shi-zuka?
I'm...
...going to an orphanage.
Wh-
What do you mean?
Why?
I hurt my aunt...
That doesn't mean they should kick you out!

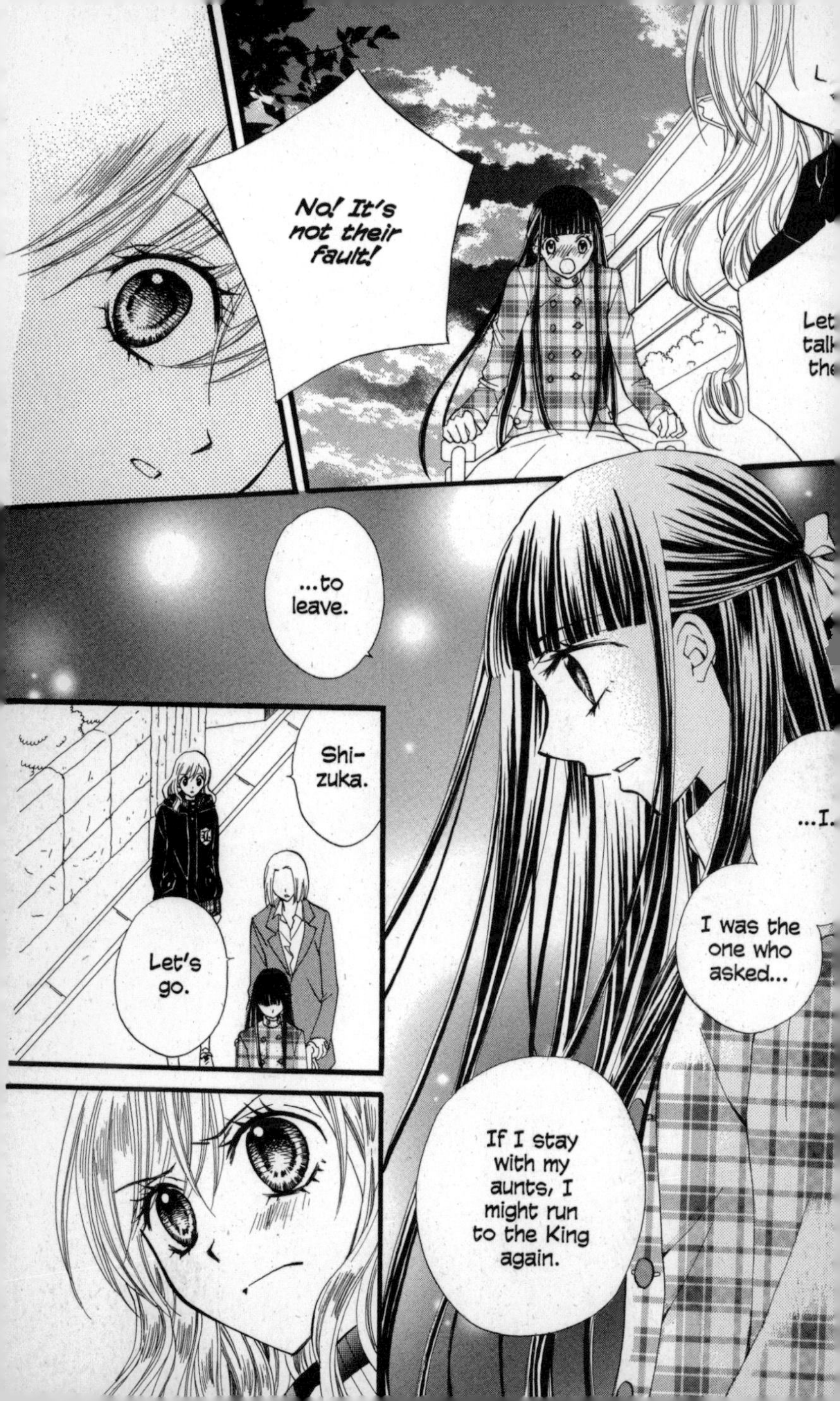
No! It's not their fault!
...I.
I was the one who asked...
...to leave.
If I stay with my aunts, I might run to the King again.
Shi-zuka.
Let's go.

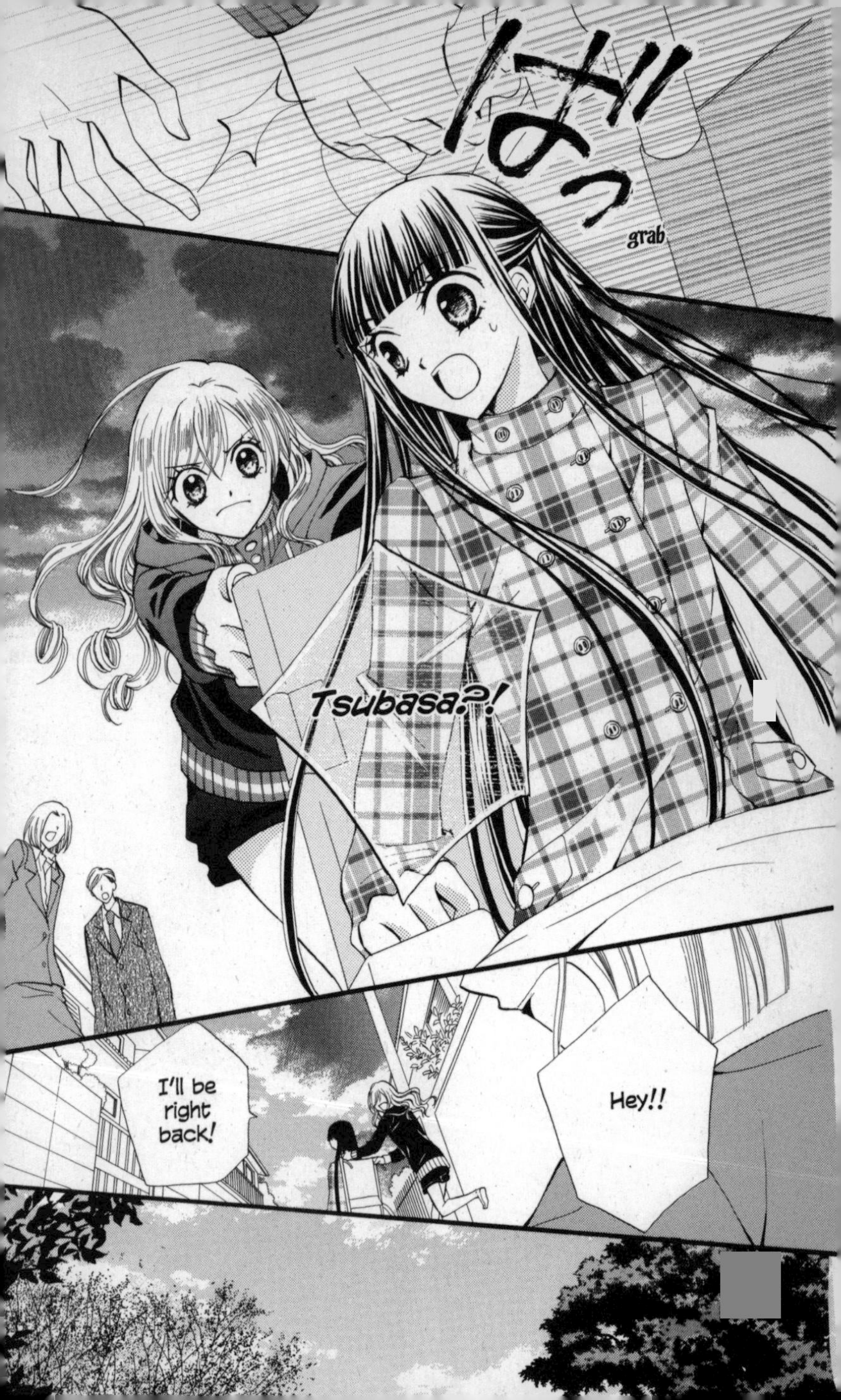
ぱっ
grab
Tsubasa?!
Hey!!
I'll be right back!

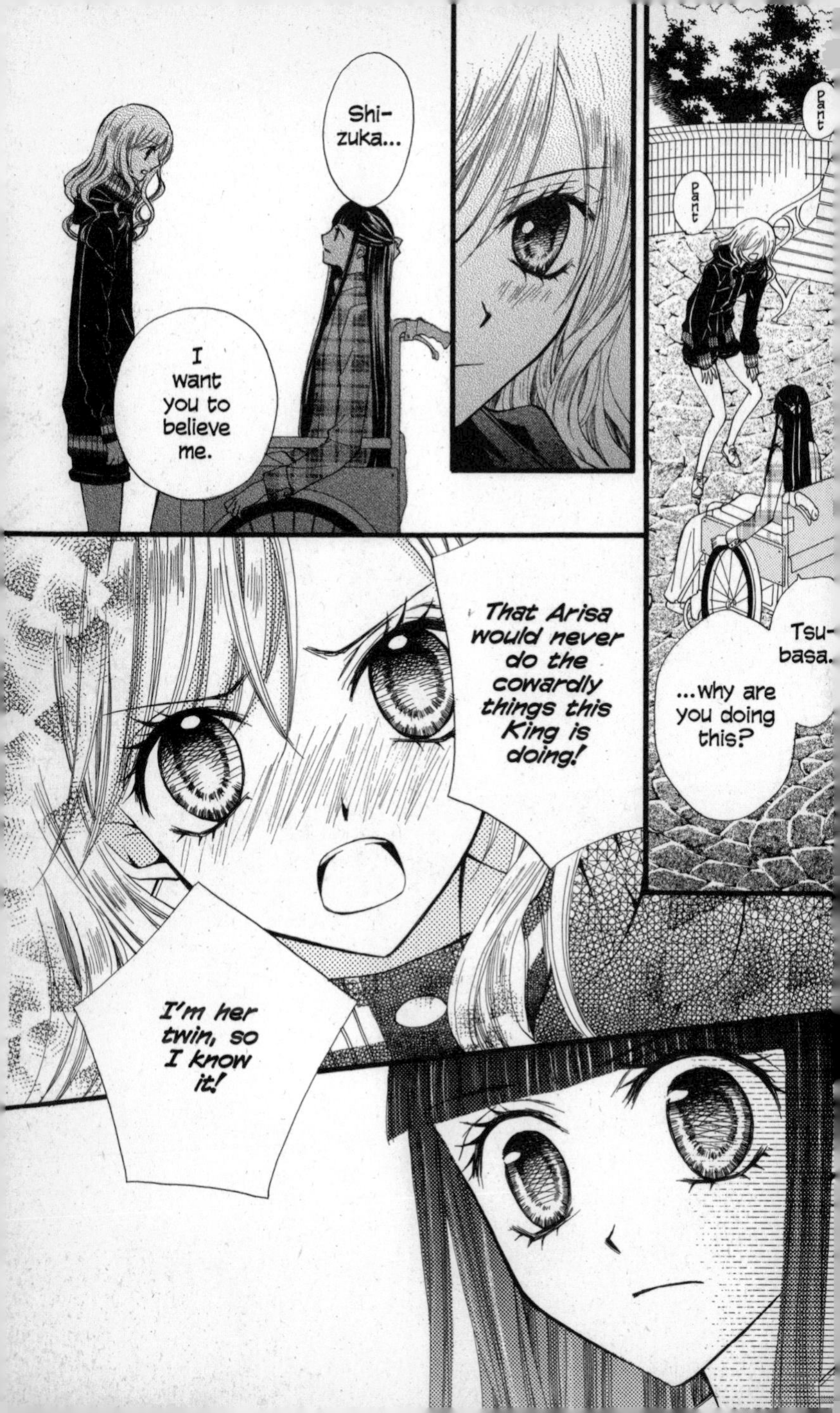

Pant
Pant
Tsu-basa.
...why are you doing this?
Shi-zuka...
I want you to believe me.
That Arisa would never do the cowardly things this King is doing!
I'm her twin, so I know it!

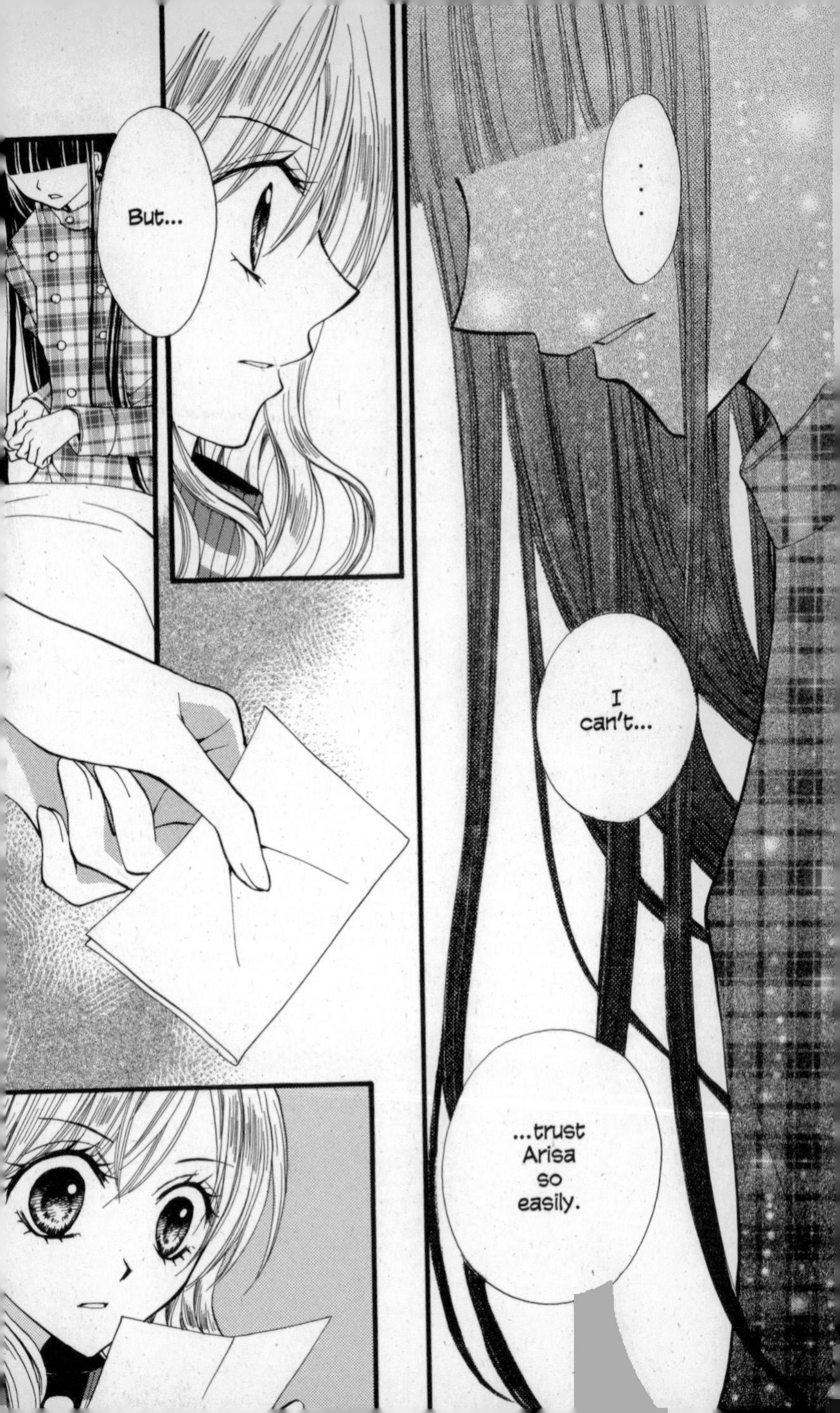
...
I can't...
...trust Arisa so easily.
But...

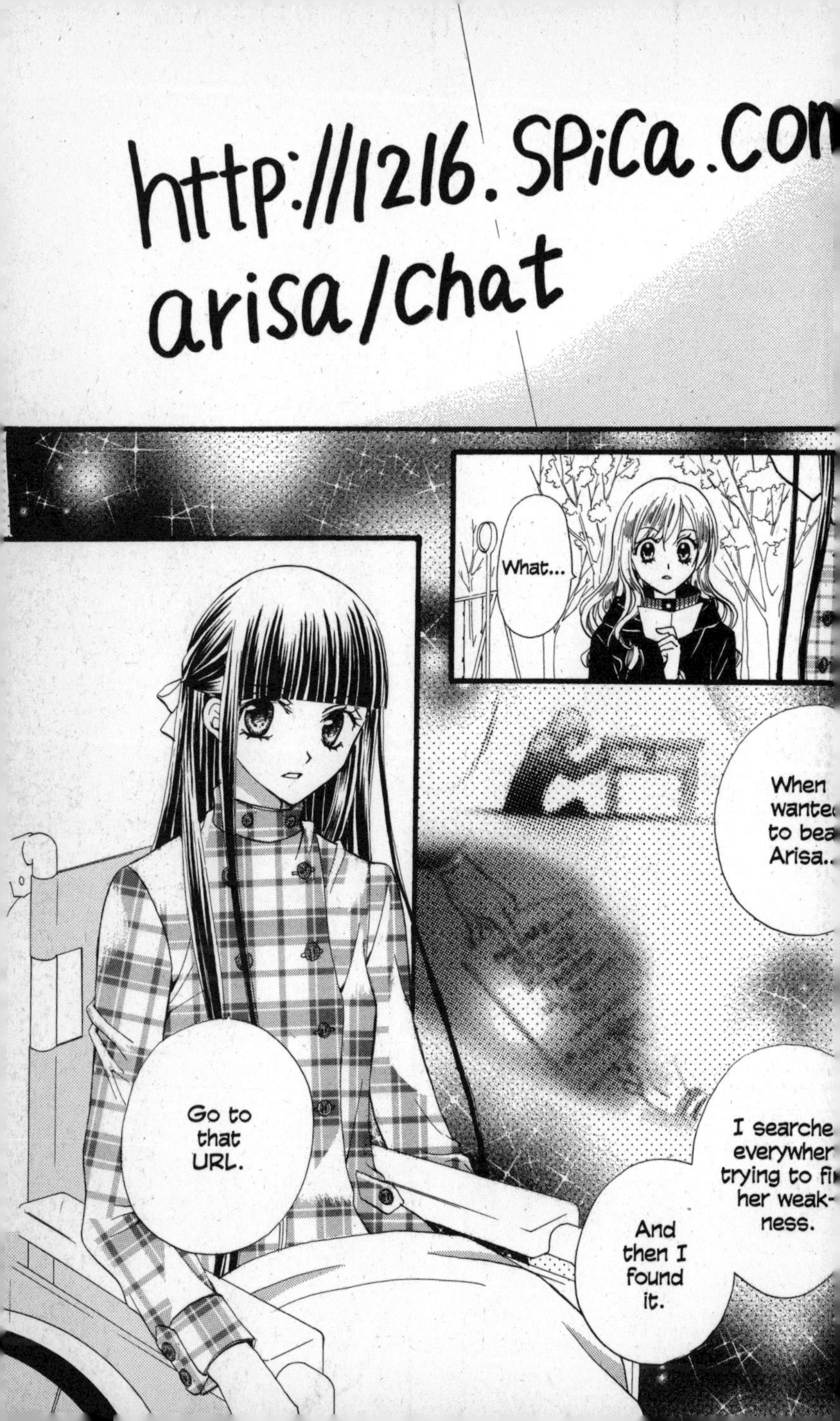
http://1216.SPiCa.com
arisa/chat
What...
When wante to bea Arisa..
I searche everywher trying to fi her weak-ness.
And then I found it.
Go to that URL.

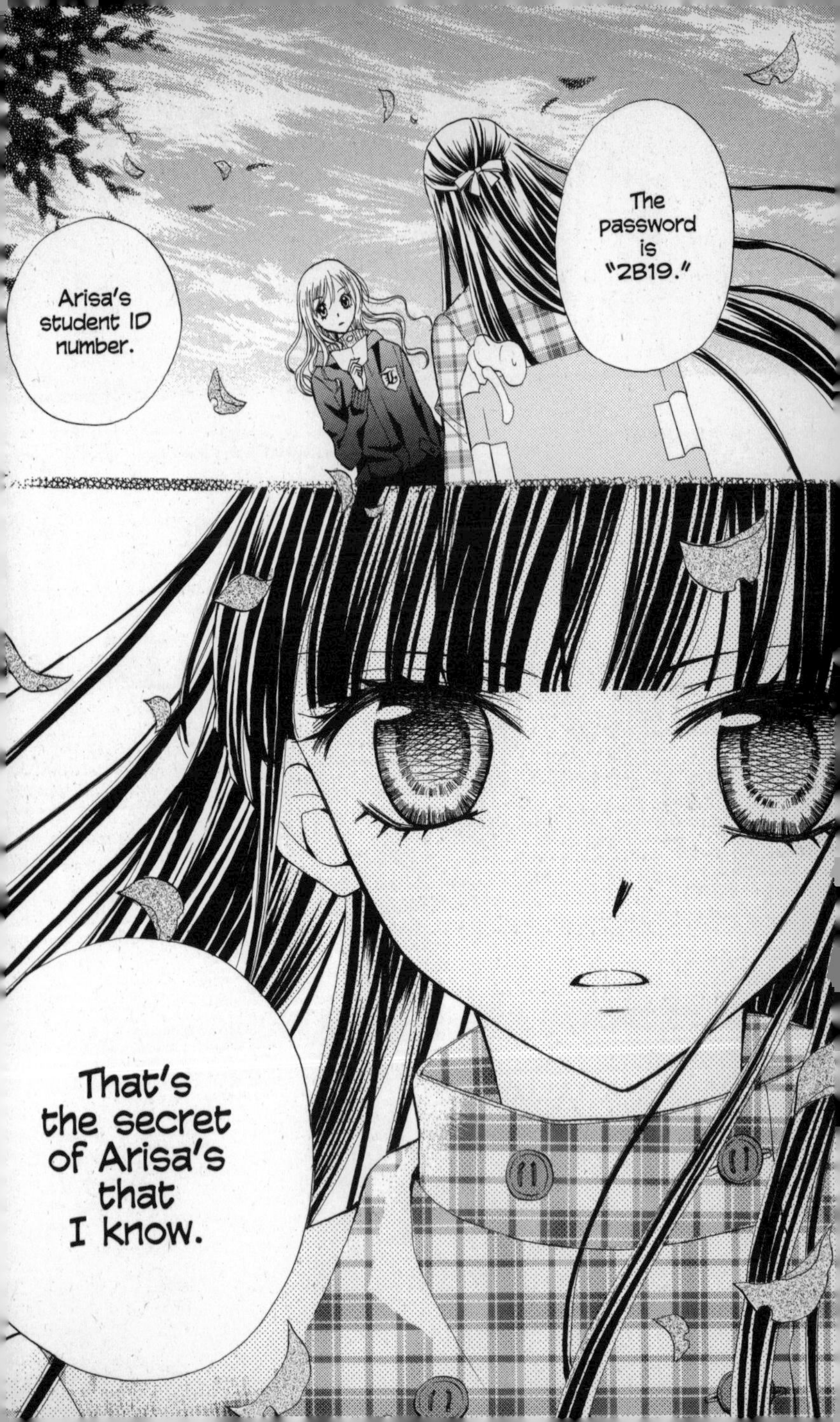
The password is "2B19."
Arisa's student ID number.
That's the secret of Arisa's that I know.

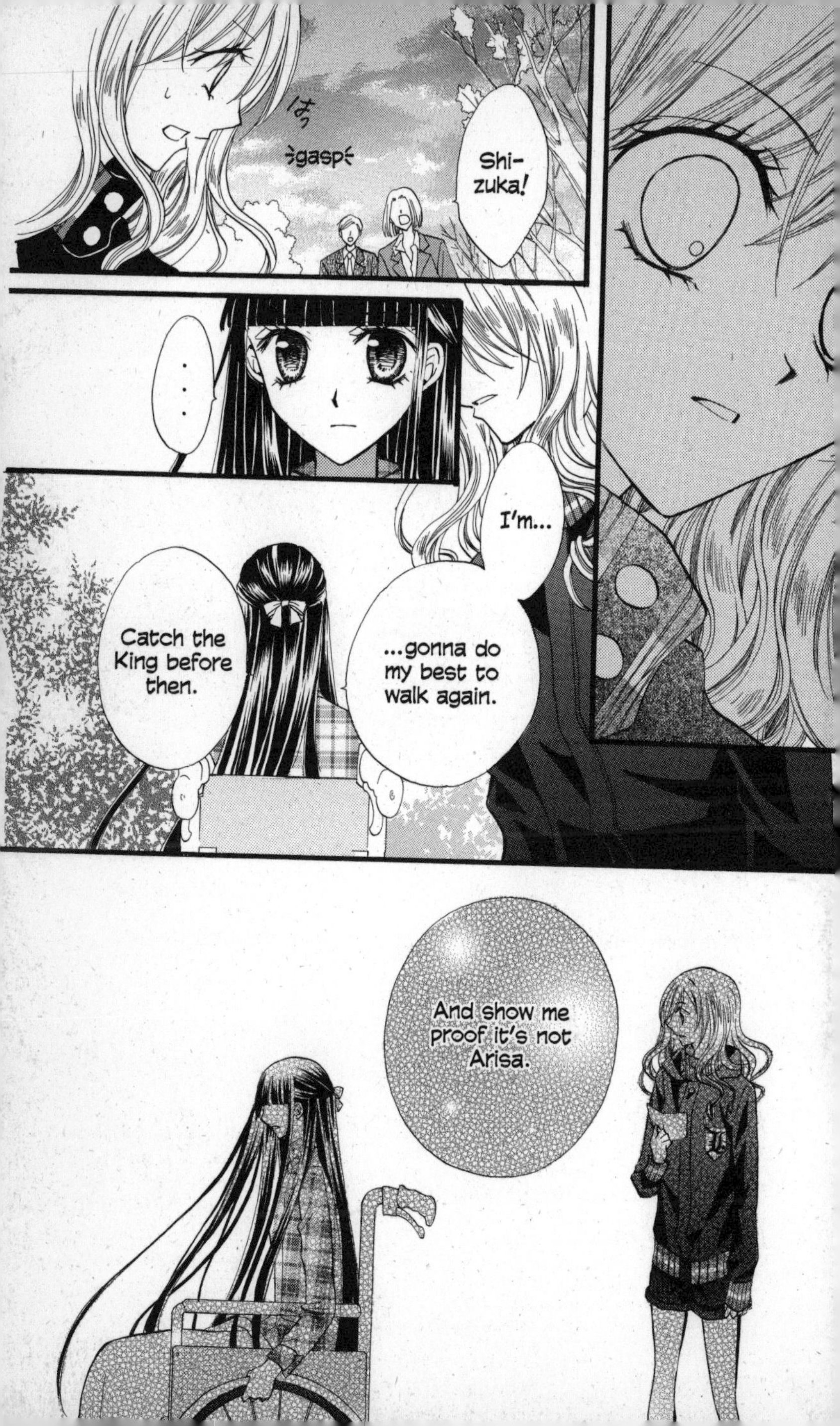
Shi-zuka!
はっ
gasp
. . .
I'm...
...gonna do my best to walk again.
Catch the King before then.
And show me proof it's not Arisa.

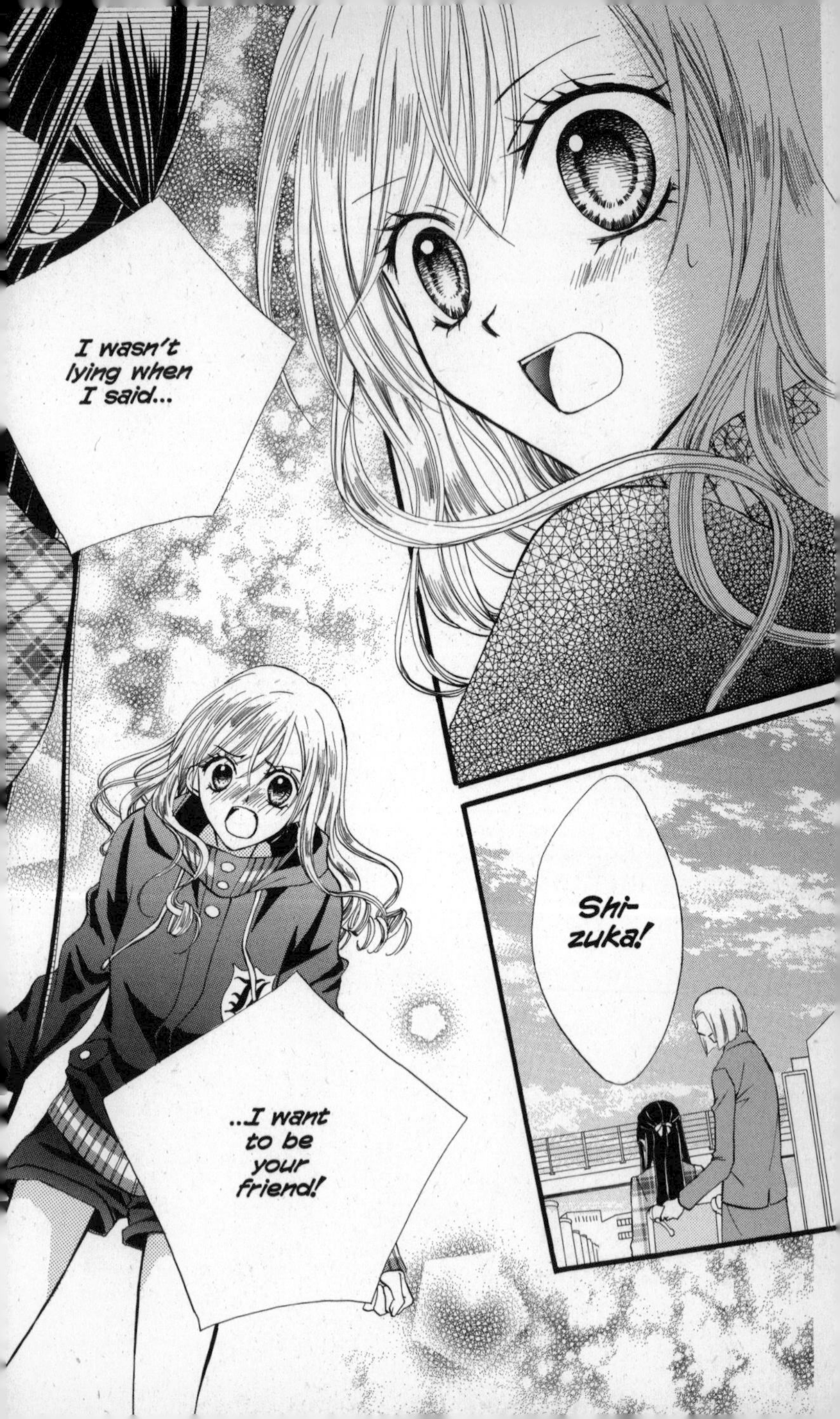
Shi-
zuka!
I wasn't lying when I said...
...I want to be your friend!

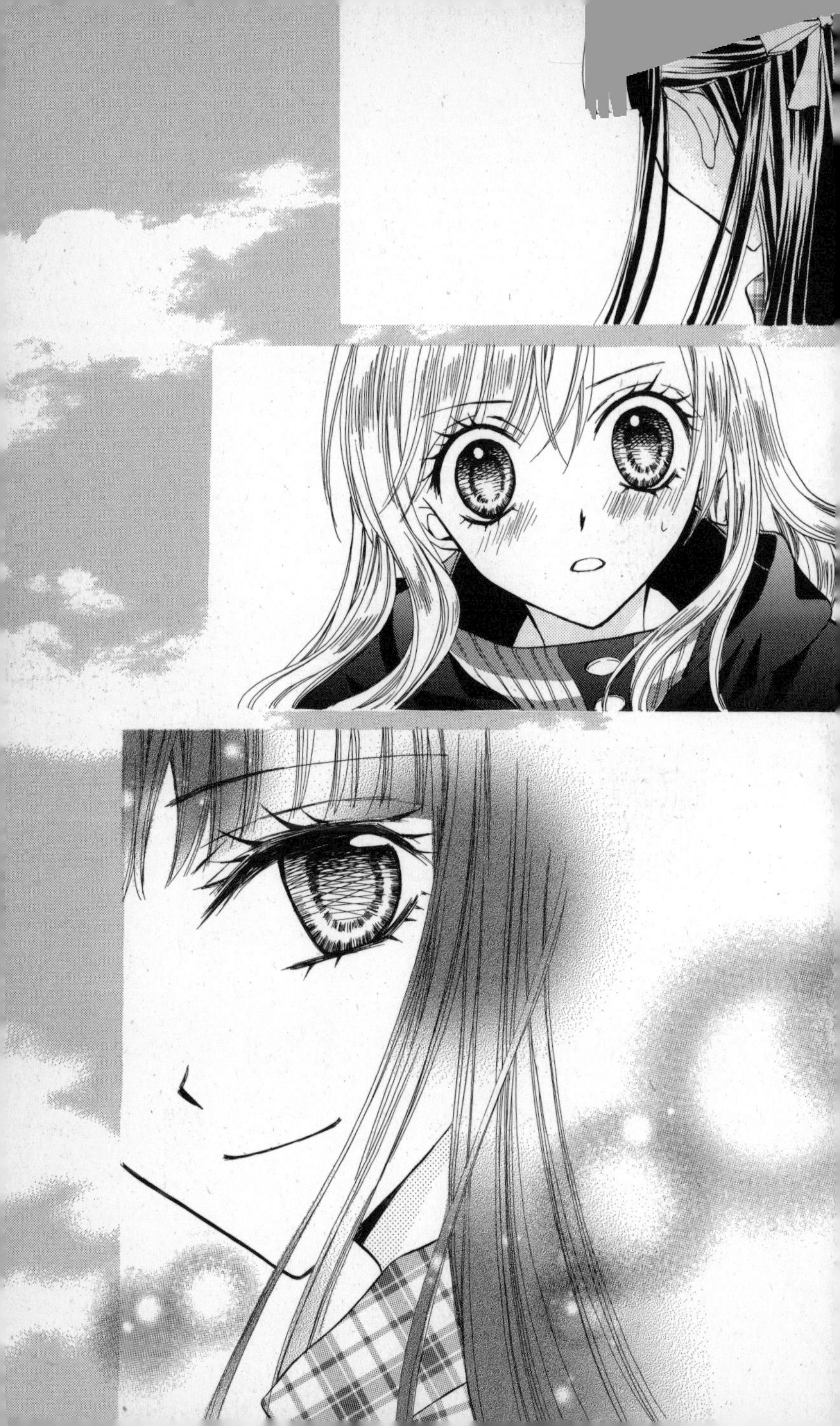

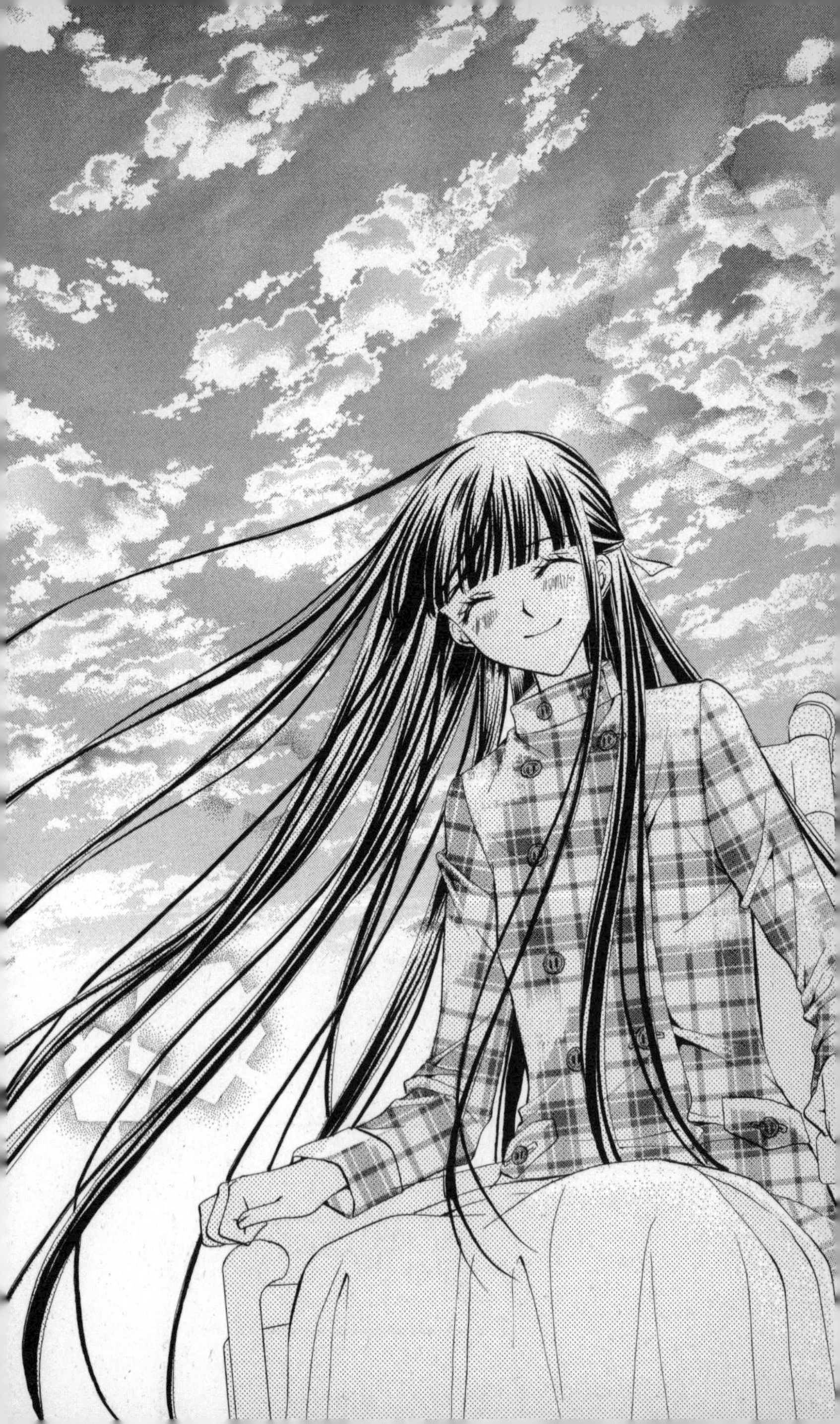

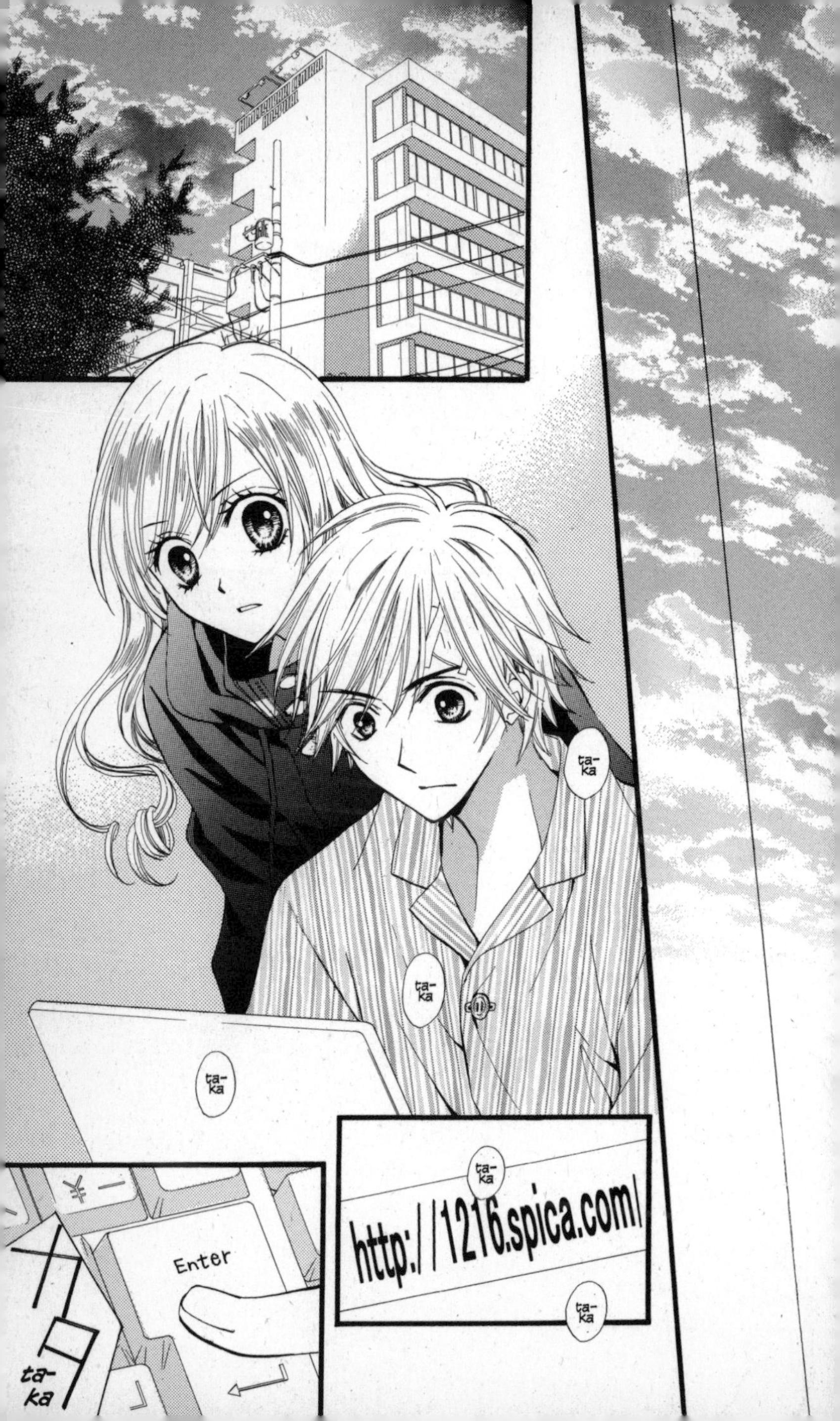
ta-ka
ta-ka
ta-ka
ta-ka
http://1216.spica.com/
ta-ka
Enter
ta-ka

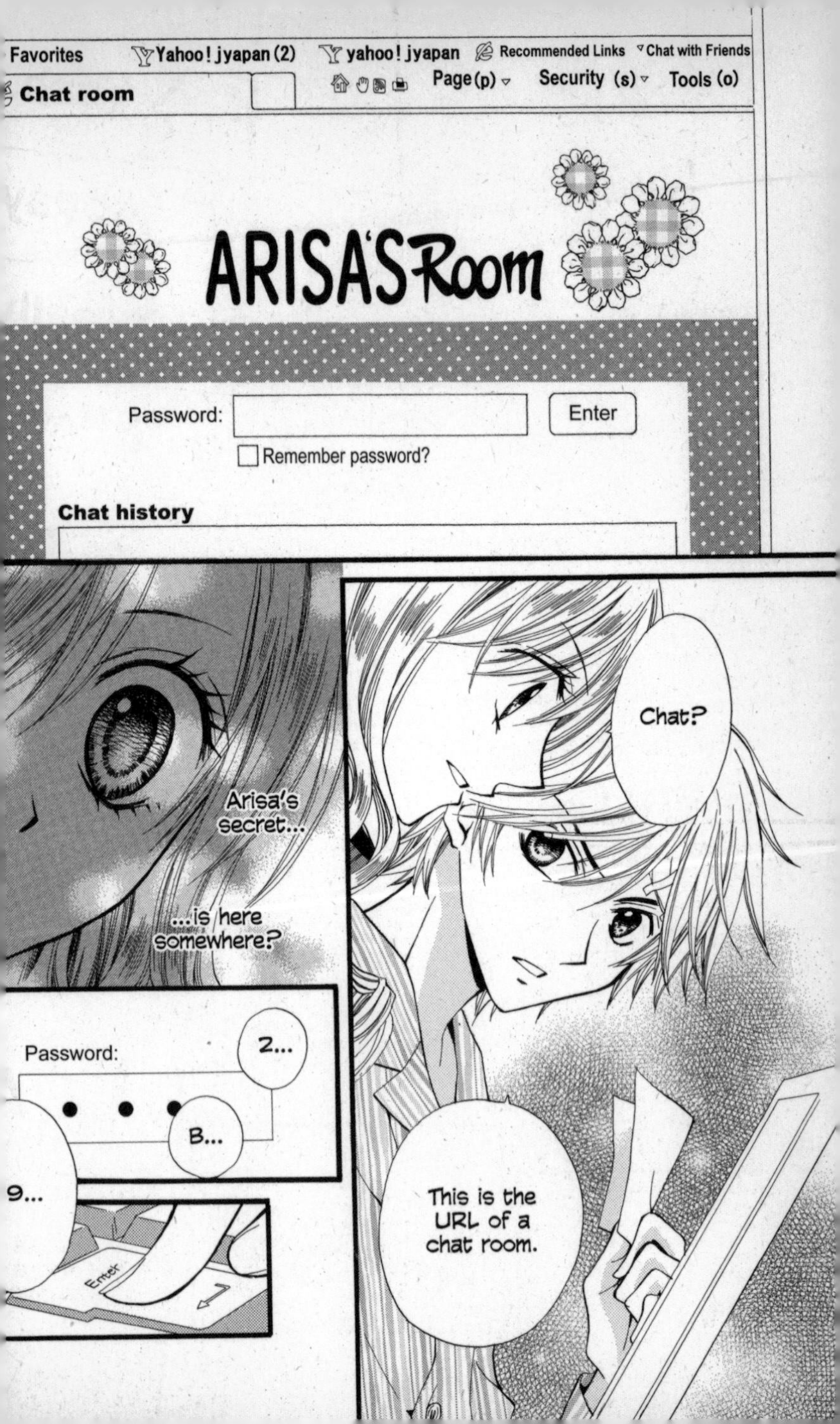
Favorites
Yahoo! jyapan (2)
yahoo! jyapan
Recommended Links
Chat with Friends
Chat room
Page (p)
Security (s)
Tools (o)
ARISA'S Room
Password:
Enter
Remember password?
Chat history
Chat?
This is the URL of a chat room.
Arisa's secret...
...is here somewhere?
Password:
2...
B...
9...
Enter

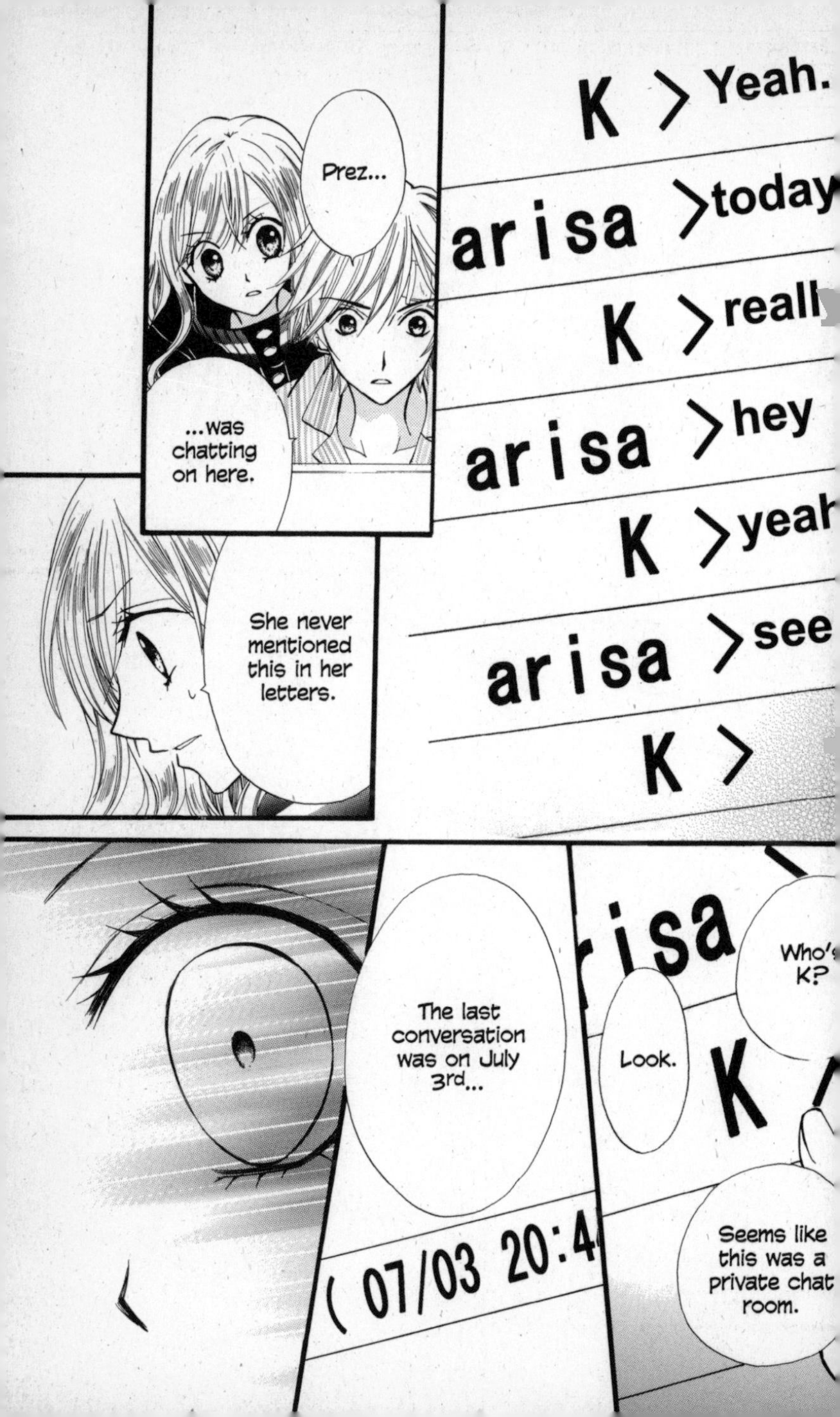

K > Yeah.
arisa >today
K >reall
arisa >hey
K >yeah
arisa >see
K >
Prez...
...was chatting on here.
She never mentioned this in her letters.
isa
Who's K?
Look.
K
Seems like this was a private chat room.
The last conversation was on July 3rd...
(07/03 20:4

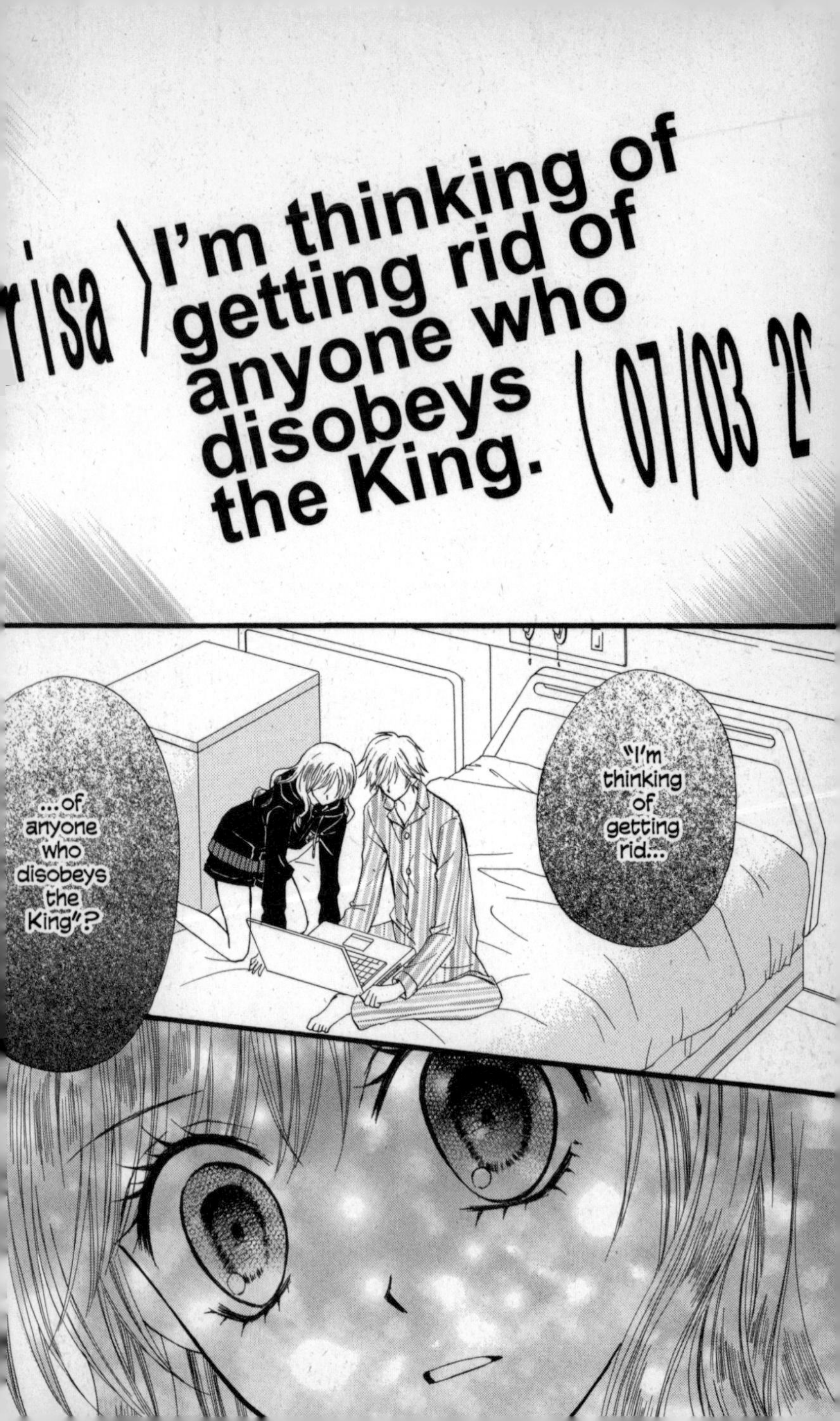
risa) I'm thinking of getting rid of anyone who disobeys the King. (07/03 2
"I'm thinking of getting rid...
...of anyone who disobeys the King"?

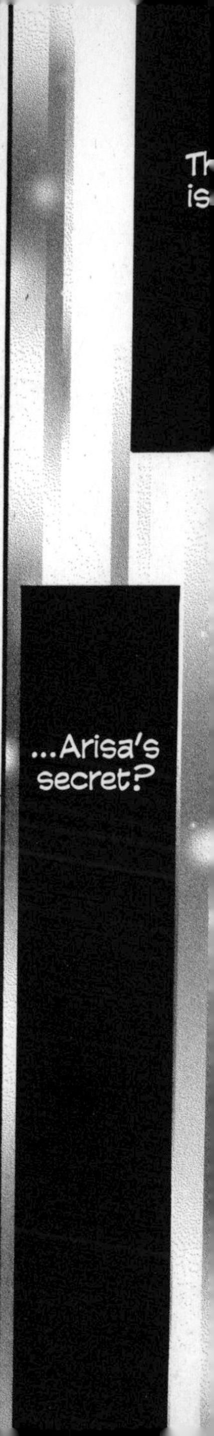
...Arisa's secret?

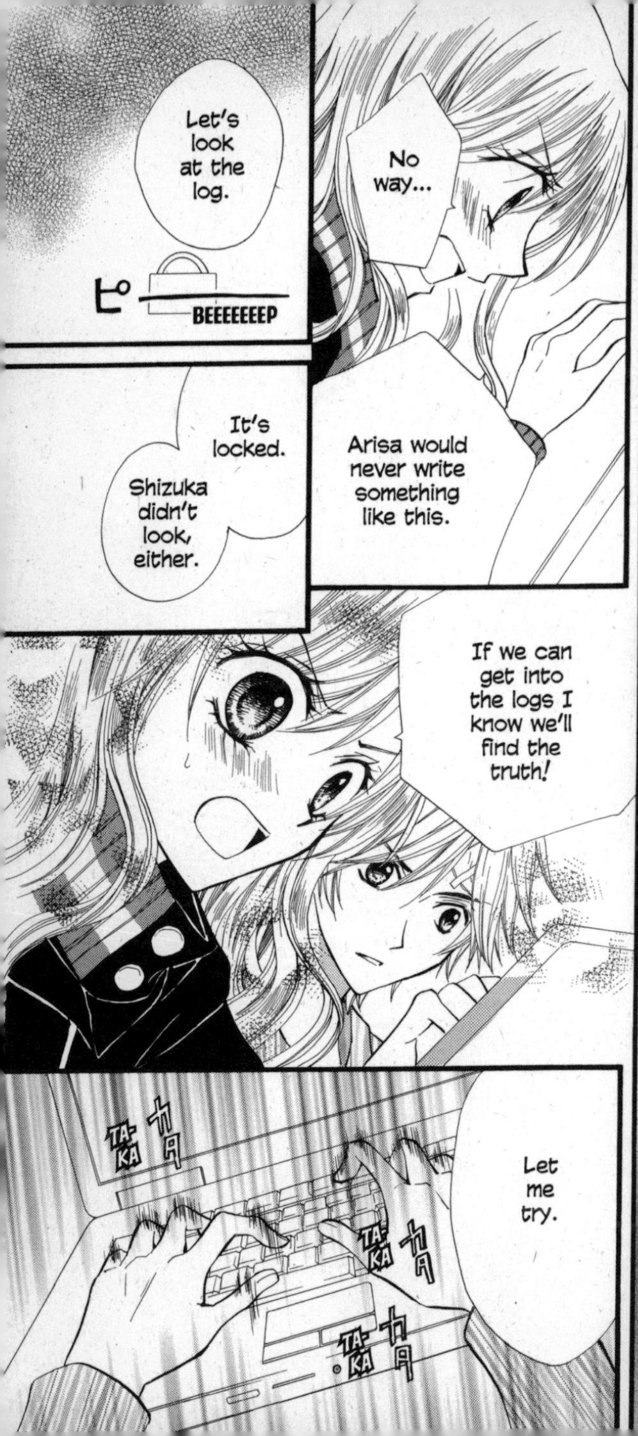
No way...
Arisa would never write something like this.
Let's look at the log.
ピー BEEEEEEEP
It's locked.
Shizuka didn't look, either.
If we can get into the logs I know we'll find the truth!
Let me try.
TA-KA カタ
TA-KA カタ
TA-KA カタ

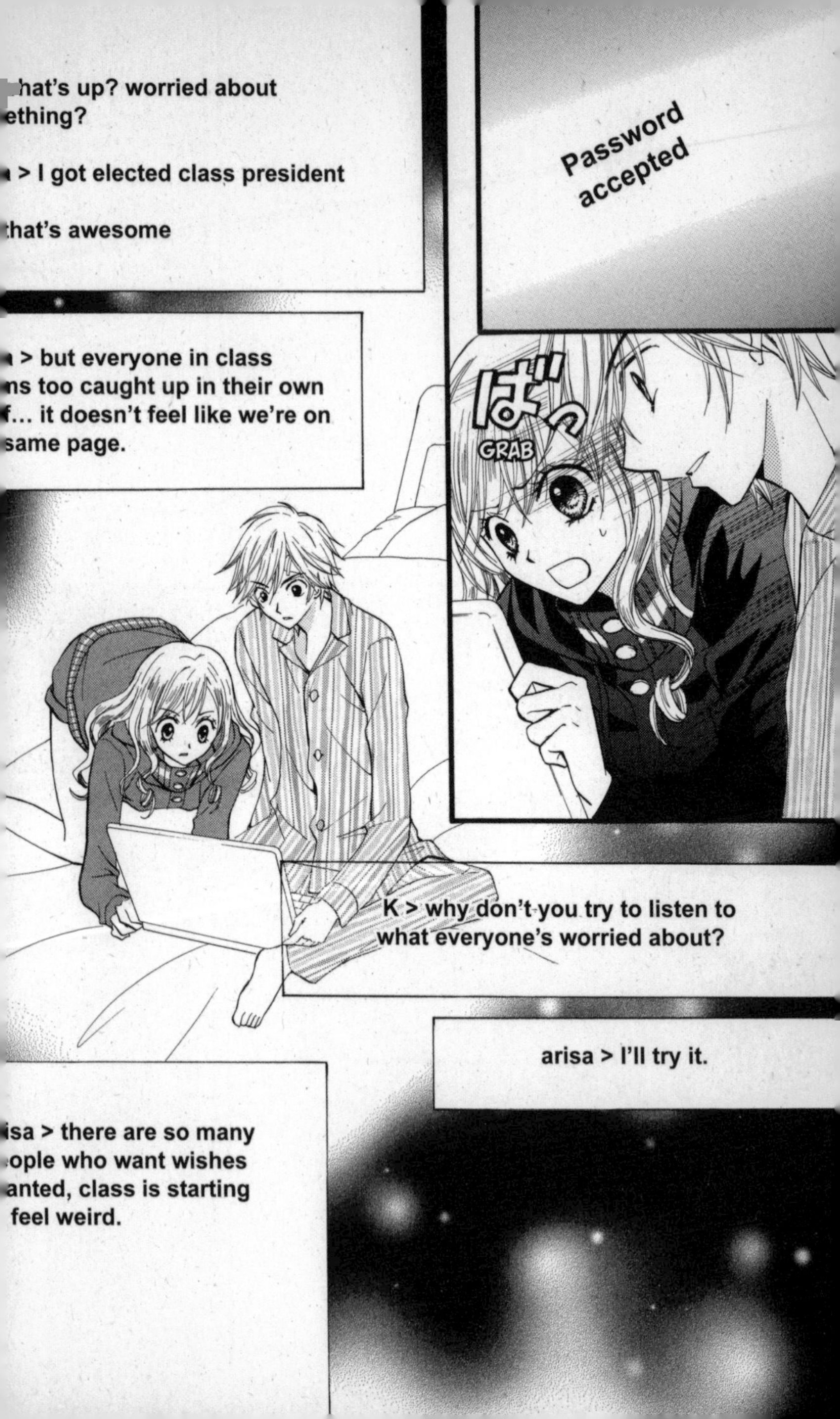
Password accepted
hat's up? worried about ething?
> I got elected class president
hat's awesome
ばっ
GRAB
> but everyone in class ns too caught up in their own f... it doesn't feel like we're on same page.
K > why don't you try to listen to what everyone's worried about?
arisa > I'll try it.
isa > there are so many ople who want wishes anted, class is starting feel weird.

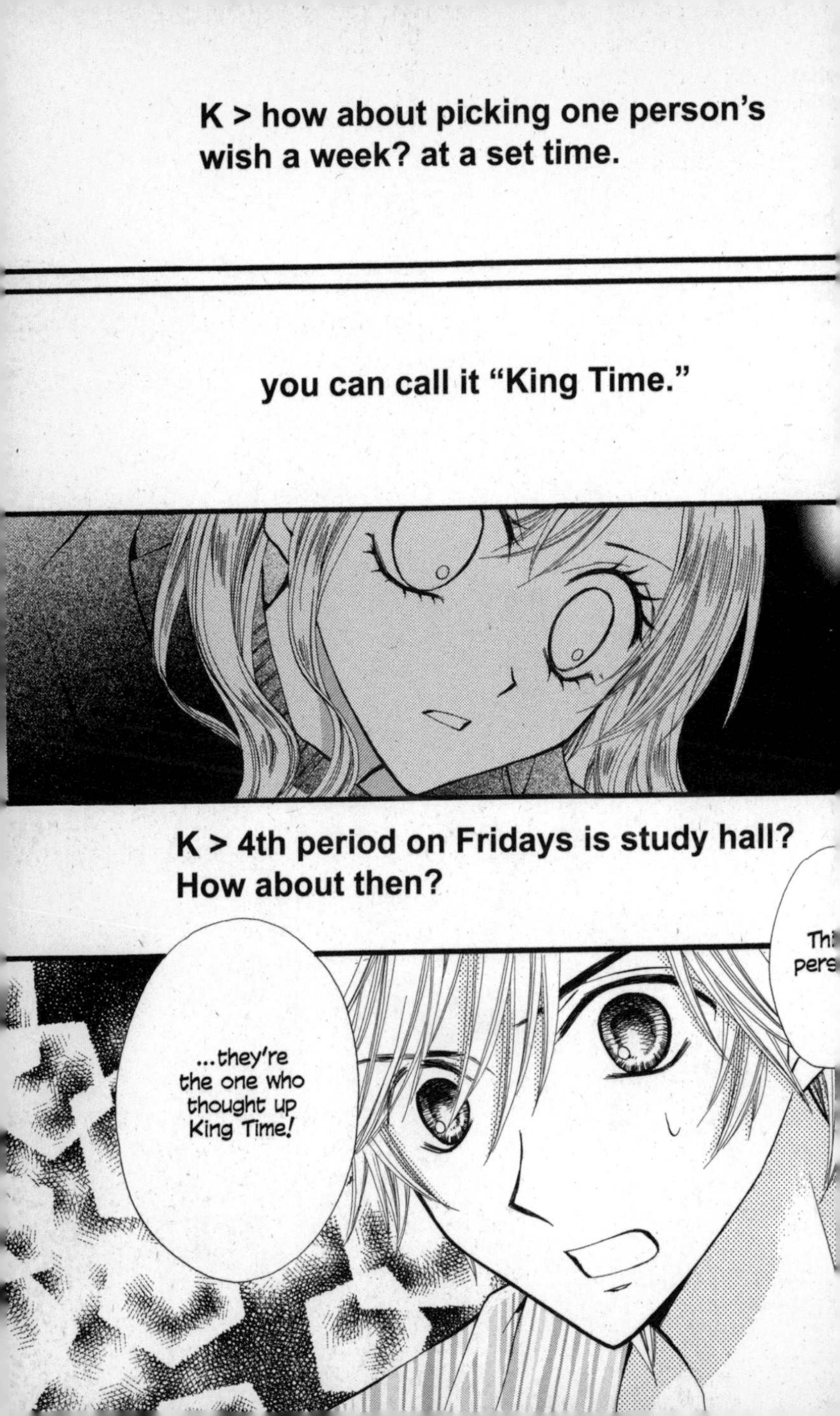
K > how about picking one person's wish a week? at a set time.
you can call it "King Time."
K > 4th period on Fridays is study hall? How about then?
...they're the one who thought up King Time!

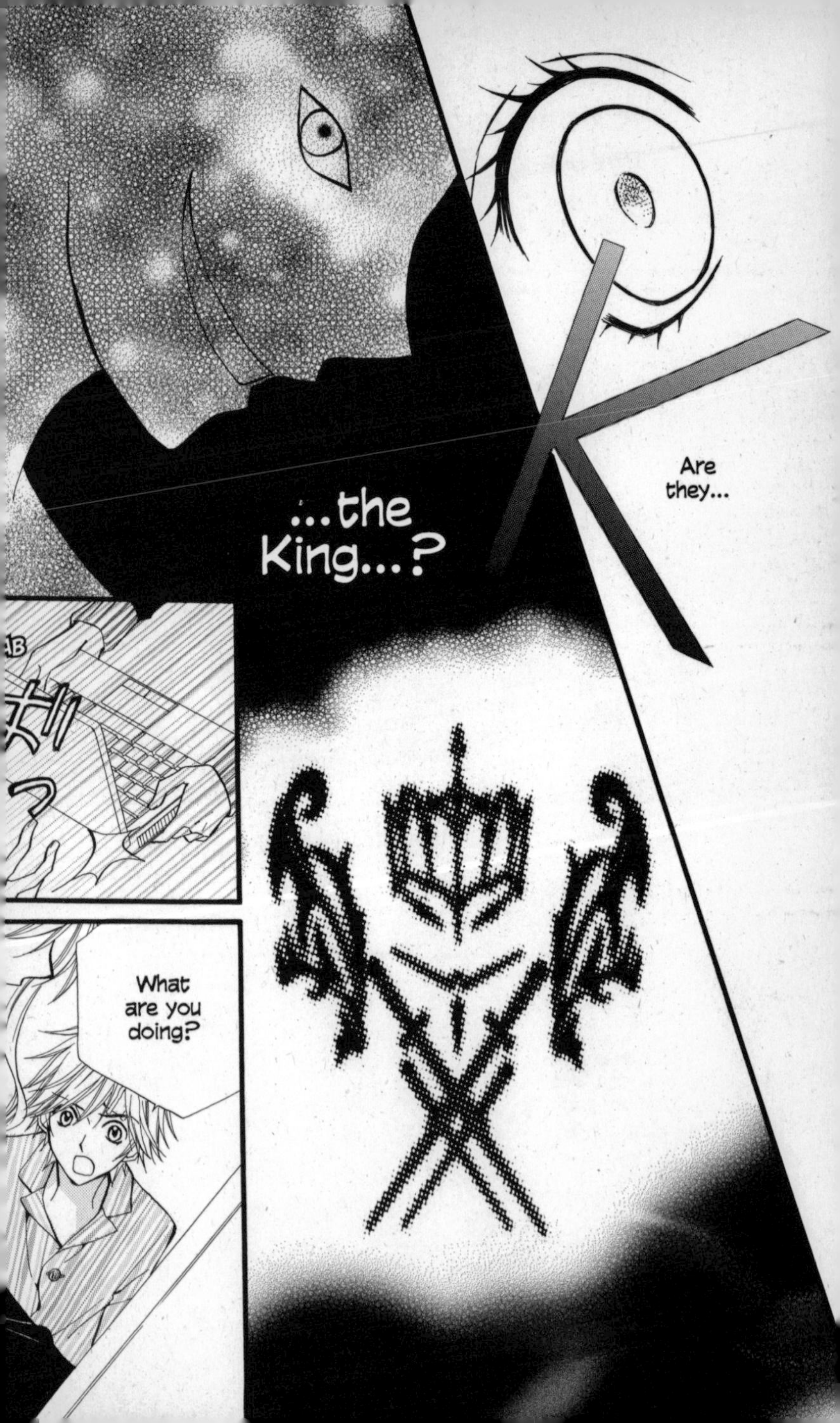
Are they...
...the King...?
What are you doing?

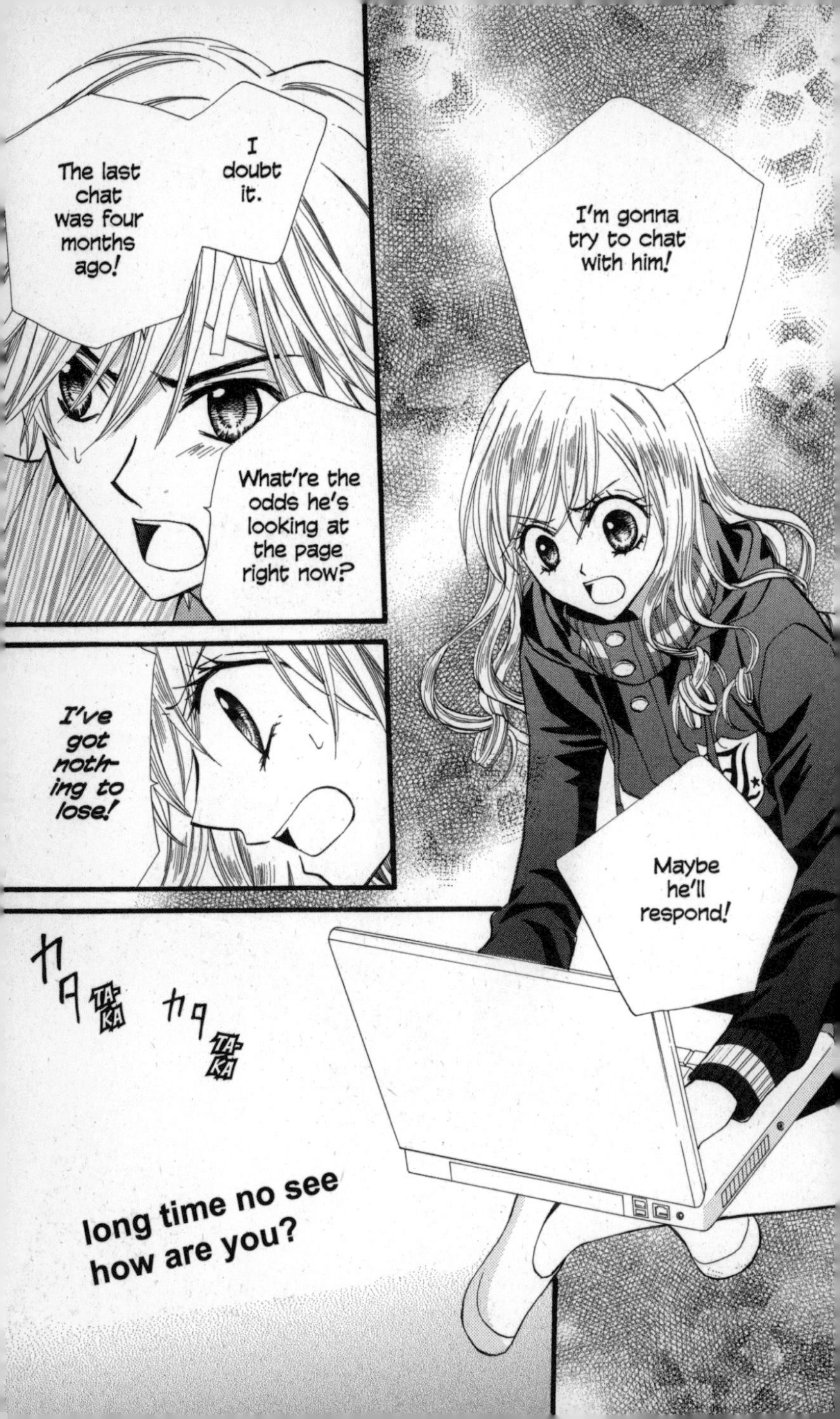
I'm gonna try to chat with him!
Maybe he'll respond!
I doubt it.
The last chat was four months ago!
What're the odds he's looking at the page right now?
I've got noth-ing to lose!
TA-KA
TA-KA
long time no see
how are you?

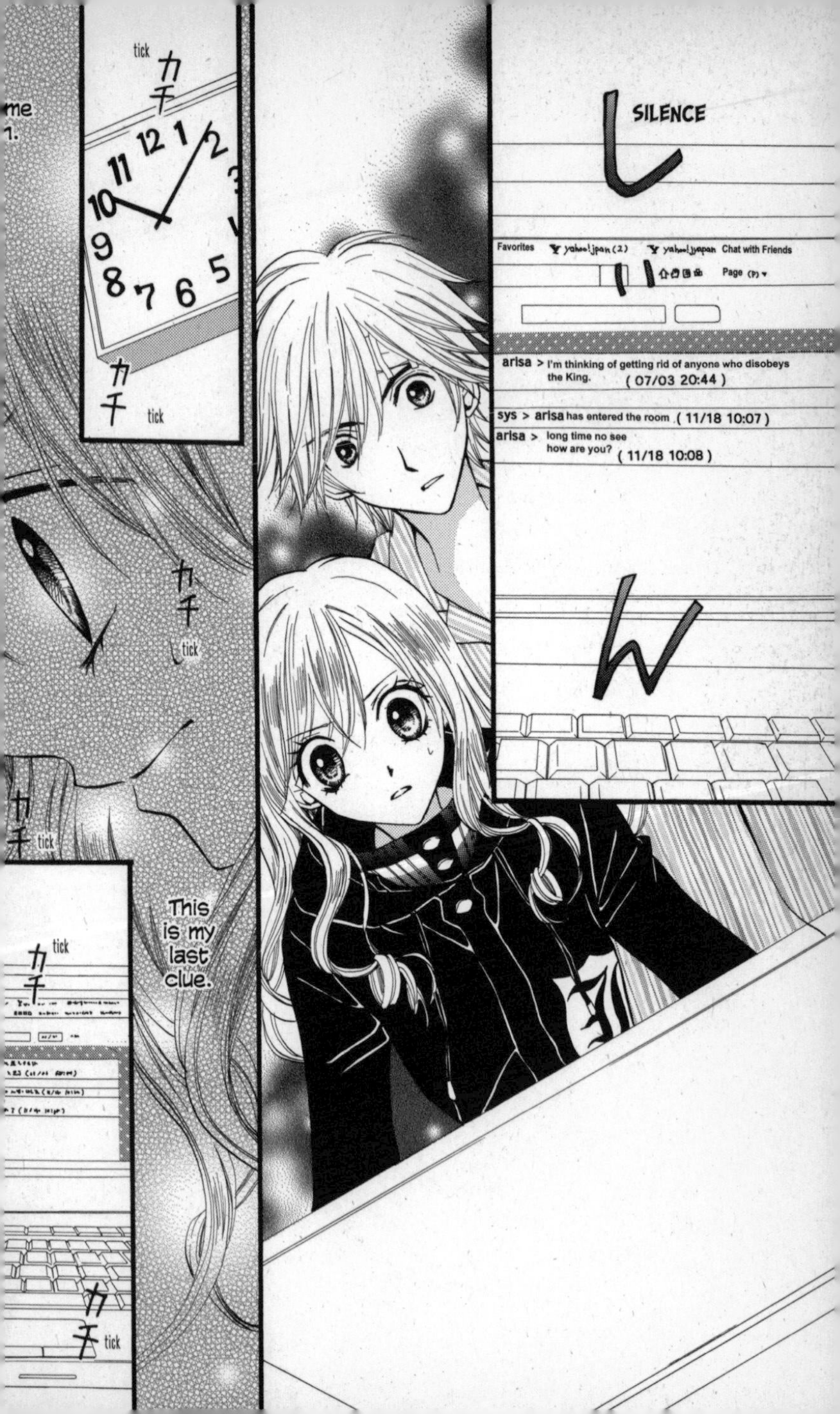
SILENCE
Favorites yahoo!japan (2) yahoo!japan Chat with Friends
Page (P)
arisa > I'm thinking of getting rid of anyone who disobeys the King. (07/03 20:44)
sys > arisa has entered the room (11/18 10:07)
arisa > long time no see how are you? (11/18 10:08)
カチ tick
カチ tick
カチ tick
カチ tick
This is my last clue.
カチ tick
カチ tick

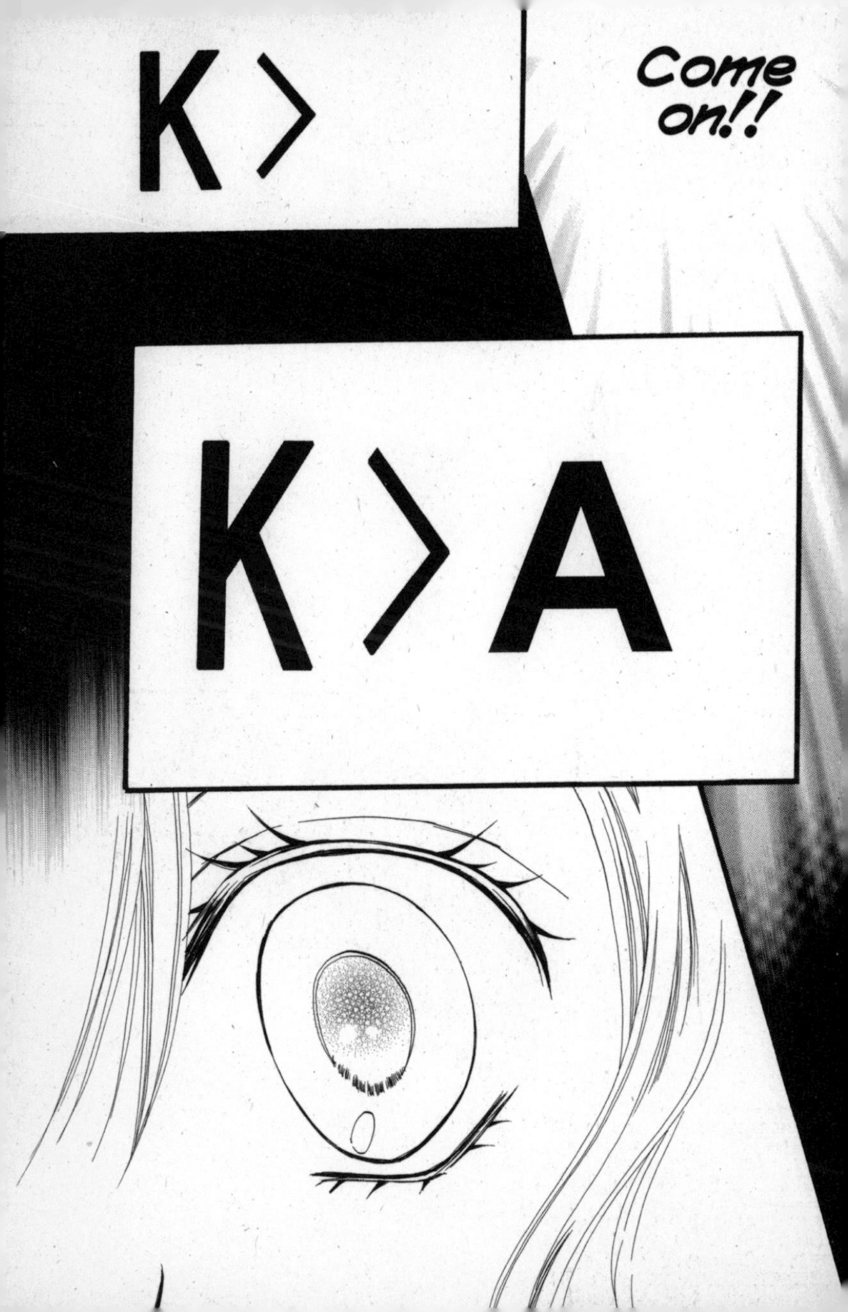
Come on!!
K>
K>A

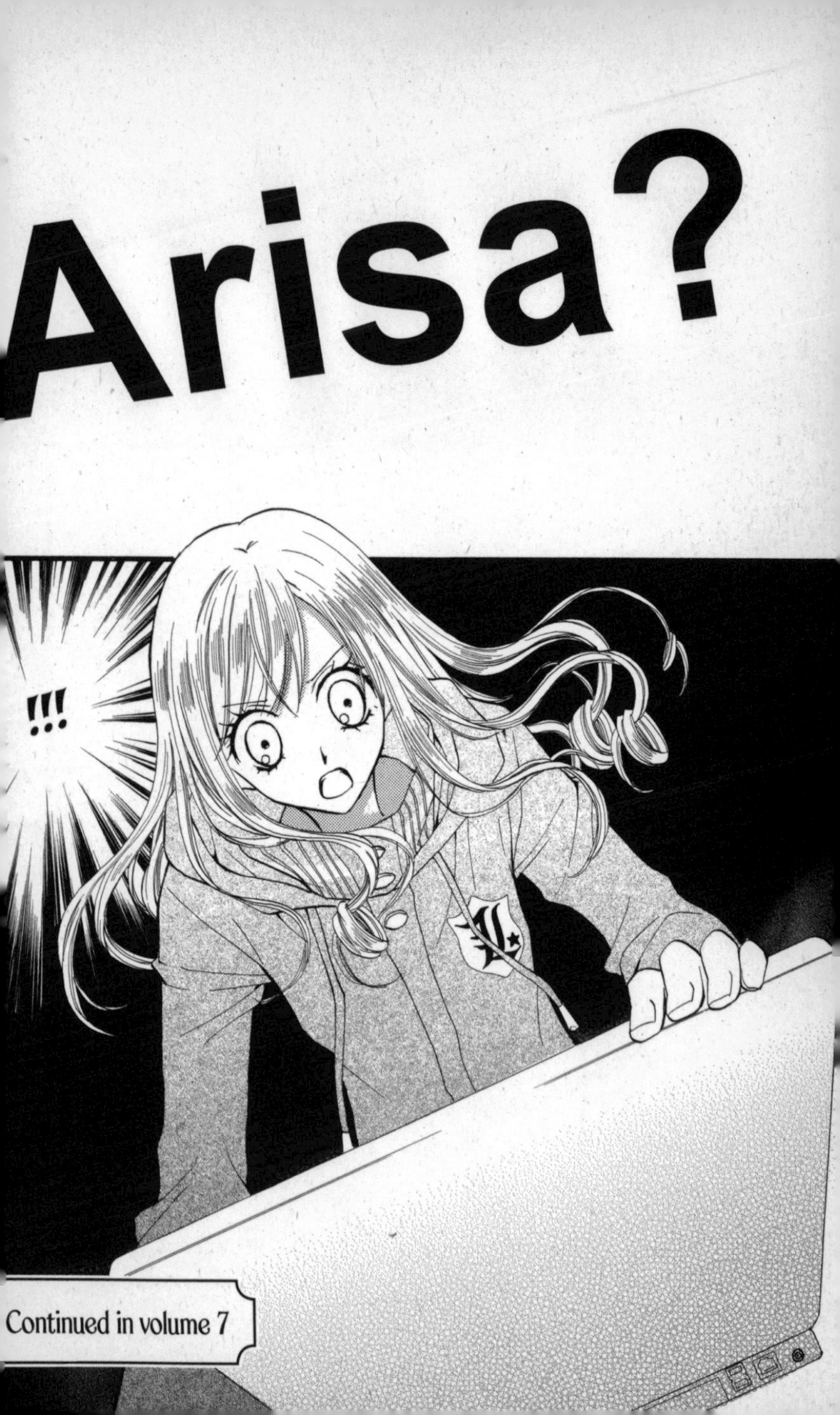

Arisa?
!!!
Continued in volume 7

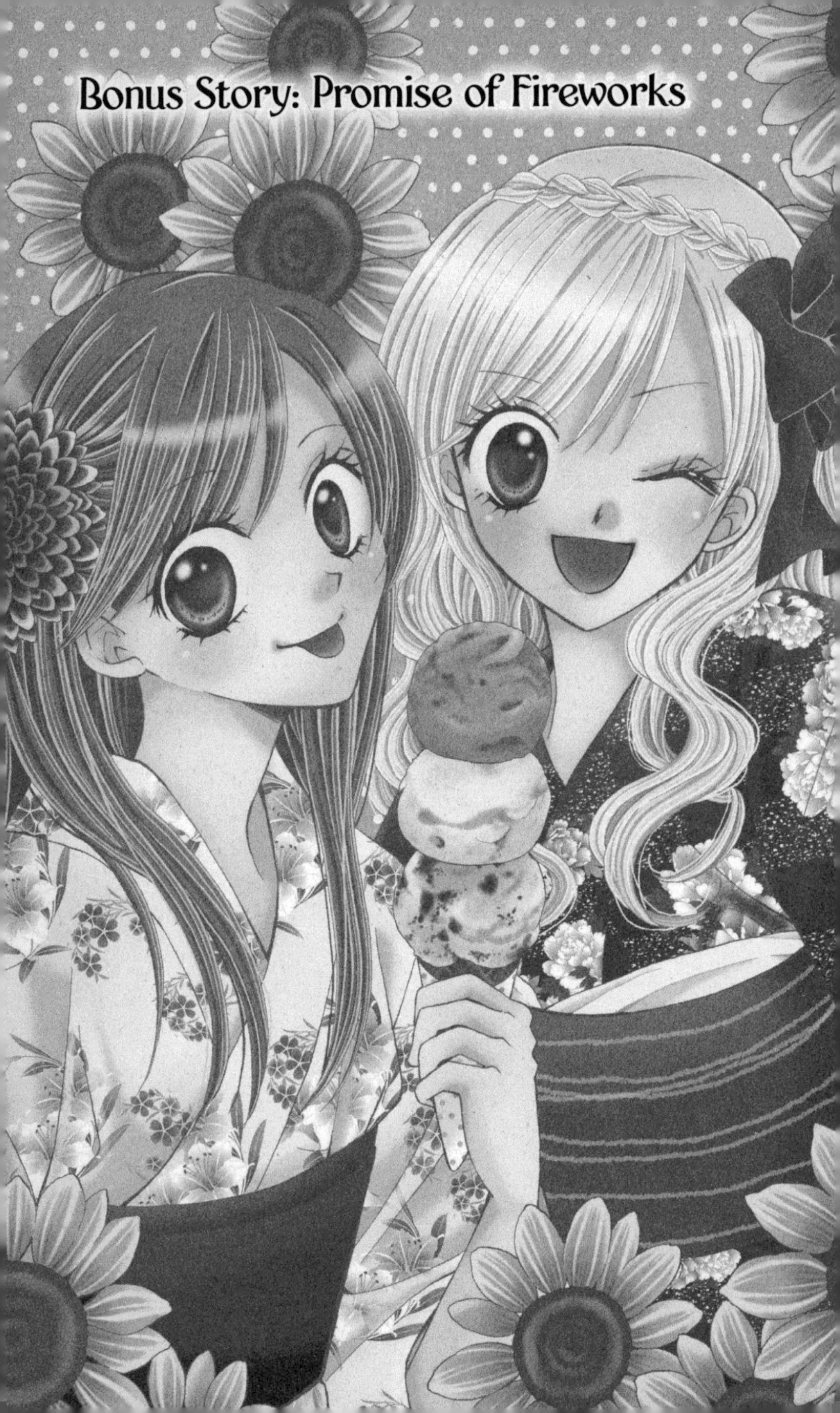
Bonus Story: Promise of Fireworks

Special Thanks:

T. Nakamura
H. Kishimoto
M. Nakata
Taki
My assistants
and editors at Nakayoshi
Takeda-sama
Red rooster
Takashi Shimoyama
GINNANSHA
Toriumi-sama

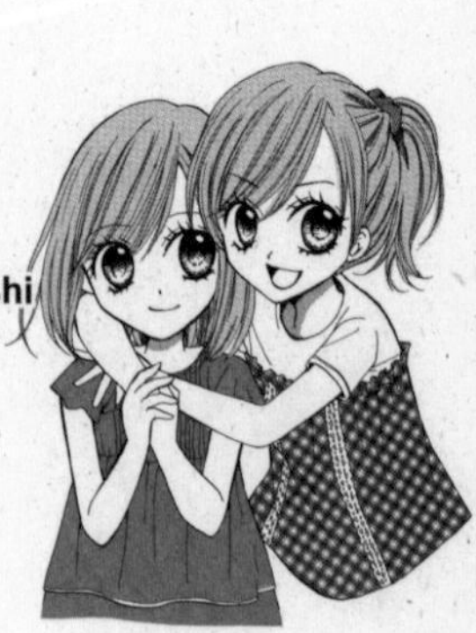

Please send mail to:

Natsumi Andō c/o
Kondansha Comics
1745 Broadway
New York, NY 10019

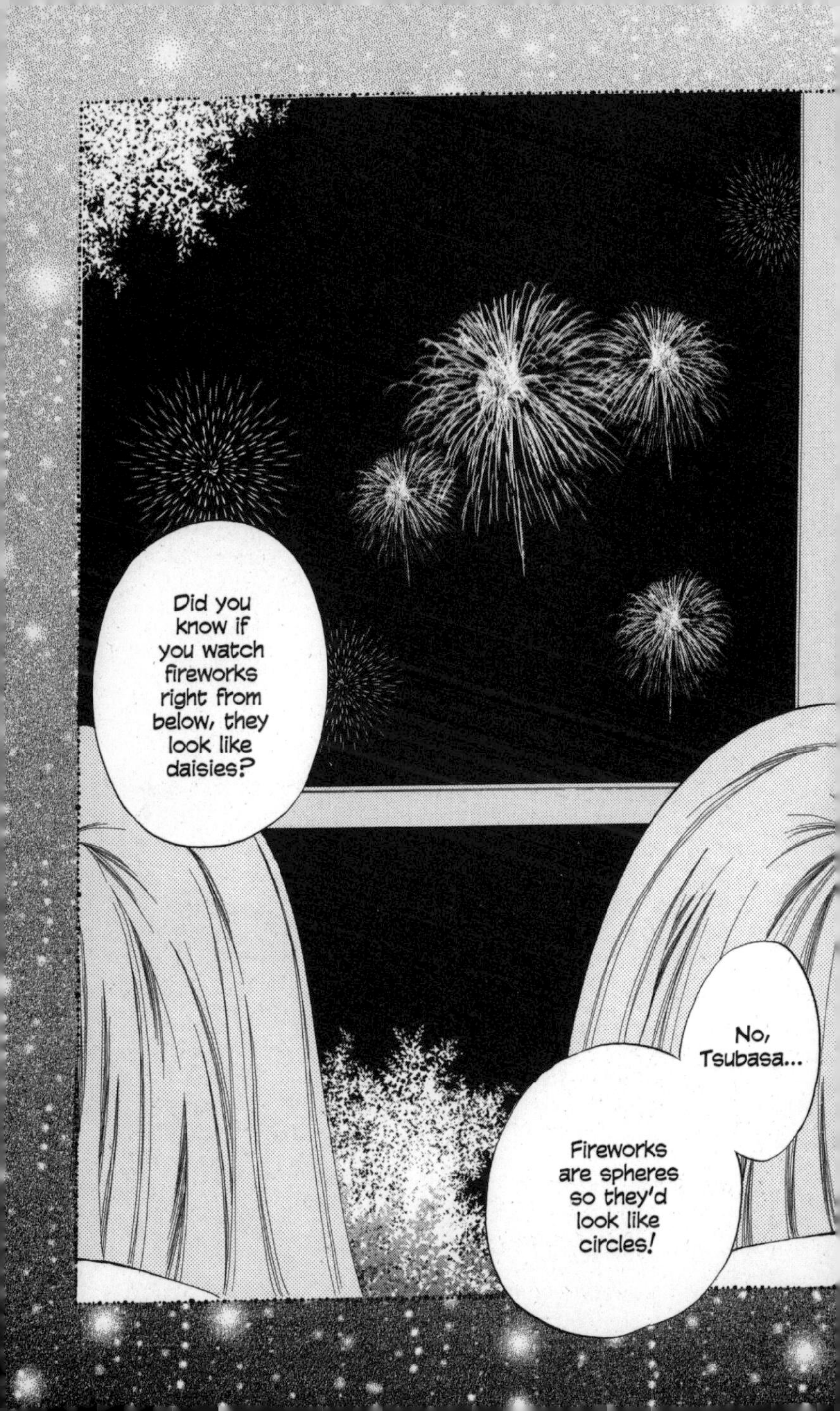
Did you know if you watch fireworks right from below, they look like daisies?
No, Tsubasa...
Fireworks are spheres so they'd look like circles!

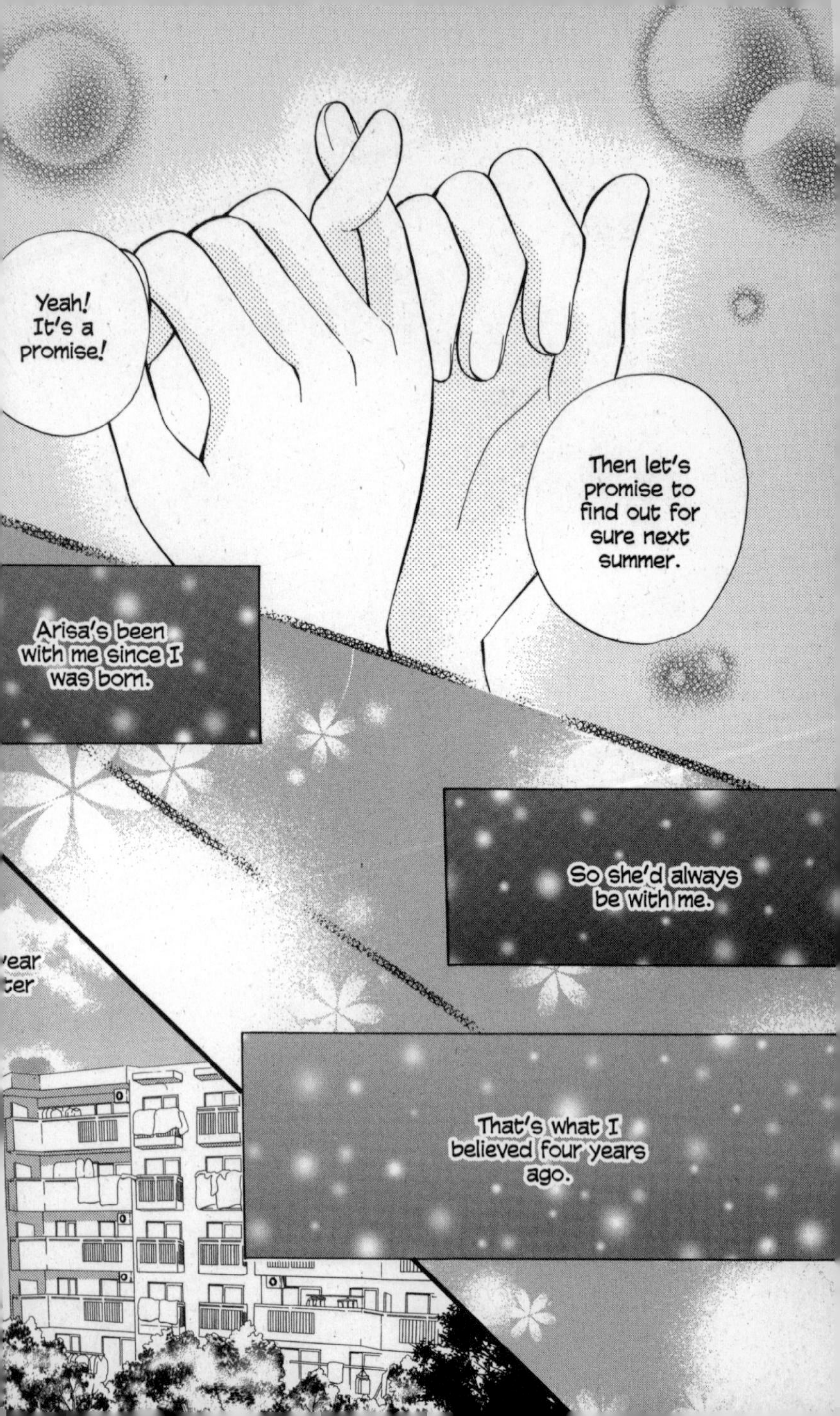
Then let's promise to find out for sure next summer.
Yeah! It's a promise!
Arisa's been with me since I was born.
So she'd always be with me.
That's what I believed four years ago.

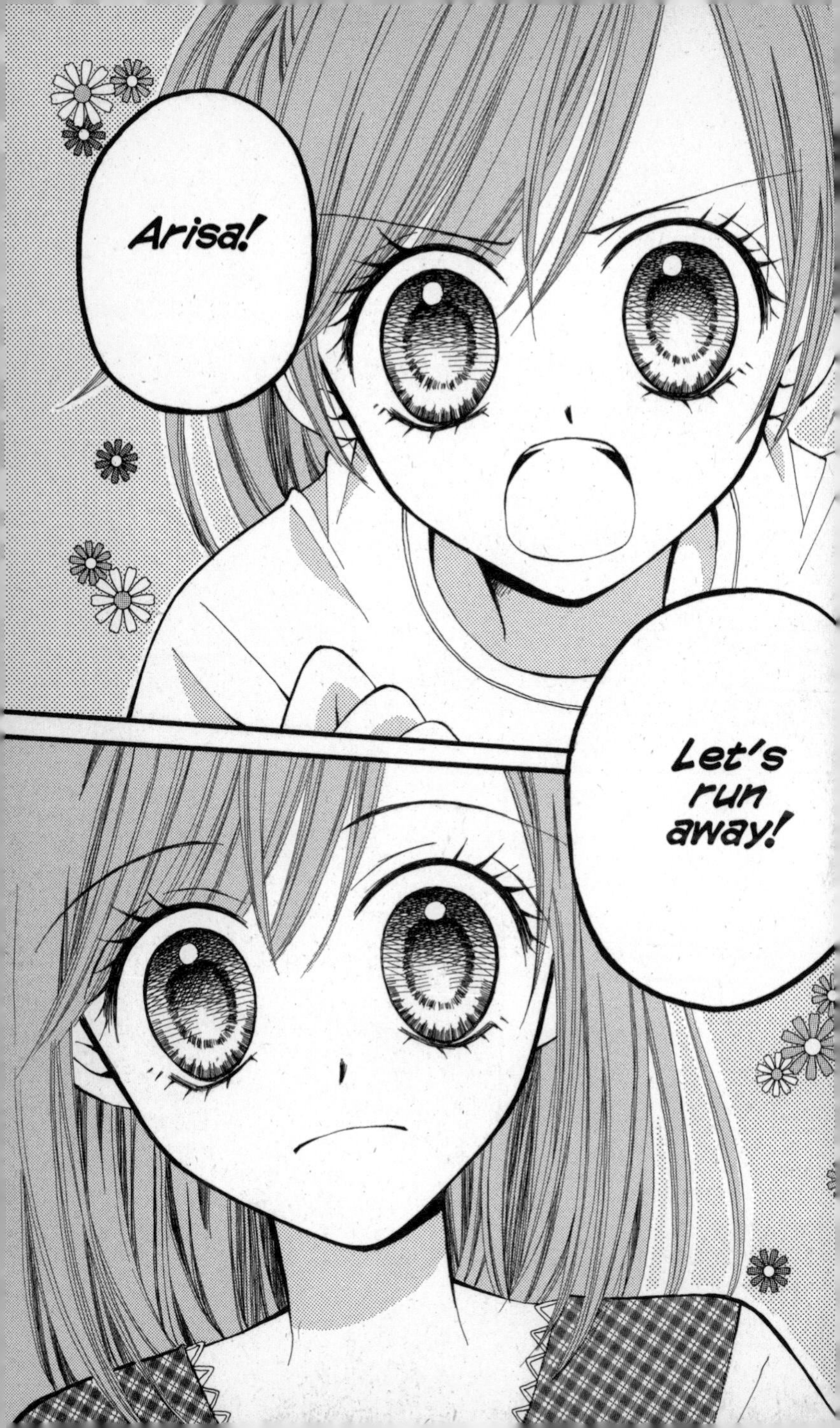
Arisa!
Let's run away!

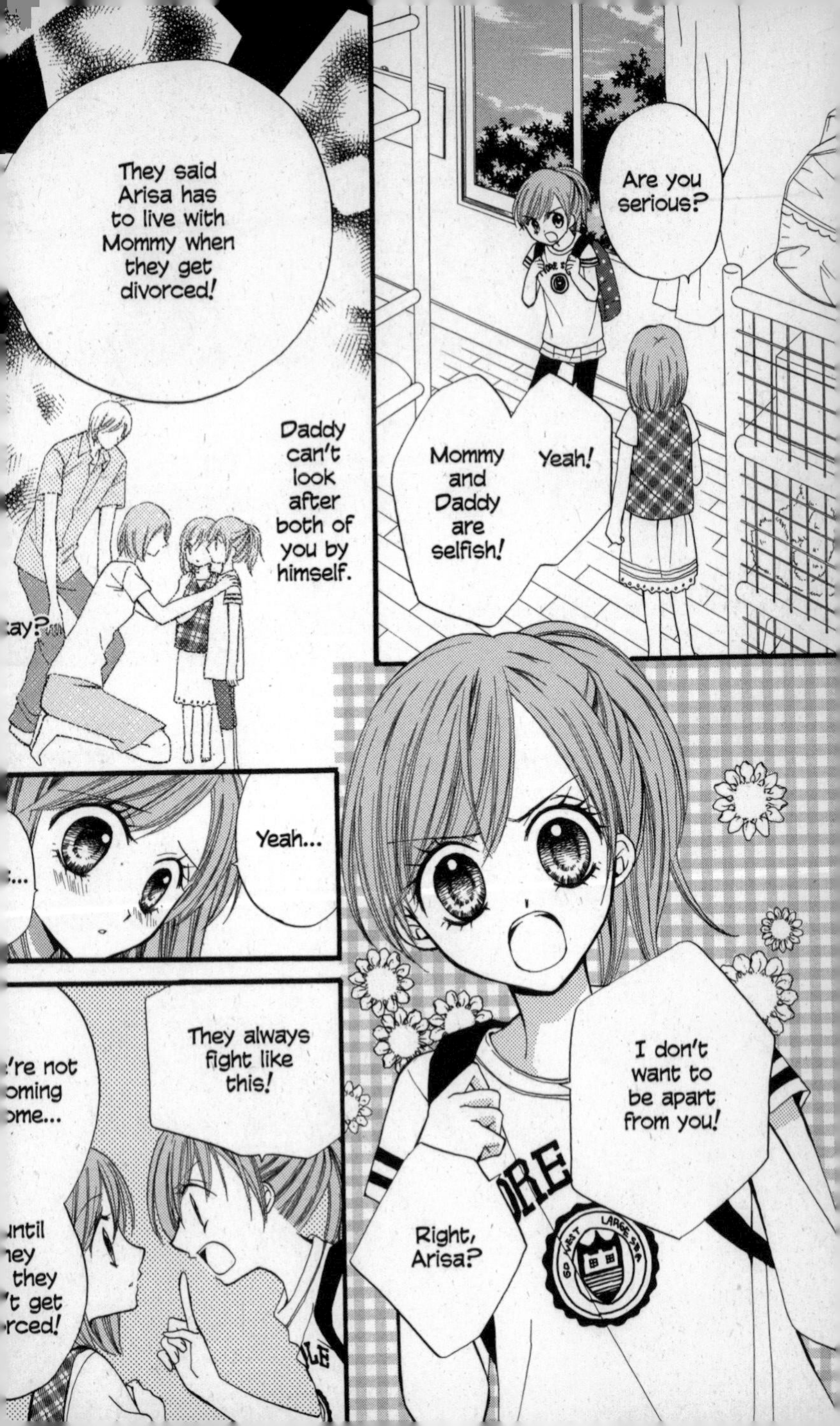

Are you serious?
Yeah!
Mommy and Daddy are selfish!
They said Arisa has to live with Mommy when they get divorced!
Daddy can't look after both of you by himself.
I don't want to be apart from you!
Right, Arisa?
Yeah...
They always fight like this!

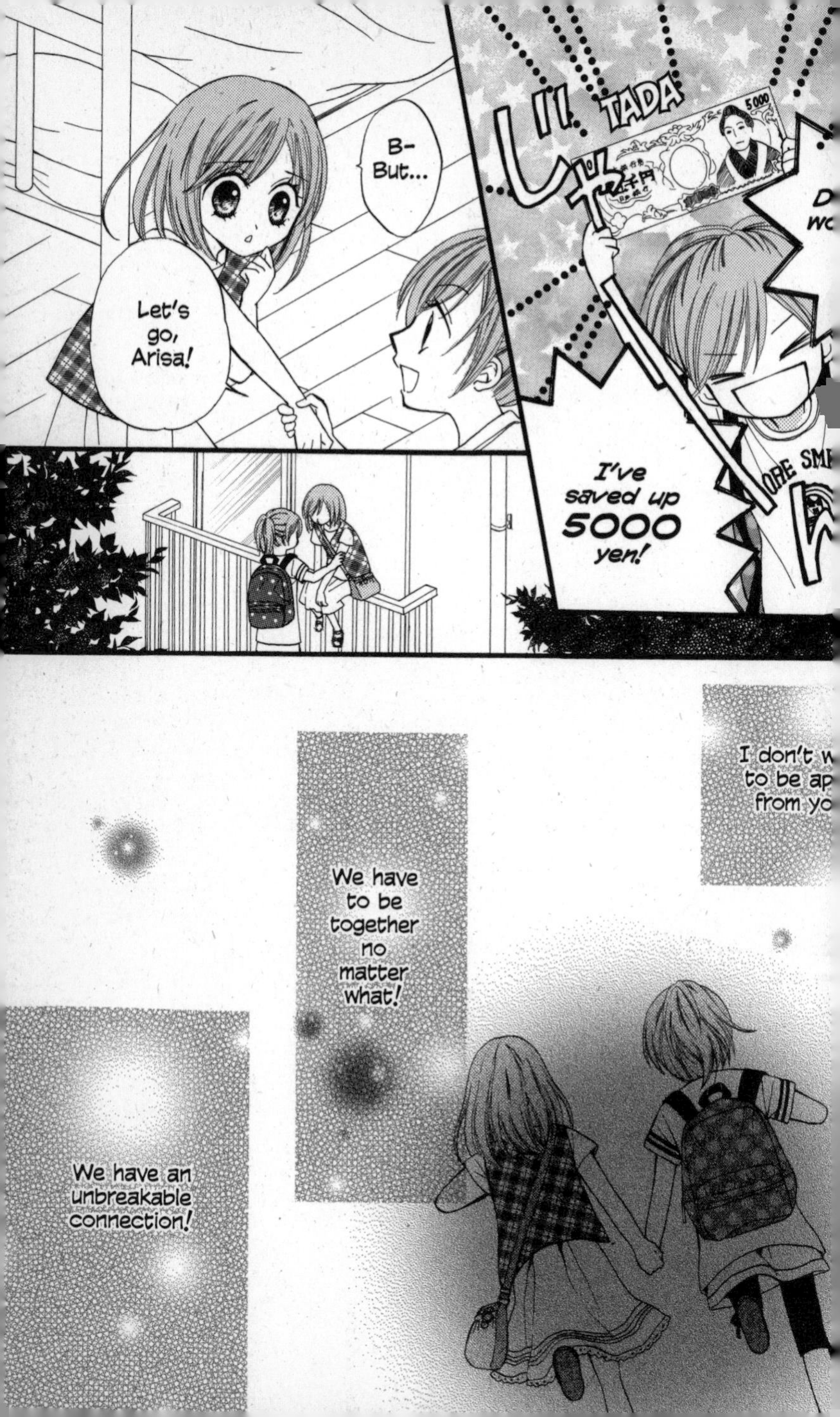

TADA
しゃ
I've saved up 5000 yen!
B-But...
Let's go, Arisa!
I don't w
to be ap
from yo
We have to be together no matter what!
We have an unbreakable connection!

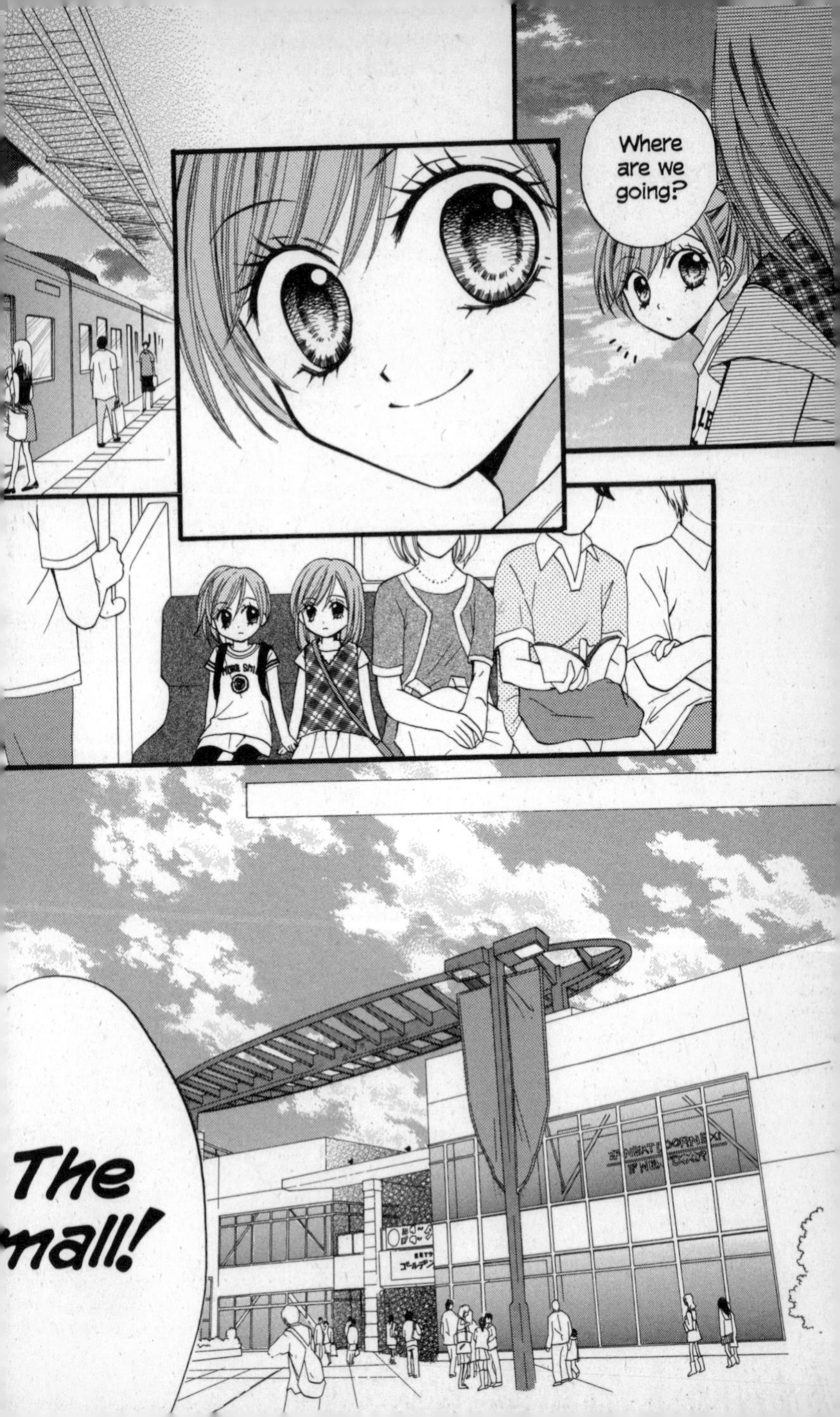
Where are we going?
The mall!

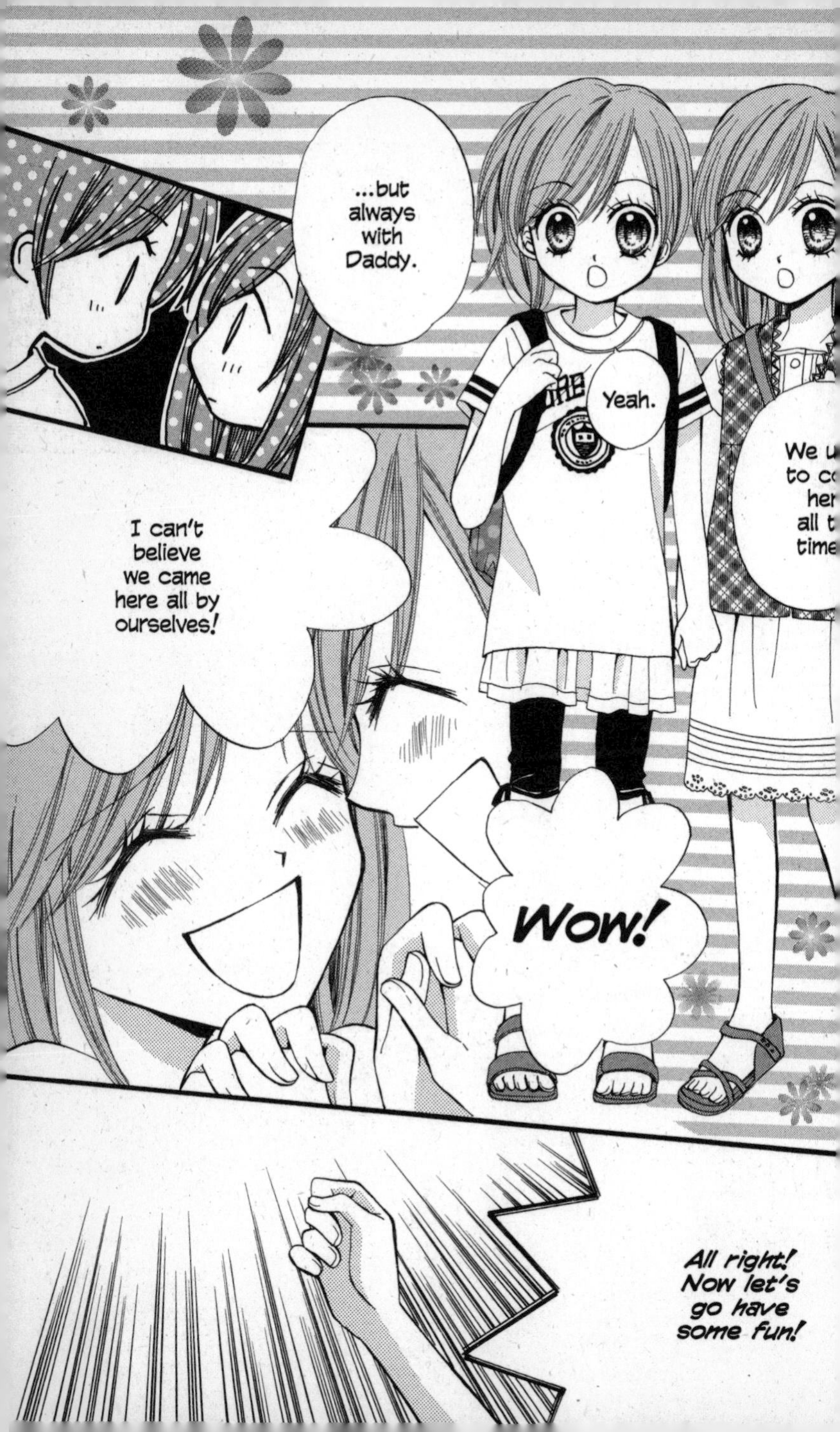

We u to co her all t time
Yeah.
...but always with Daddy.
WOW!
I can't believe we came here all by ourselves!
All right! Now let's go have some fun!

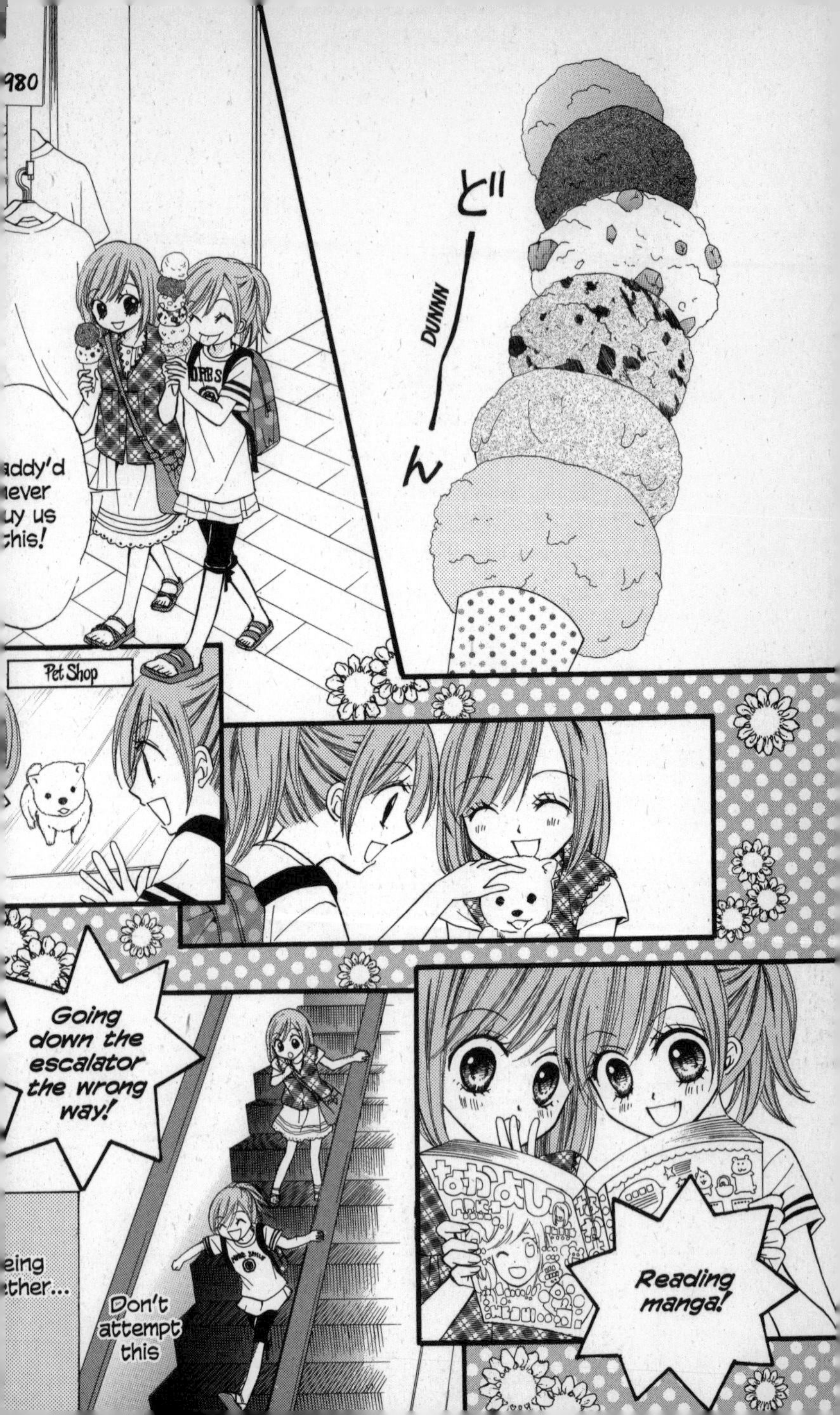

どーん
DUNNN
980
addy'd
never
uy us
his!
Pet Shop
Reading manga!
Going down the escalator the wrong way!
Don't attempt this
eing
ether...

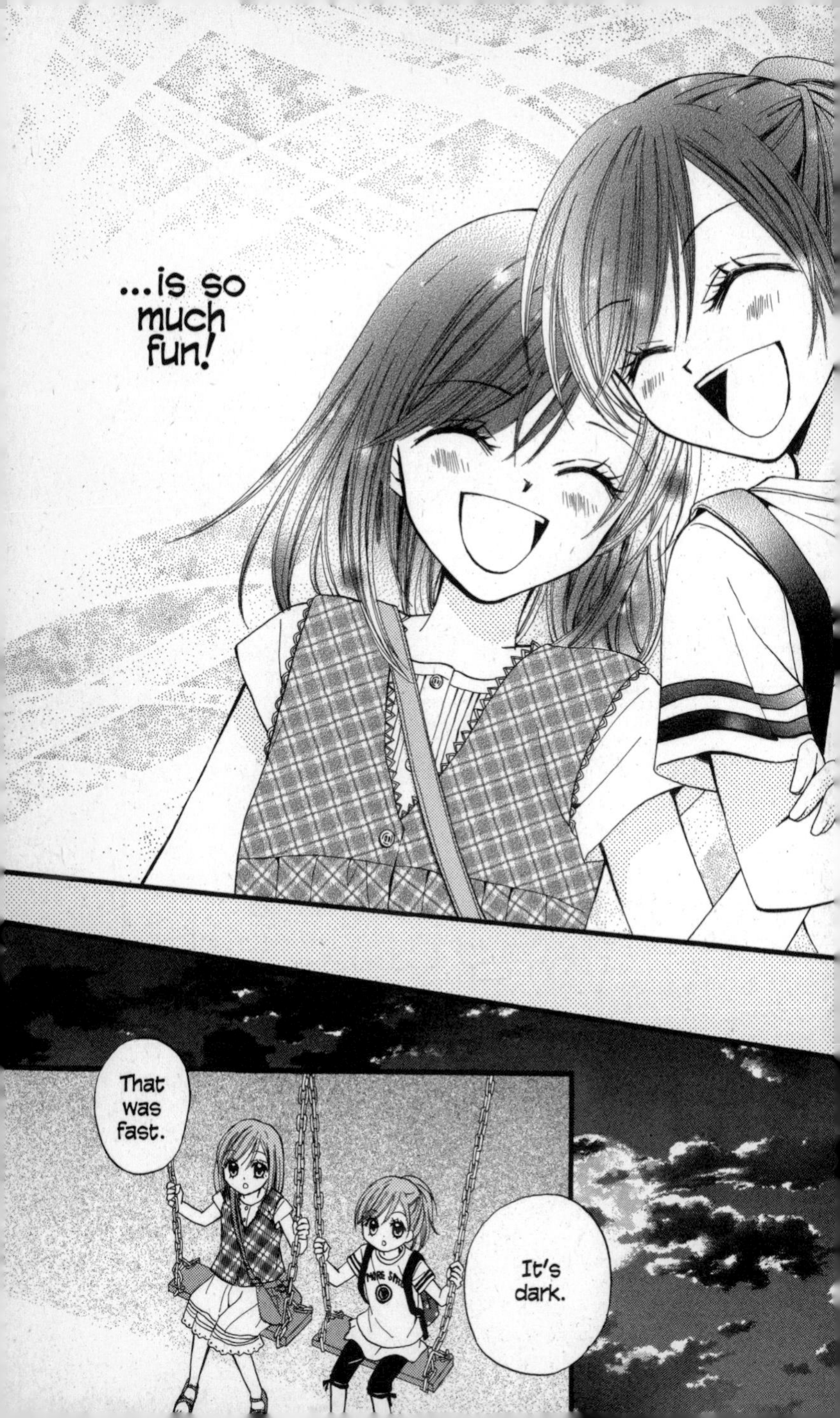
...is so much fun!
It's dark.
That was fast.

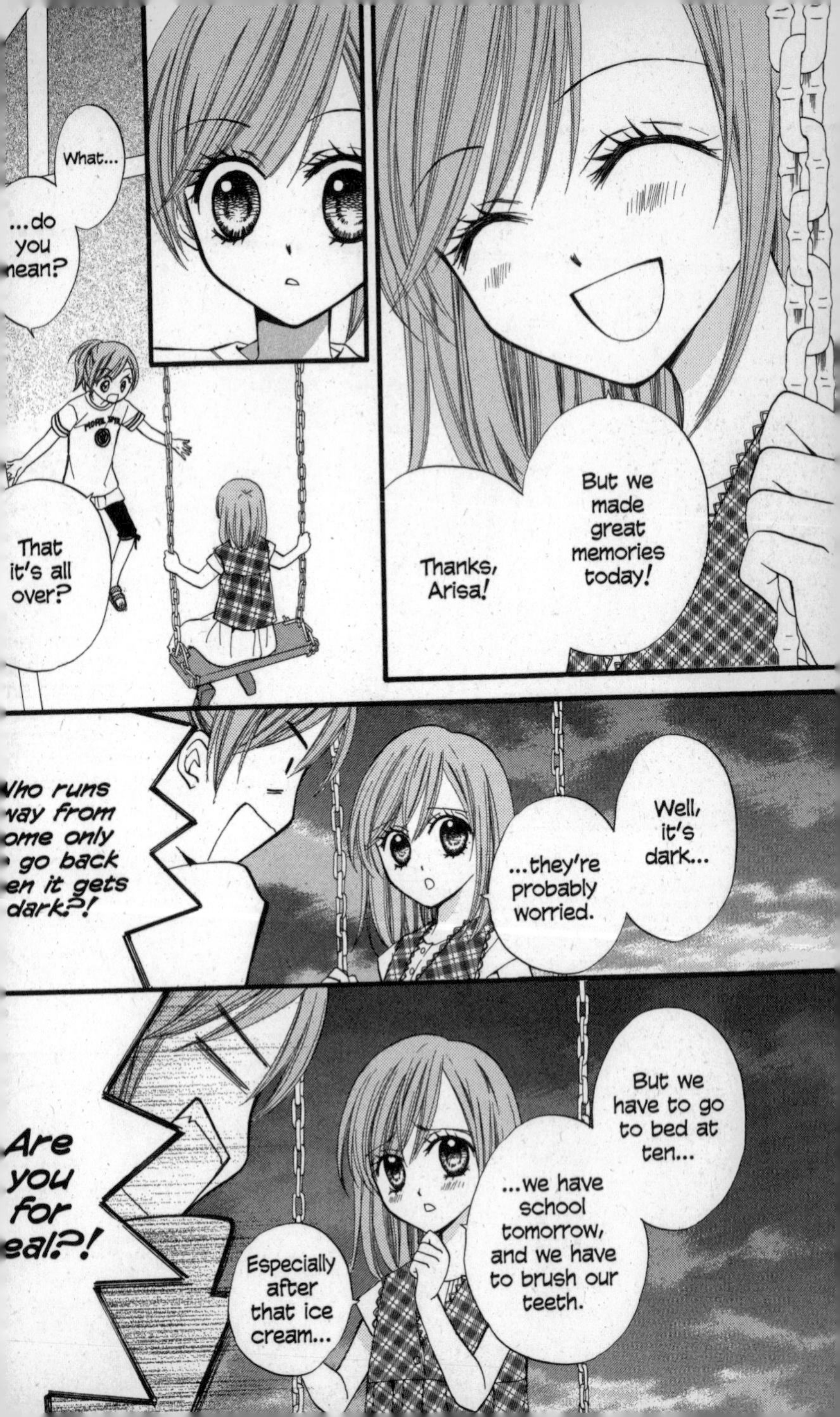

But we made great memories today!
Thanks, Arisa!
What...
...do you nean?
That it's all over?
Well, it's dark...
...they're probably worried.
Vho runs vay from ome only go back en it gets dark?!
But we have to go to bed at ten...
...we have school tomorrow, and we have to brush our teeth.
Especially after that ice cream...
Are you for eal?!

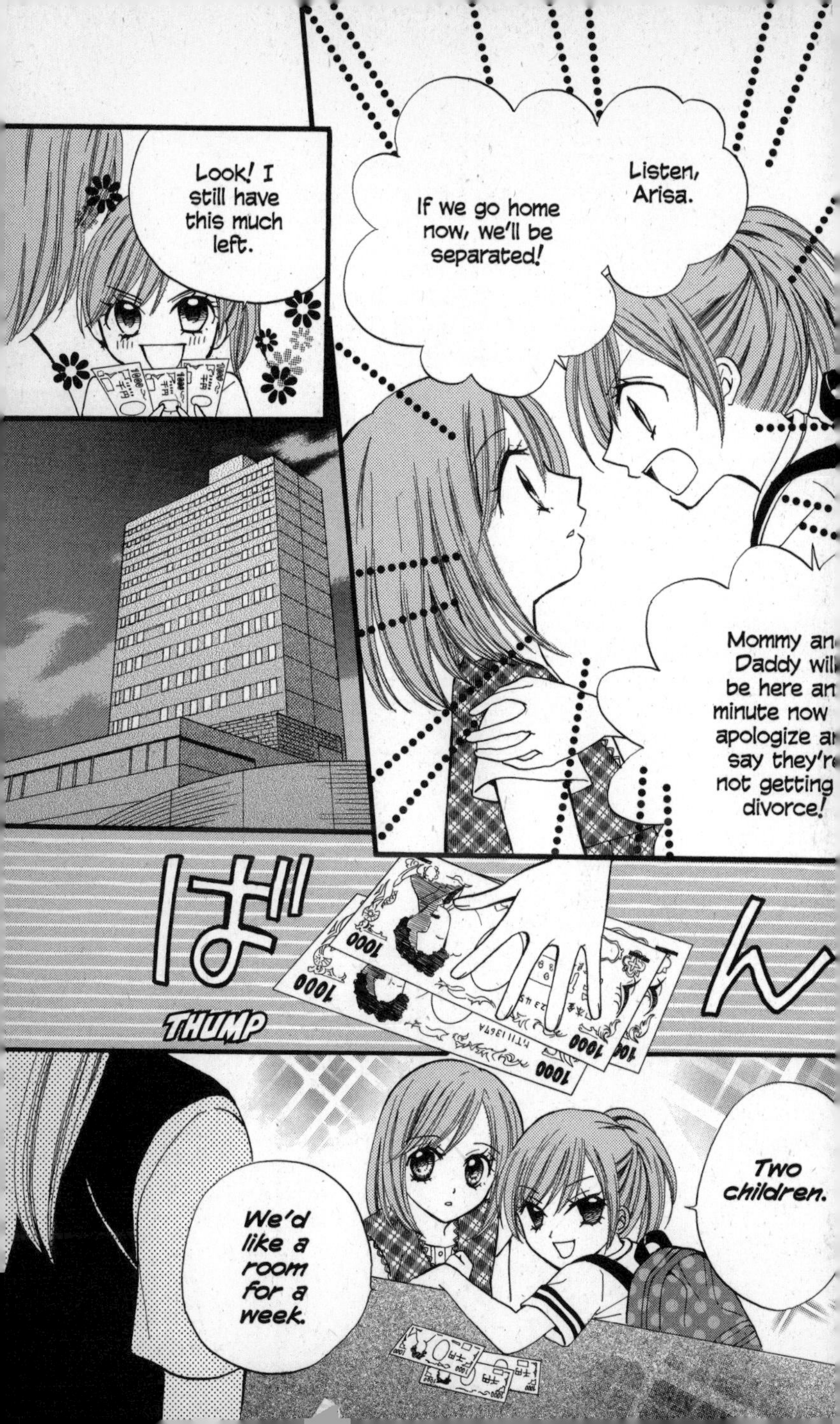

Listen, Arisa.
If we go home now, we'll be separated!
Mommy an Daddy wil be here an minute now apologize ar say they'r not getting divorce!
Look! I still have this much left.
ばん
THUMP
Two children.
We'd like a room for a week.

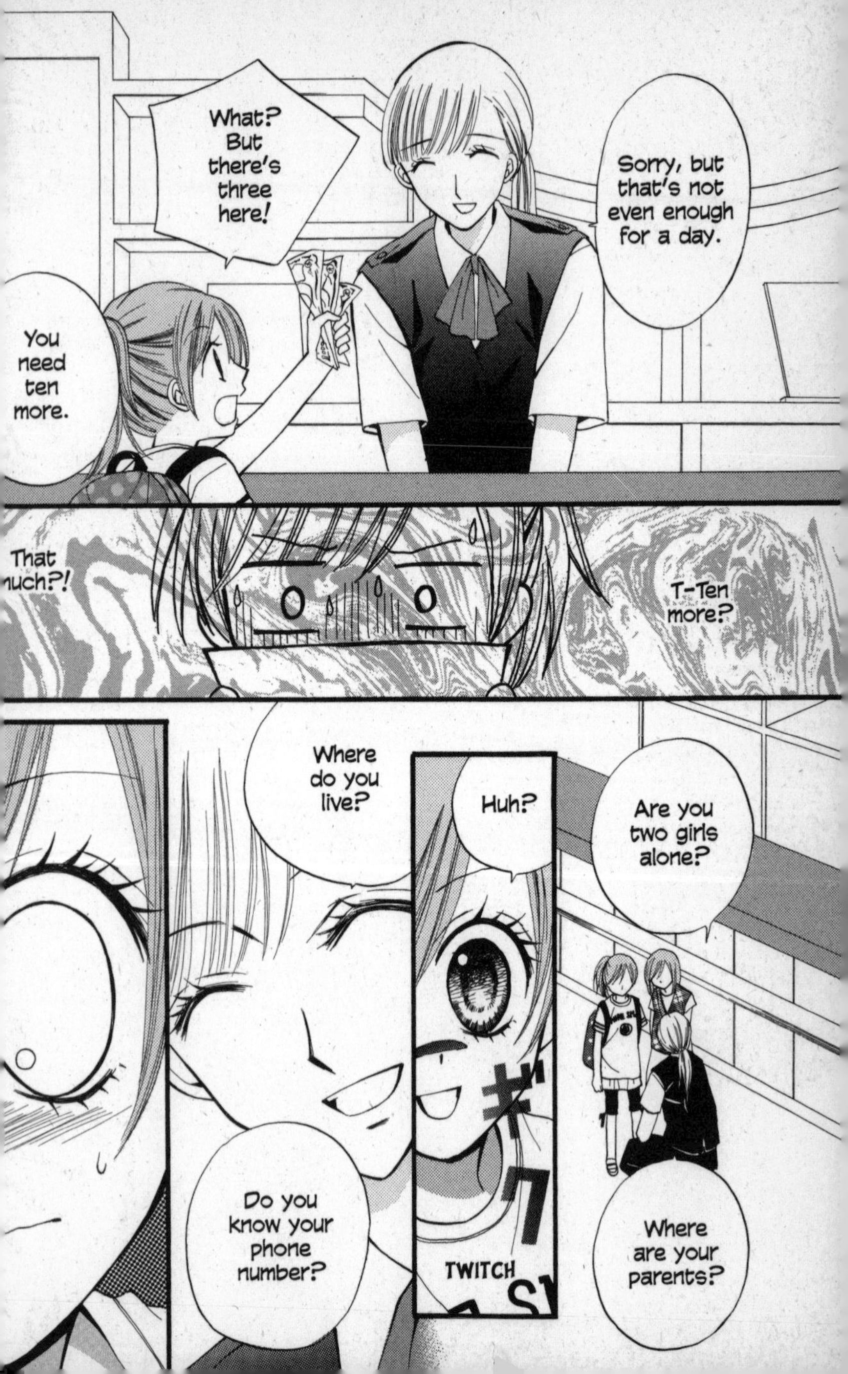
Sorry, but that's not even enough for a day.
What? But there's three here!
You need ten more.
T-Ten more?
That much?!
Are you two girls alone?
Where are your parents?
Huh?
TWITCH
Where do you live?
Do you know your phone number?

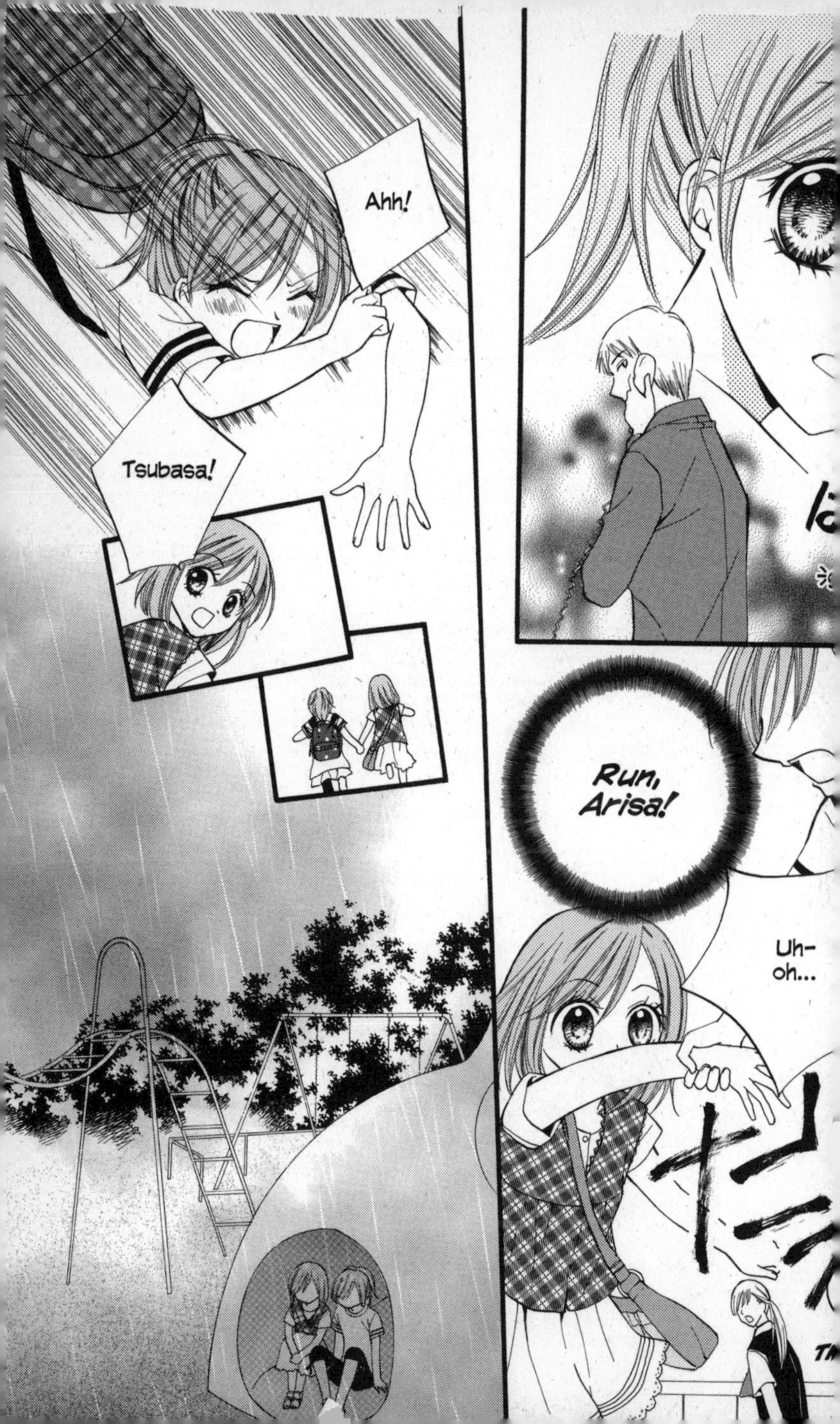
Run, Arisa!
Uh-oh...
Ahh!
Tsubasa!

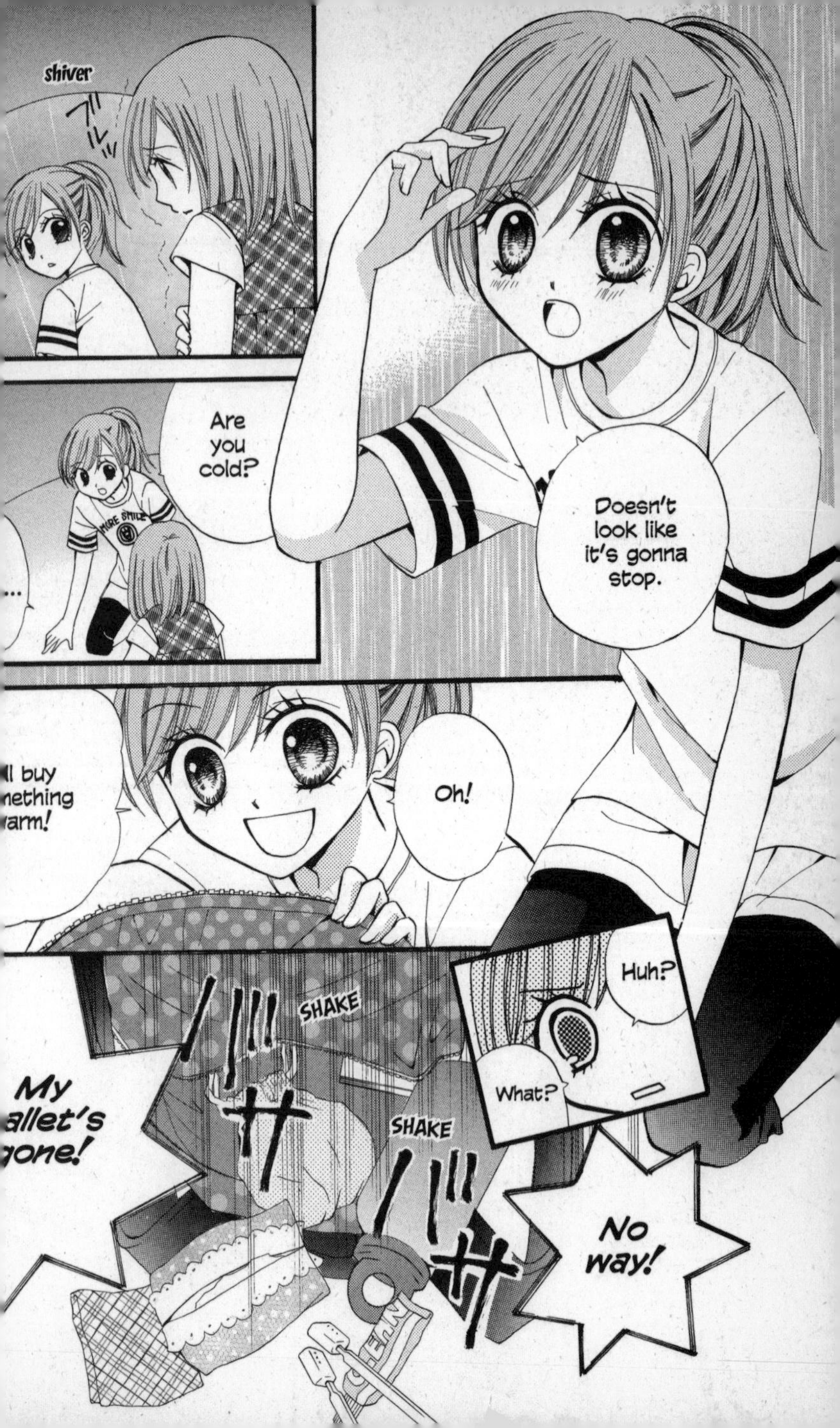
Doesn't look like it's gonna stop.
shiver
ブルッ
Are you cold?
...
Oh!
ll buy nething arm!
Huh?
What?
SHAKE
SHAKE
No way!
My allet's gone!

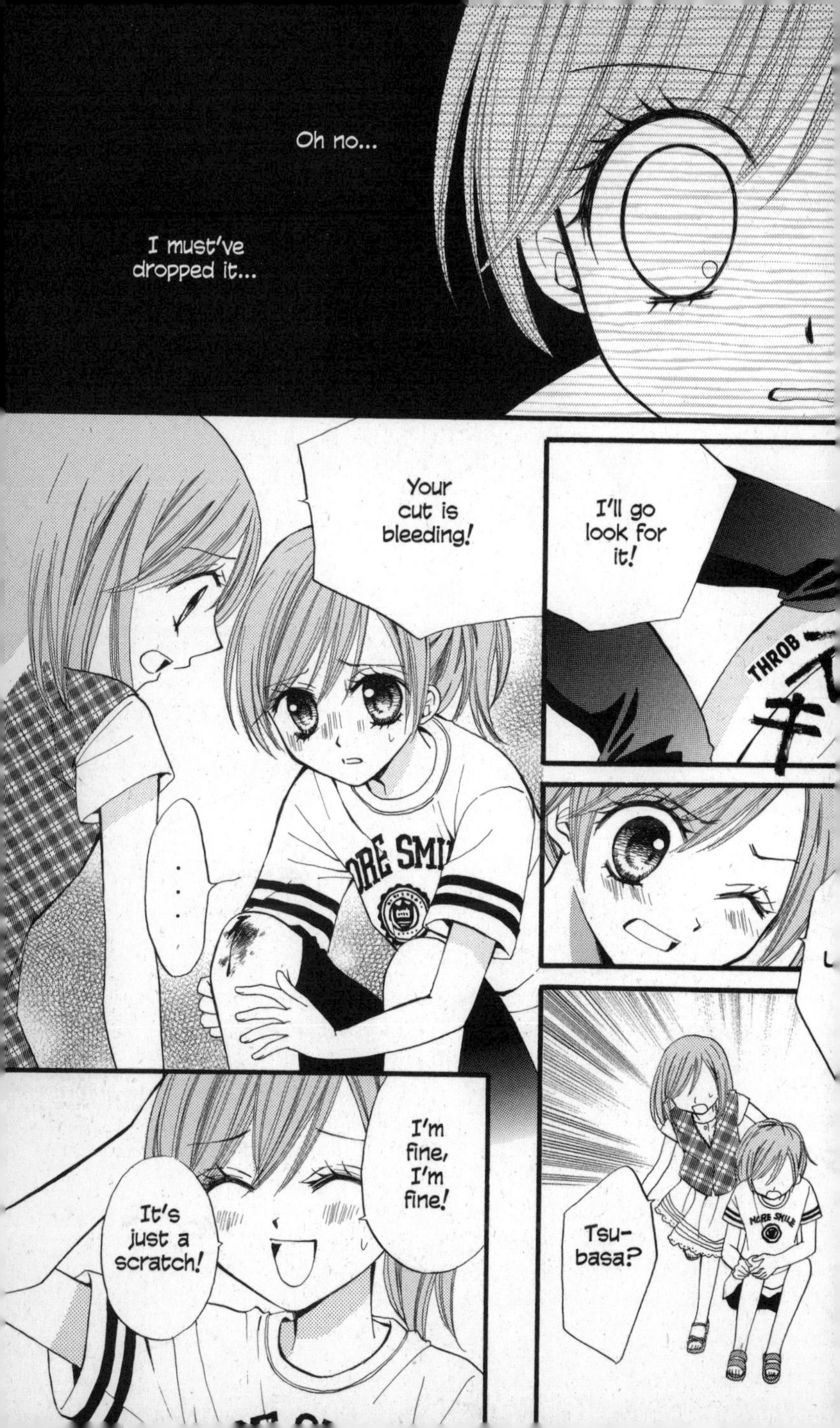
Oh no...
I must've dropped it...
I'll go look for it!
THROB
Tsu-basa?
Your cut is bleeding!
...
I'm fine, I'm fine!
It's just a scratch!

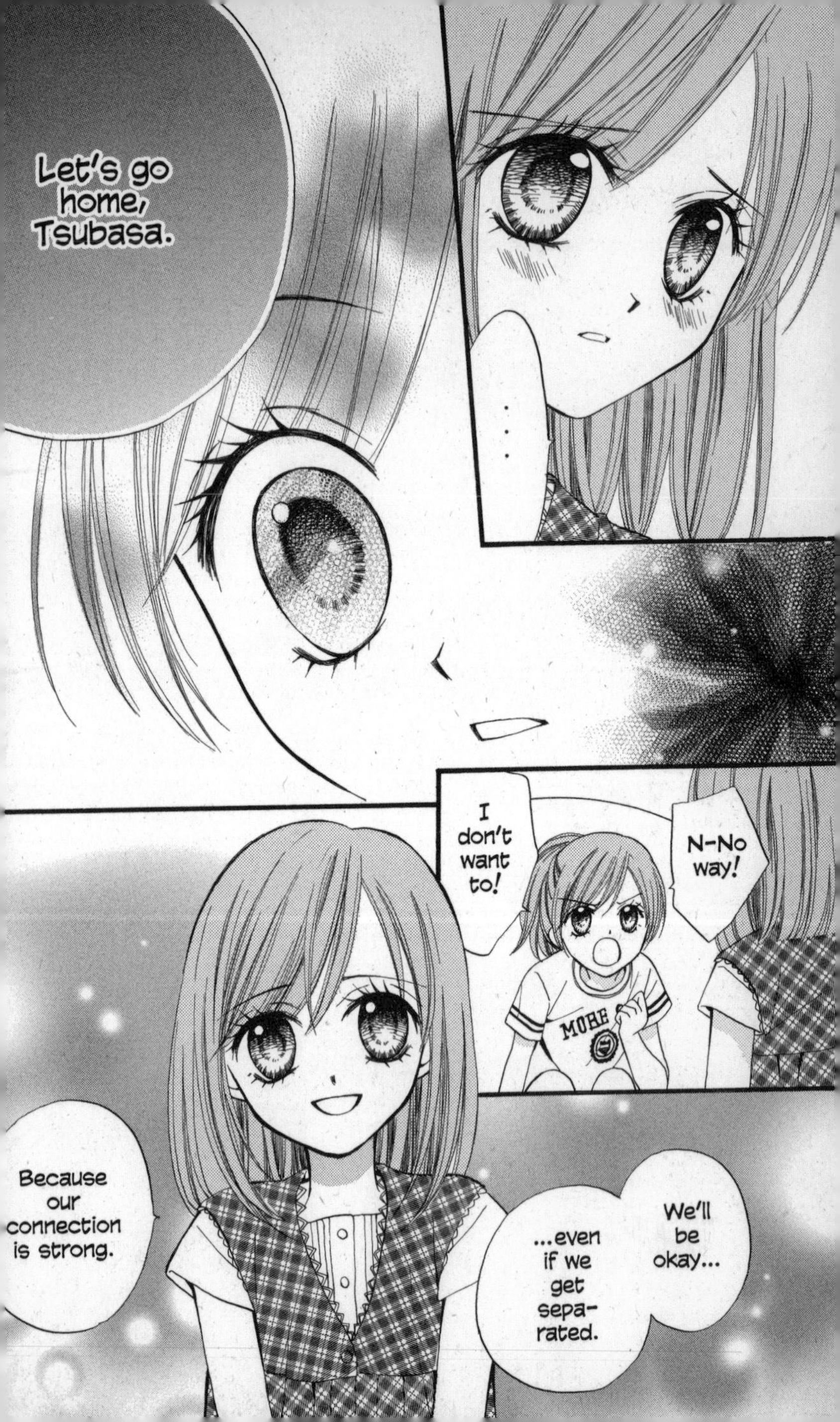
Let's go home, Tsubasa.
N-No way!
I don't want to!
We'll be okay...
...even if we get sepa-rated.
Because our connection is strong.

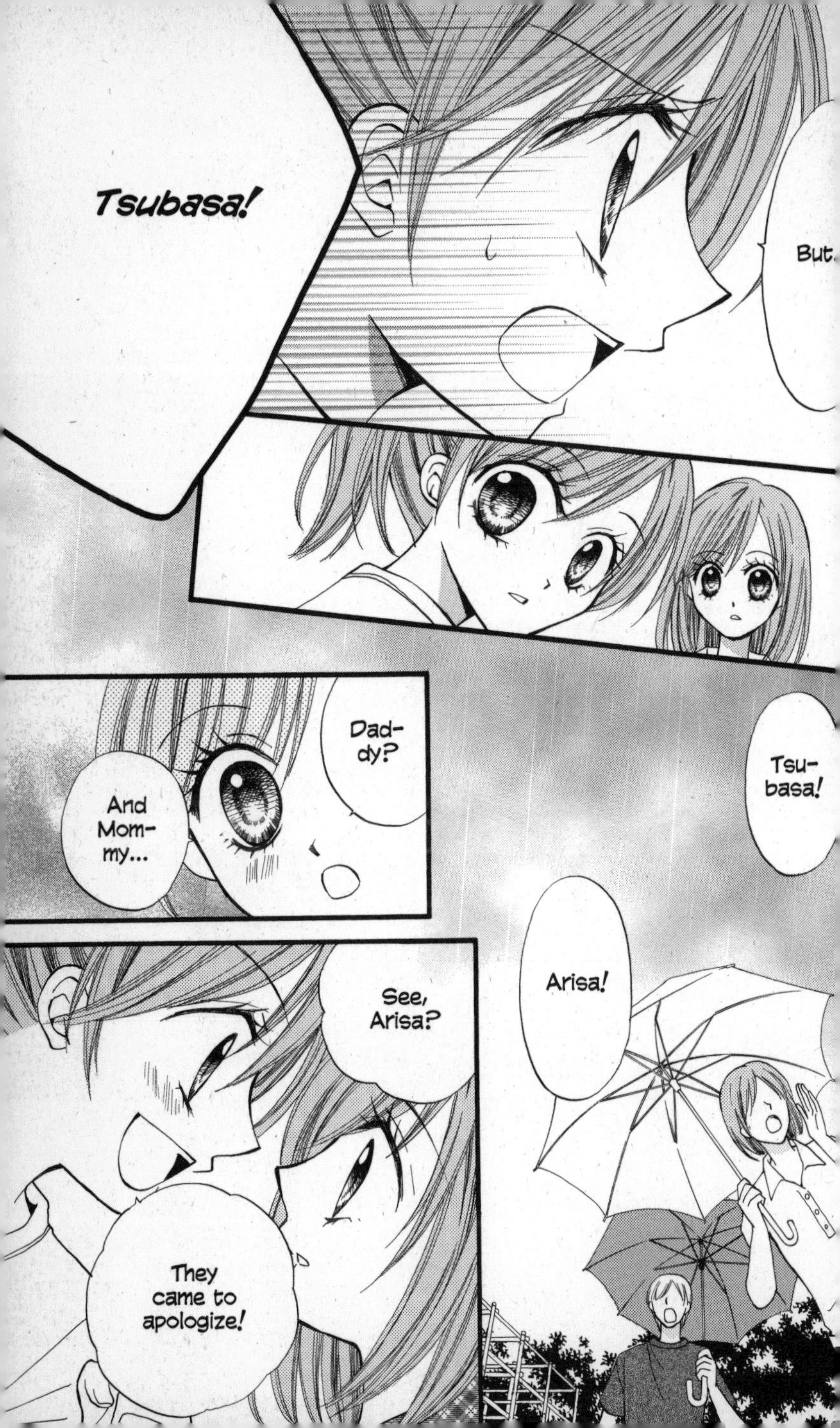
But.
Tsubasa!
Tsu-basa!
Arisa!
Dad-dy?
And Mom-my...
See, Arisa?
They came to apologize!

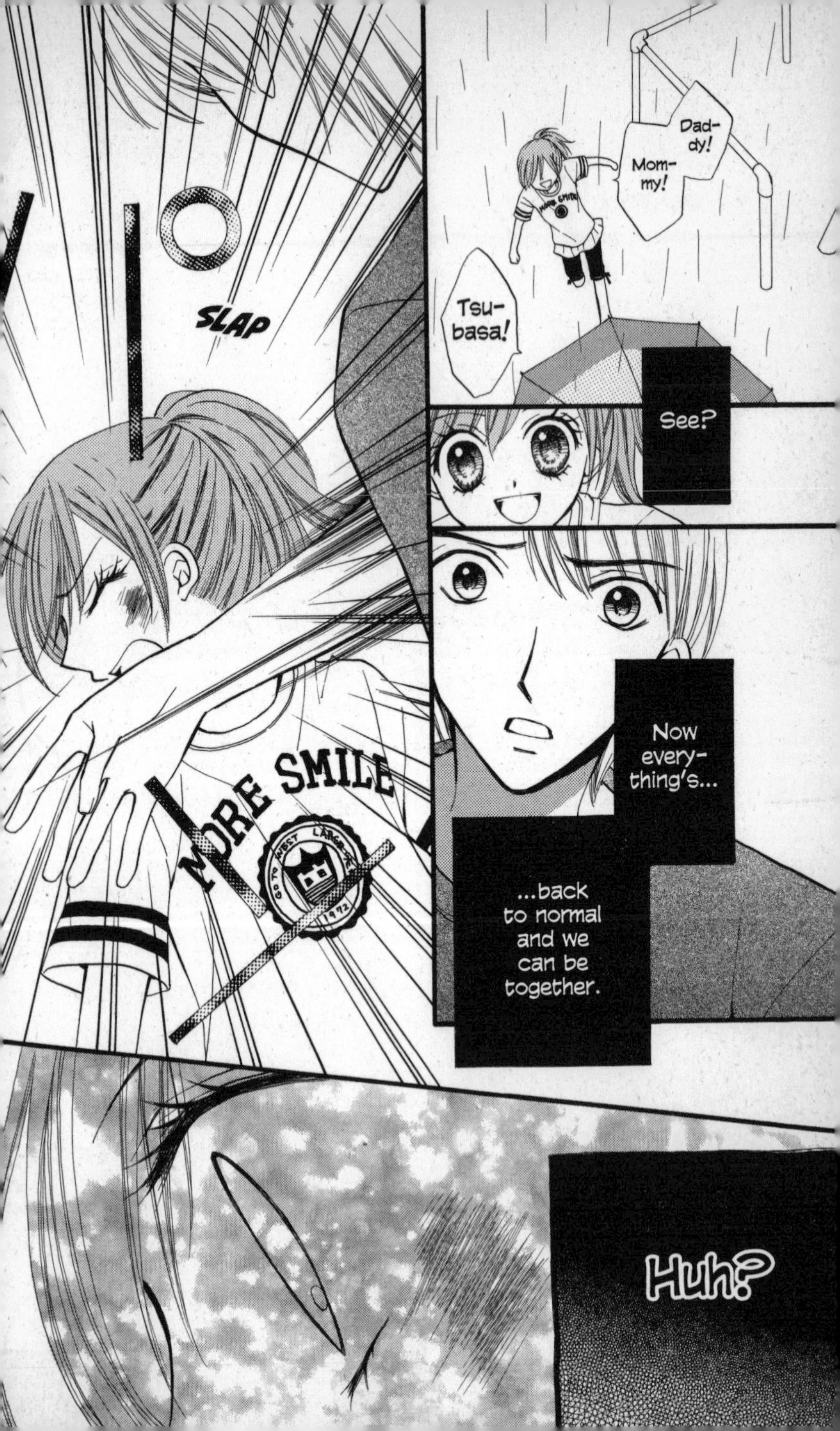
Dad-dy!
Mom-my!
Tsu-basa!
See?
Now every-thing's...
...back to normal and we can be together.
SLAP
MORE SMILE
Huh?

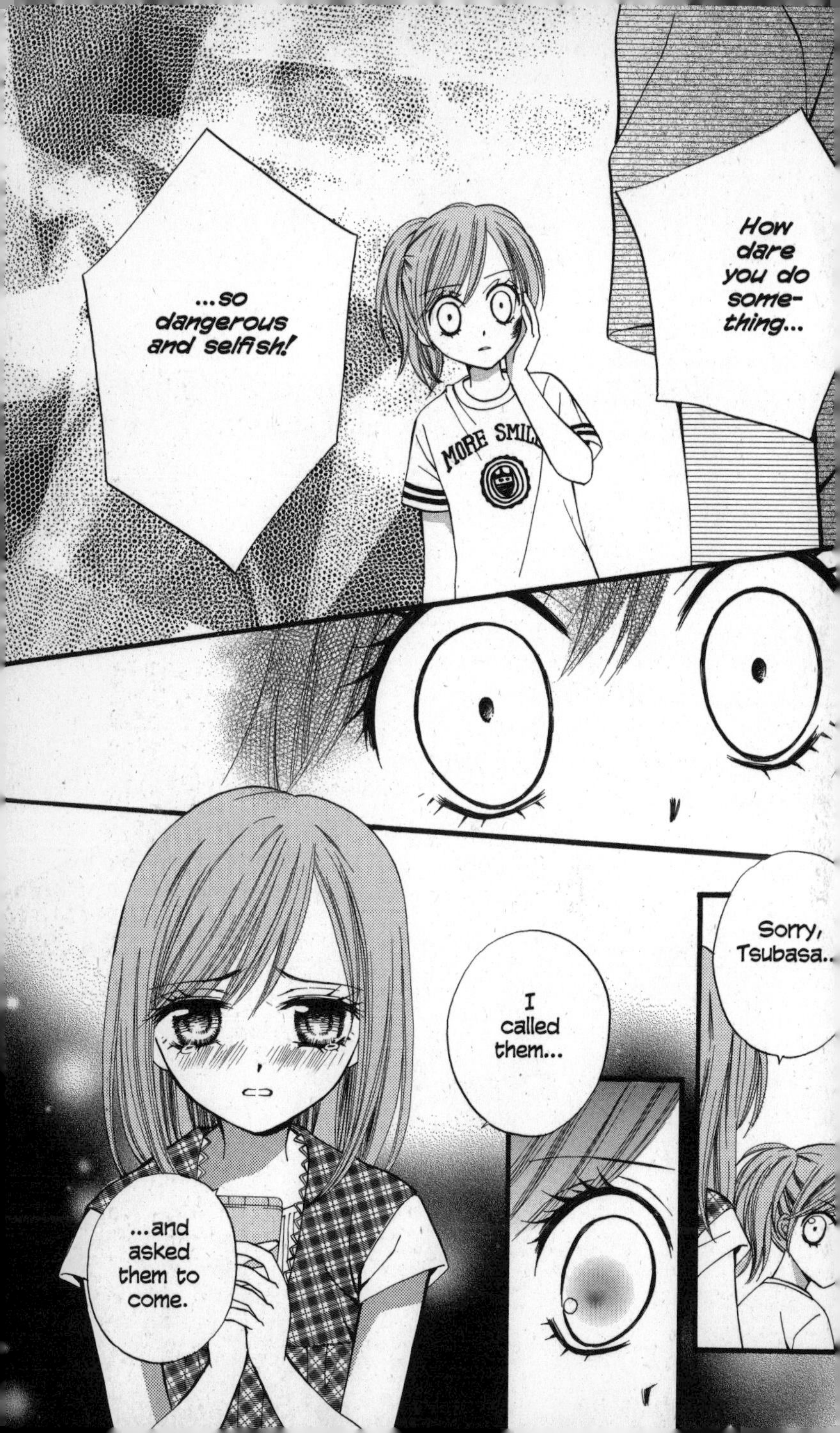
How dare you do some-thing...
...so dangerous and selfish!
Sorry, Tsubasa...
I called them...
...and asked them to come.

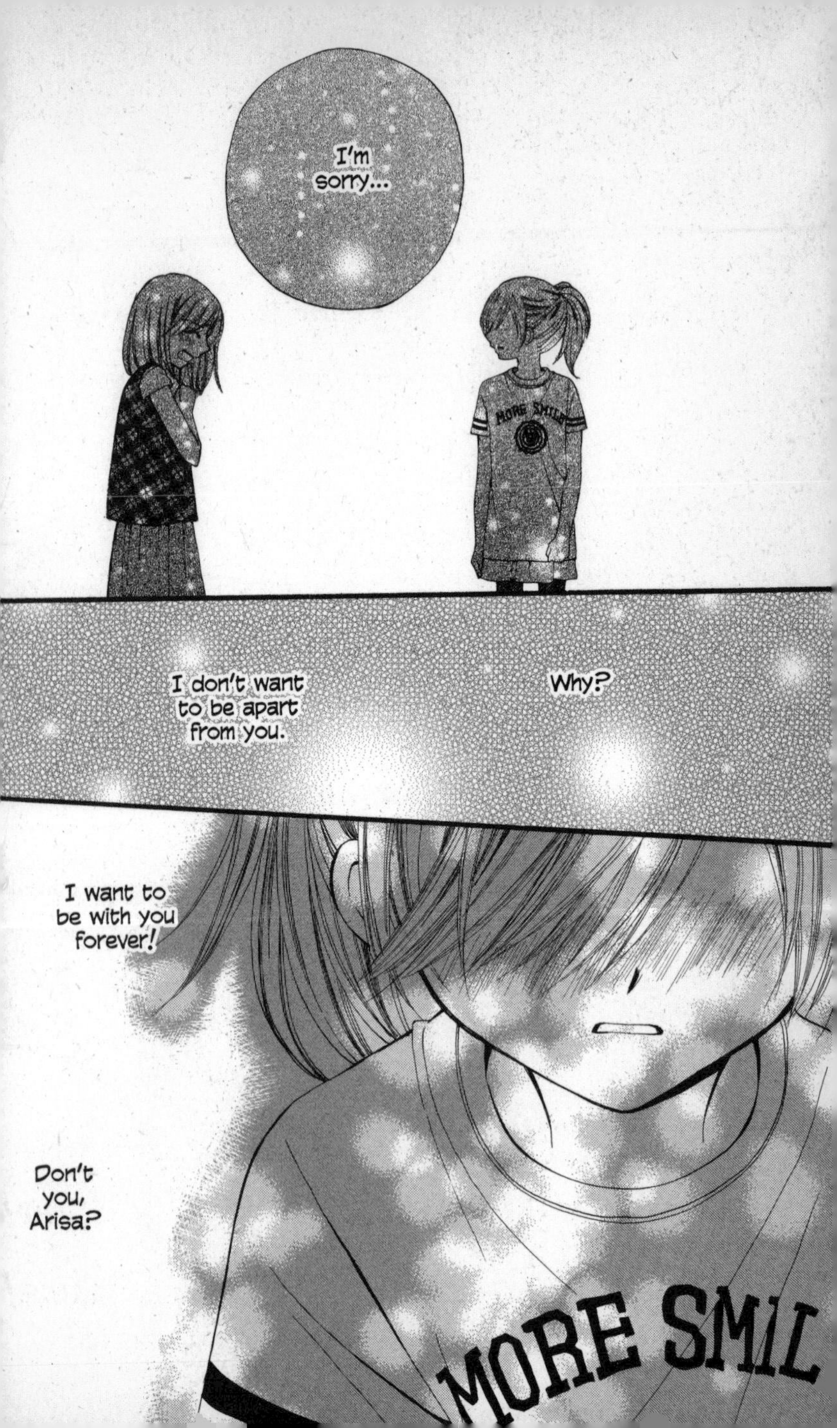
I'm sorry...
Why?
I don't want to be apart from you.
I want to be with you forever!
Don't you, Arisa?
MORE SMIL

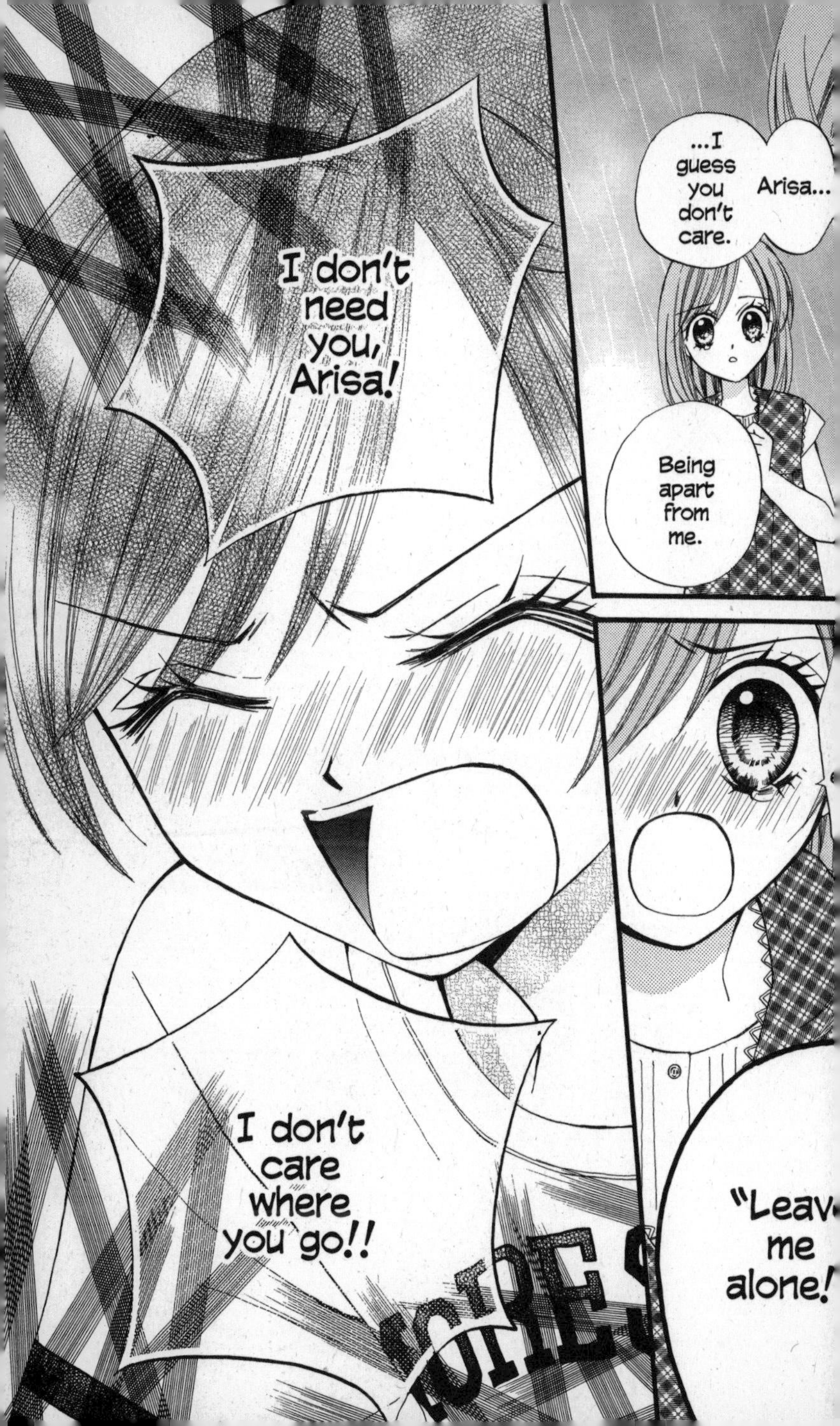
Arisa...
...I guess you don't care.
Being apart from me.
"Leav me alone!
I don't need you, Arisa!
I don't care where you go!!

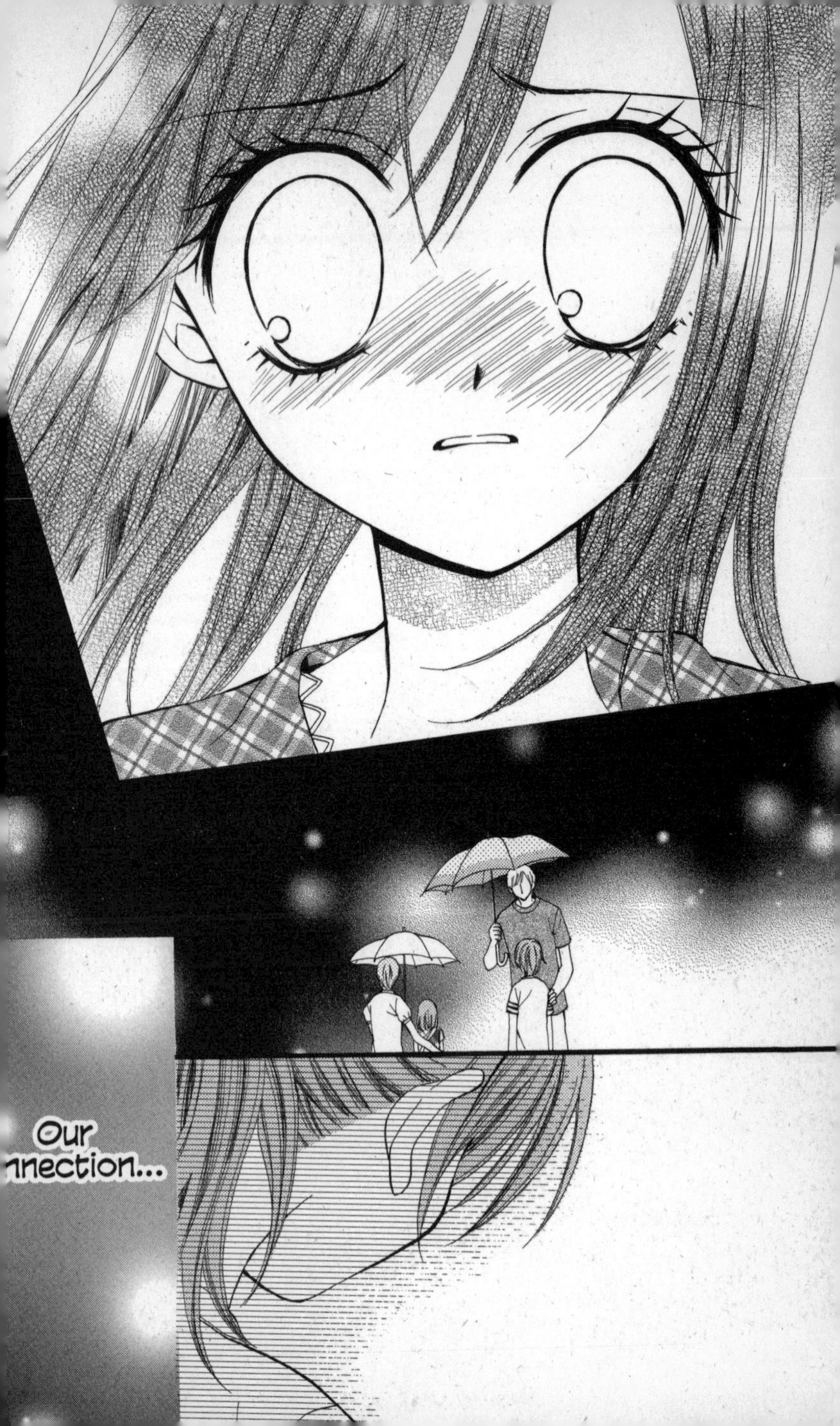
Our
nnection...

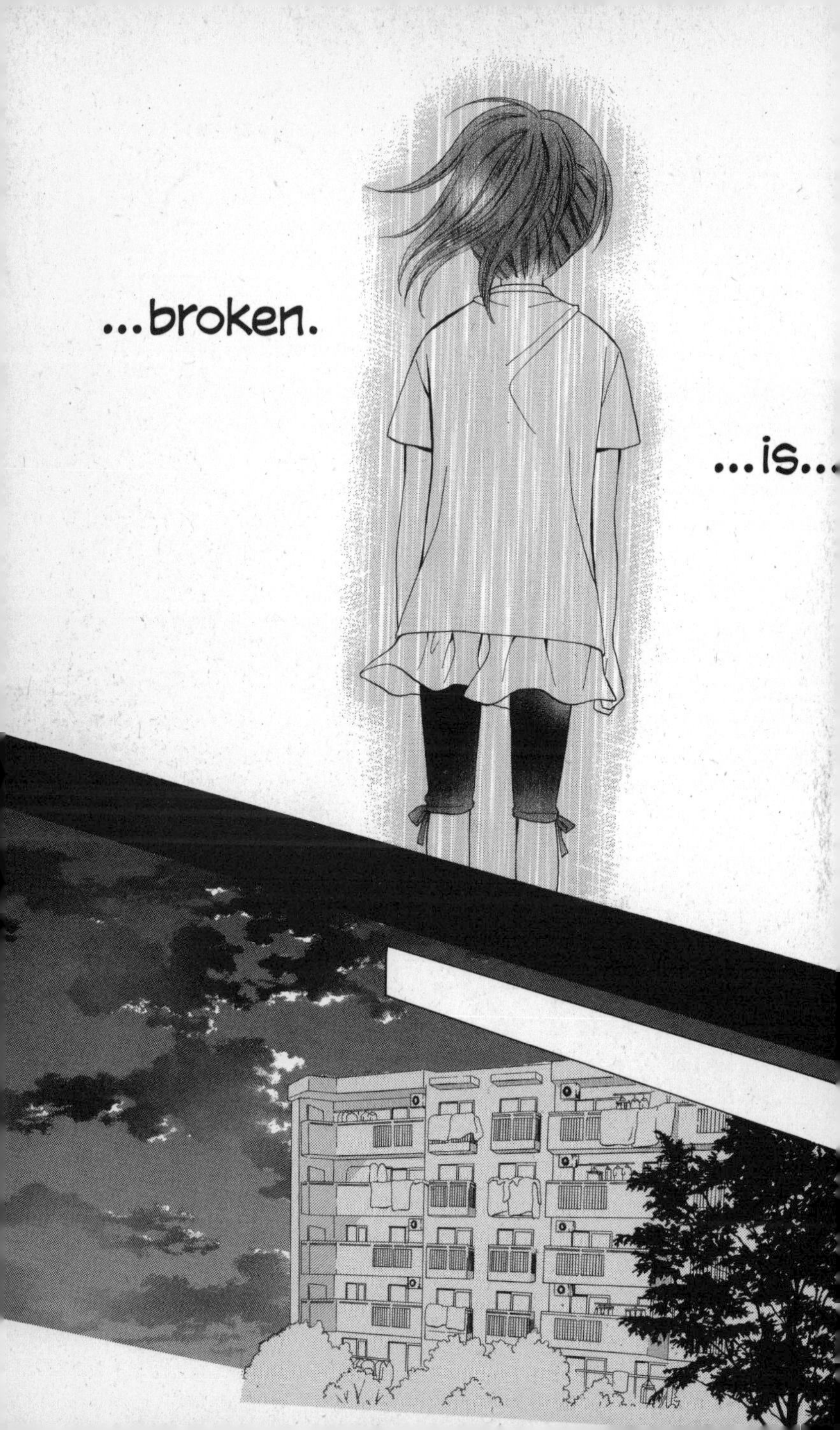
...is...
...broken.

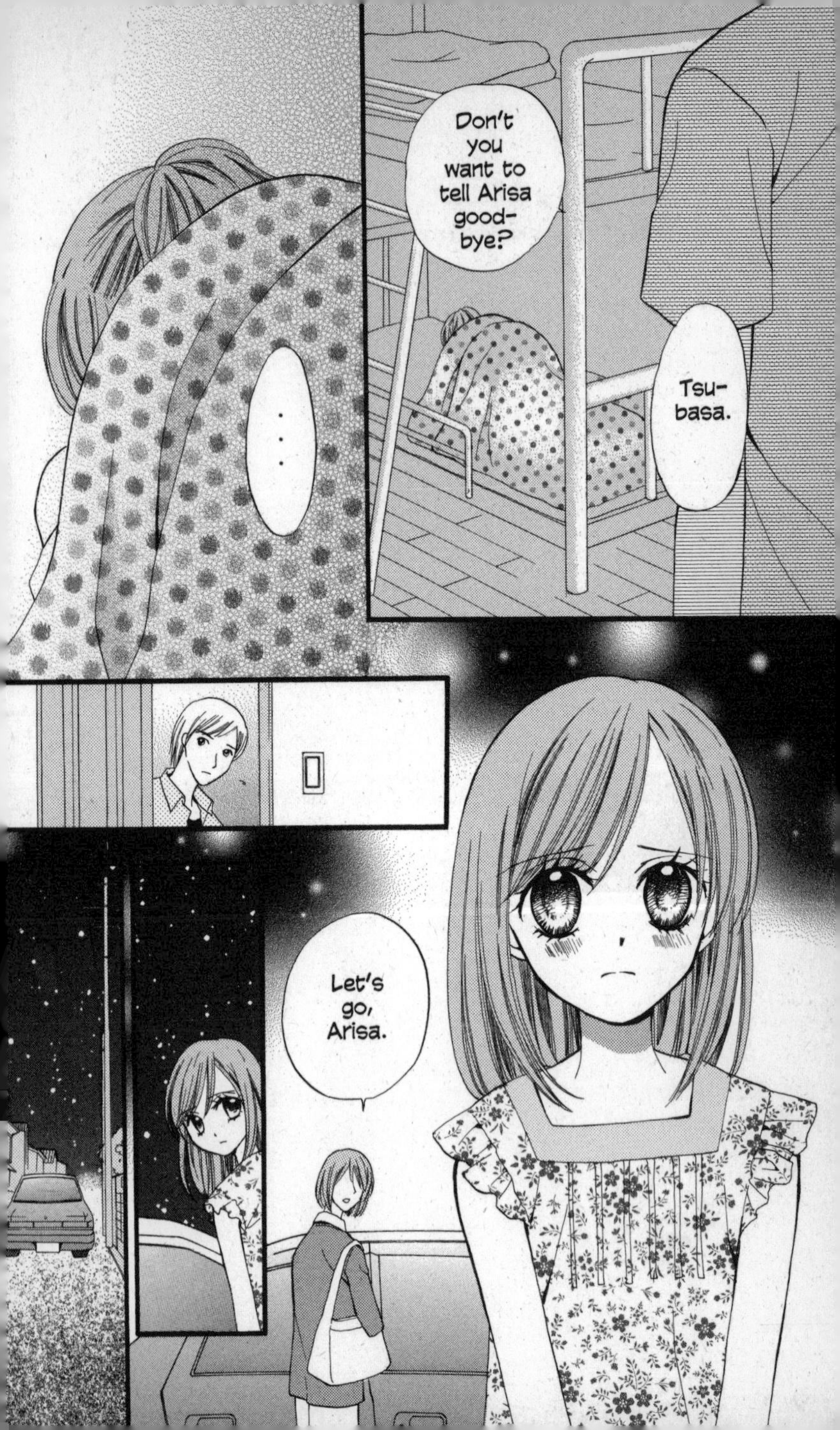
Don't you want to tell Arisa good-bye?
Tsu-basa.
. . .
Let's go, Arisa.

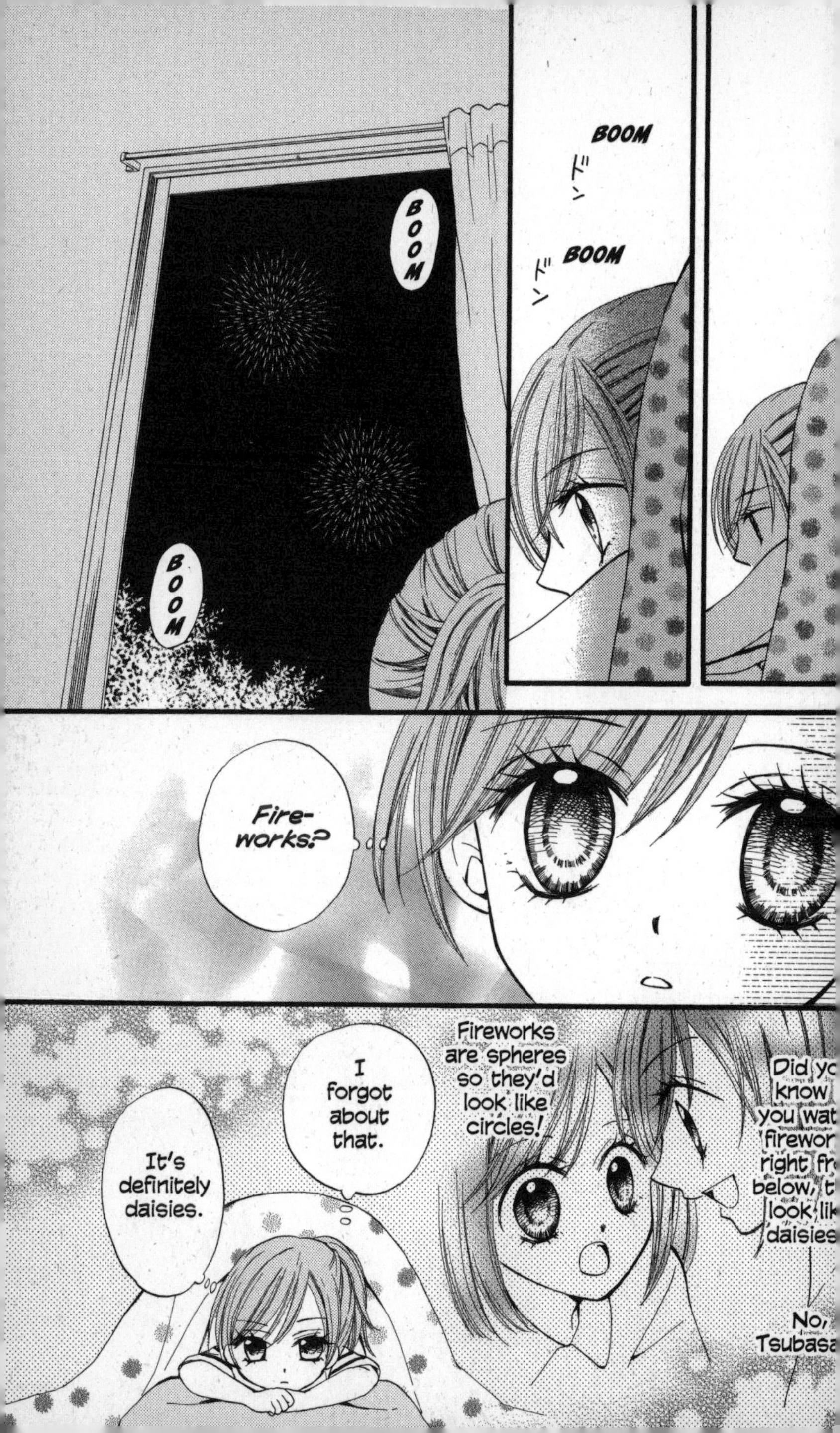
BOOM
ドン
BOOM
ドン
BOOM
BOOM
Fire-works?
Did yo know you wat firewor right fr below, t look lik daisies
No, Tsubasa
Fireworks are spheres so they'd look like circles!
I forgot about that.
It's definitely daisies.

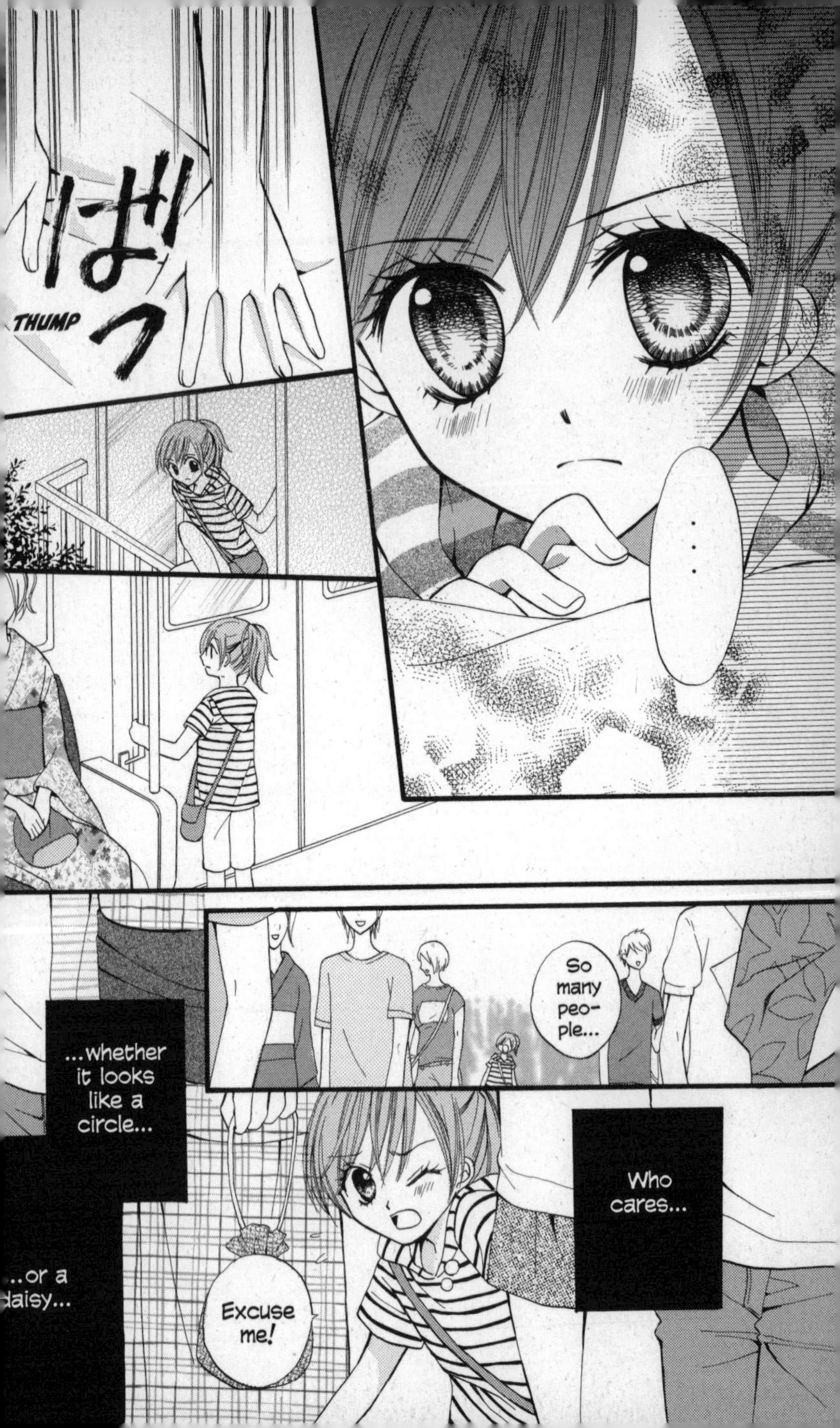

...
ぱっ
THUMP
So many peo-ple...
Who cares...
...whether it looks like a circle...
...or a daisy...
Excuse me!

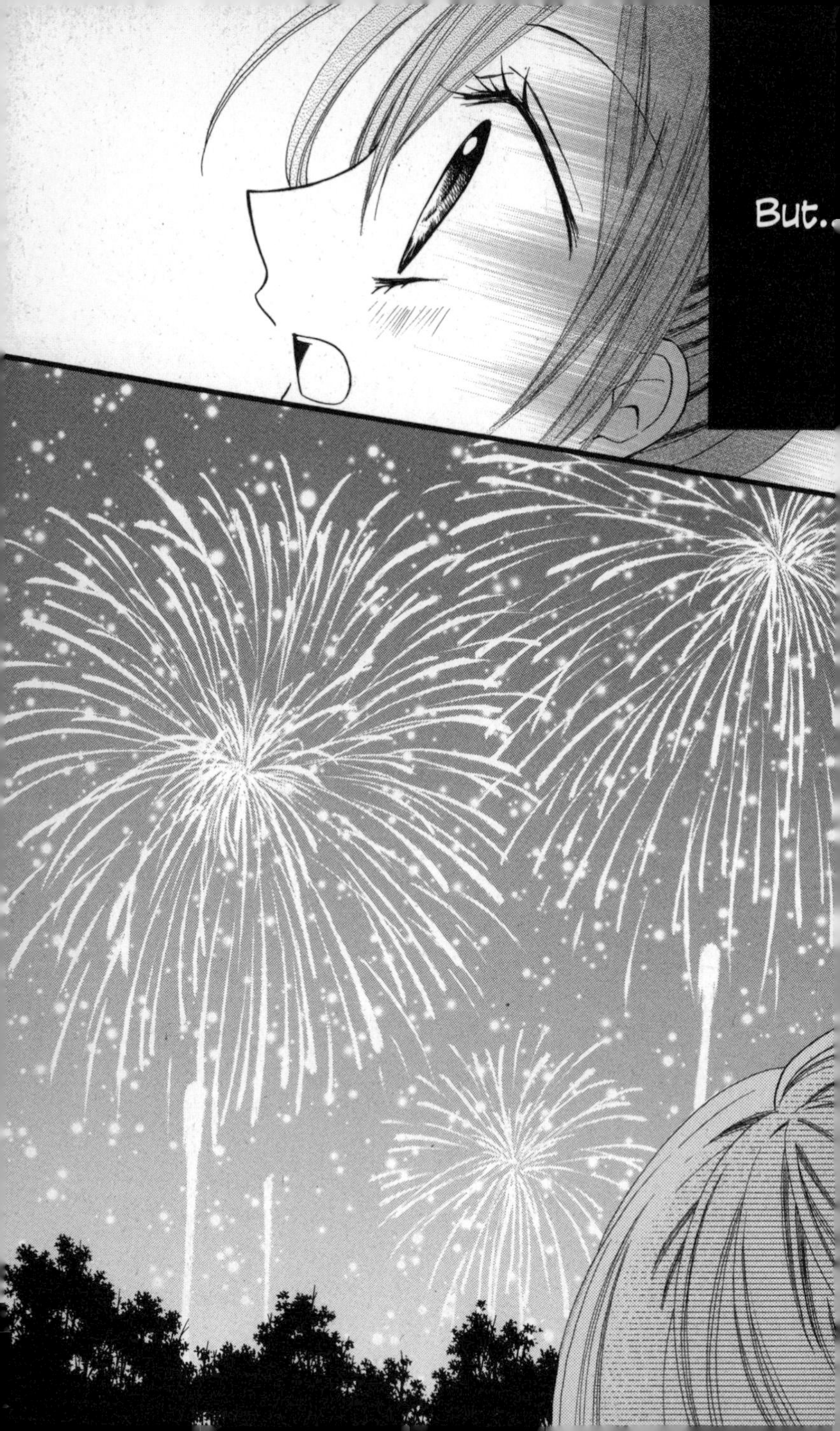
But..

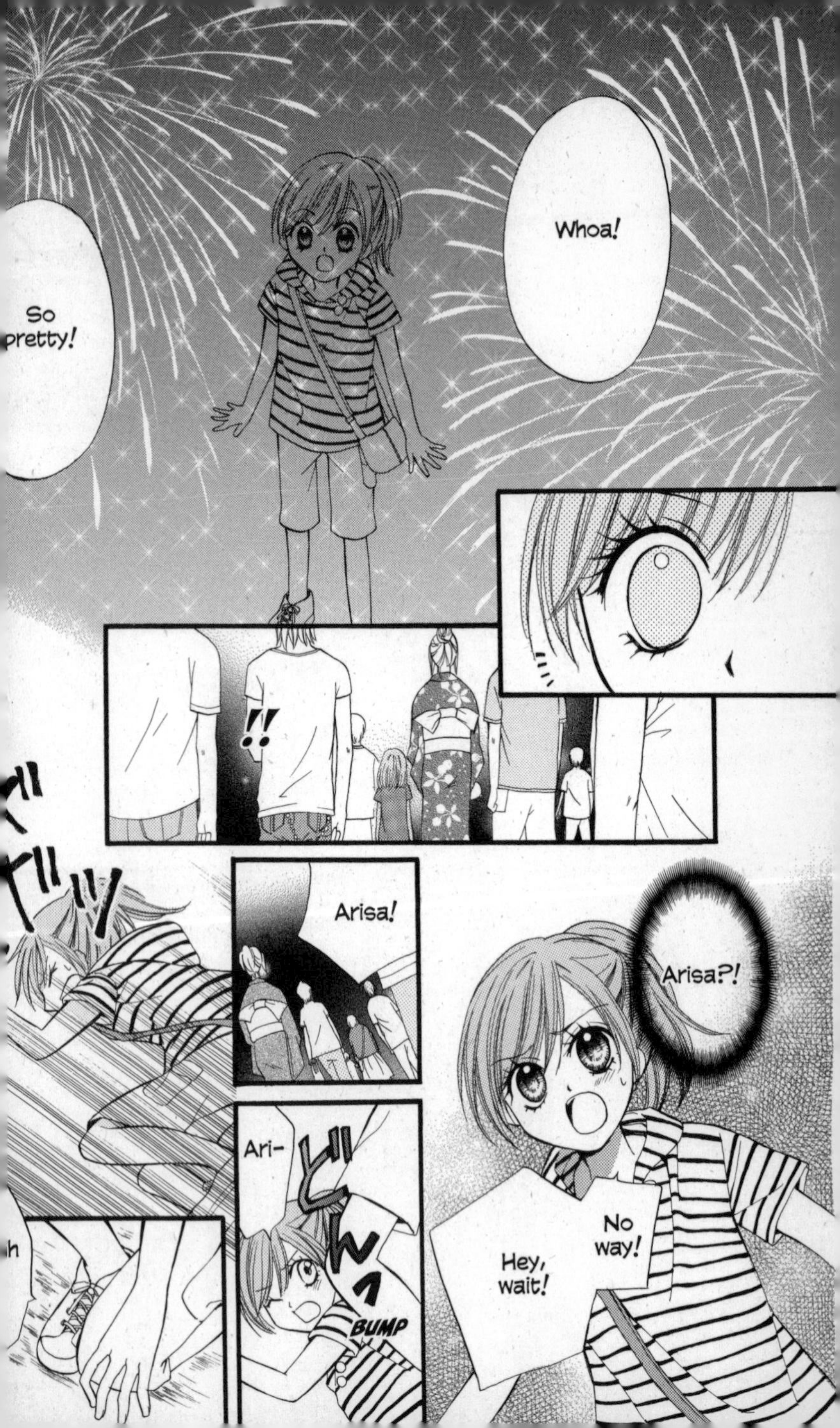
Whoa!
So pretty!
!!
Arisa?!
No way!
Hey, wait!
Arisa!
Ari-
BUMP

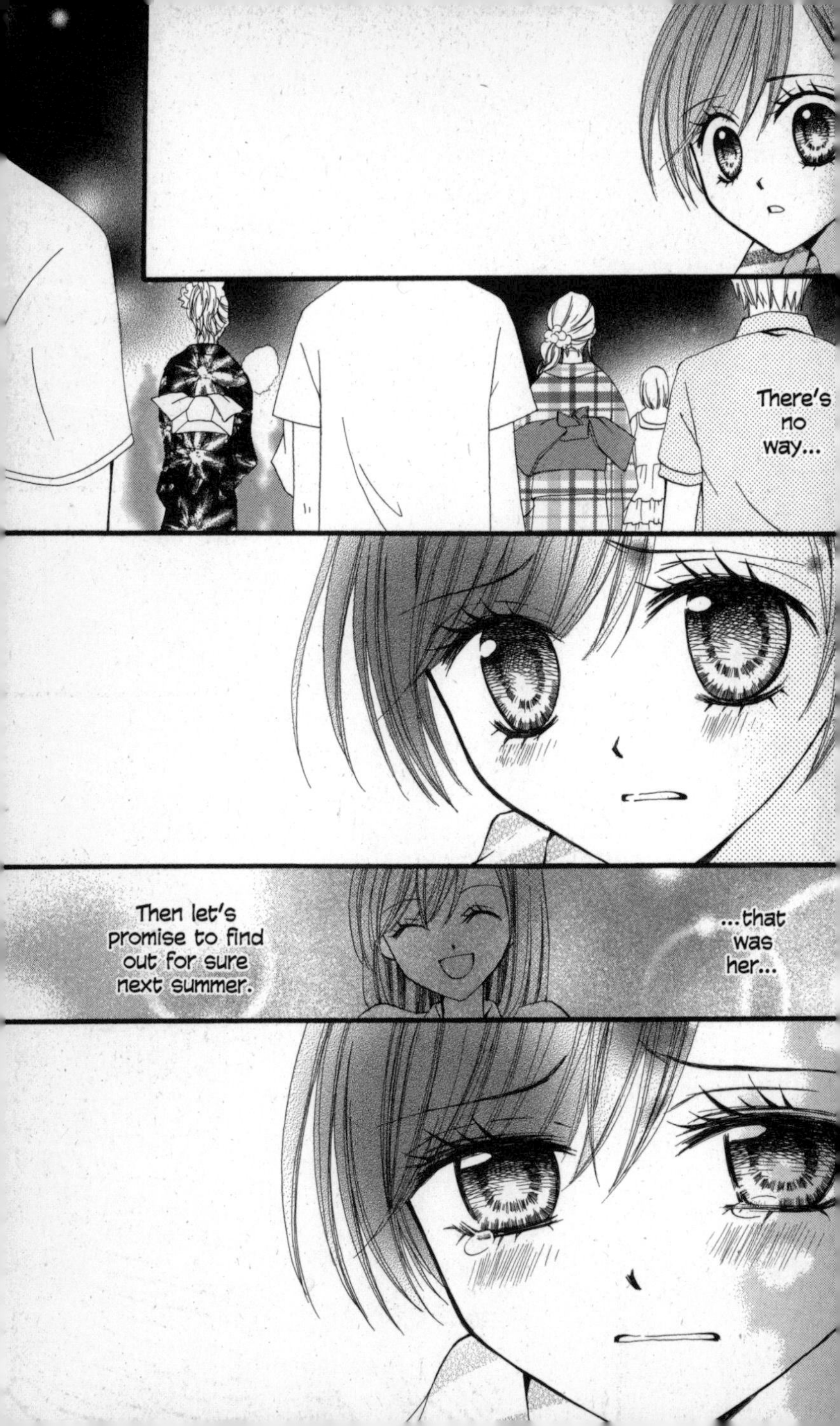
There's no way...
...that was her...
Then let's promise to find out for sure next summer.

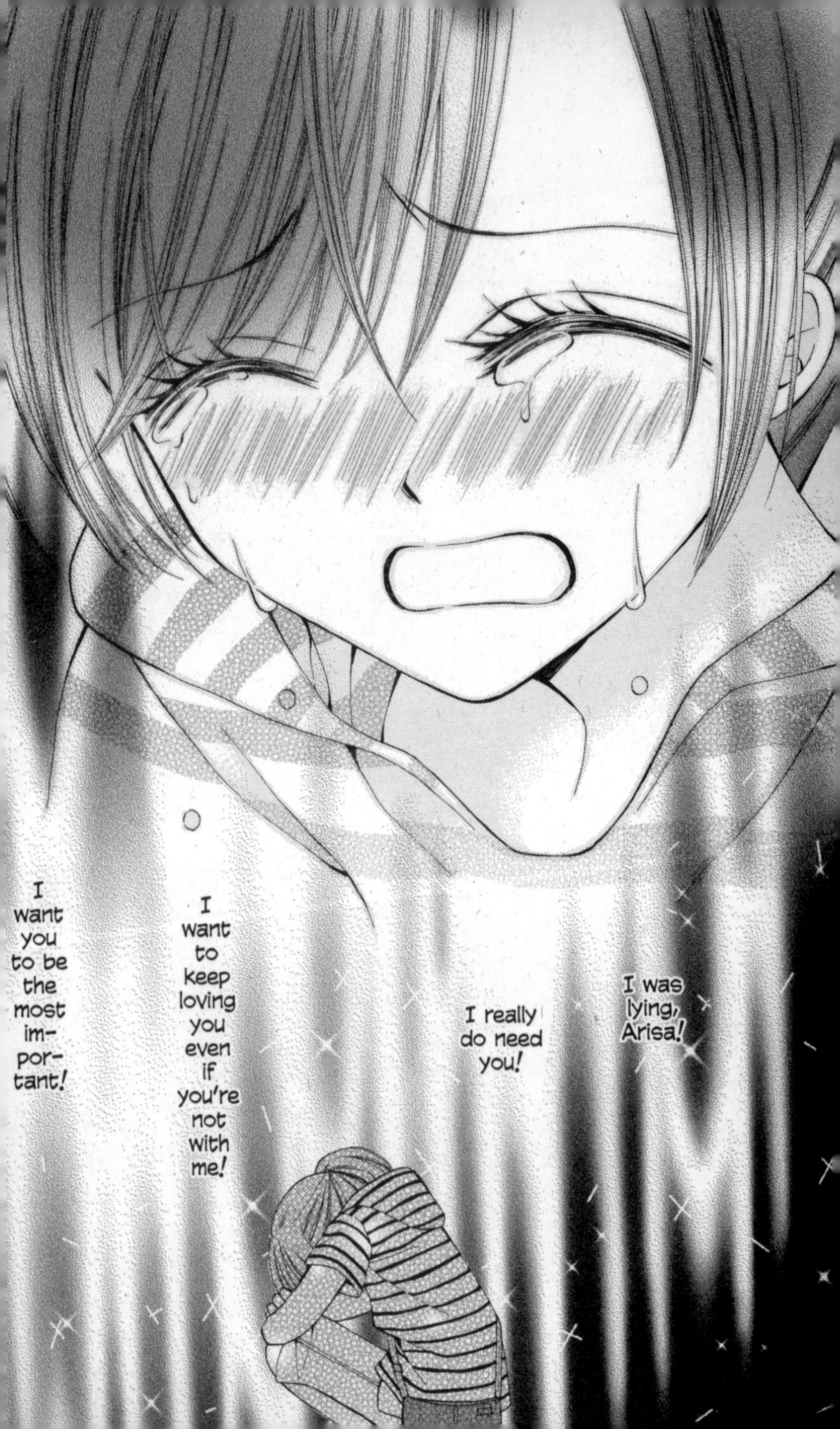
I was lying, Arisa!
I really do need you!
I want to keep loving you even if you're not with me!
I want you to be the most im-portant!

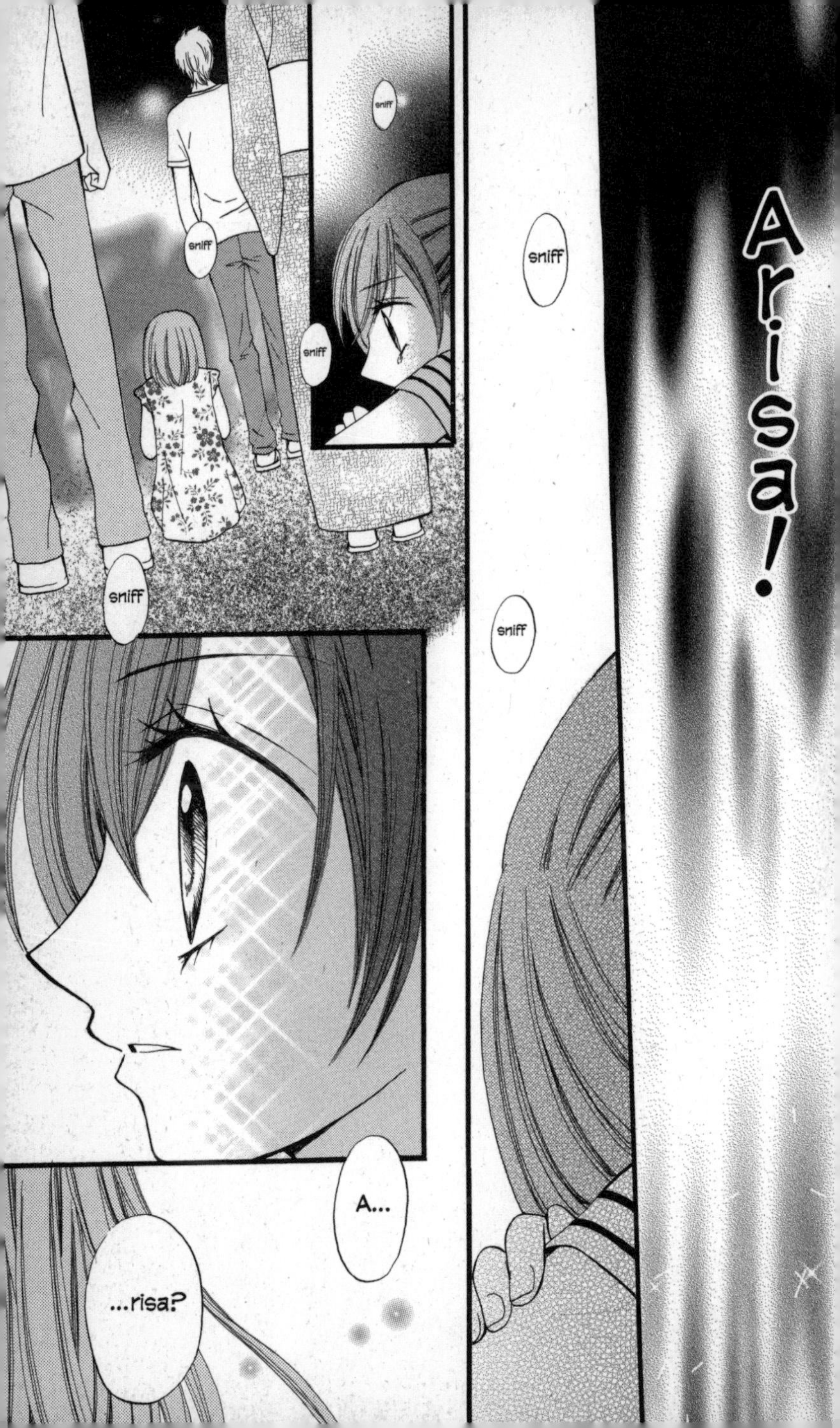

Ari-sa!
sniff
sniff
sniff
sniff
sniff
sniff
A...
...risa?

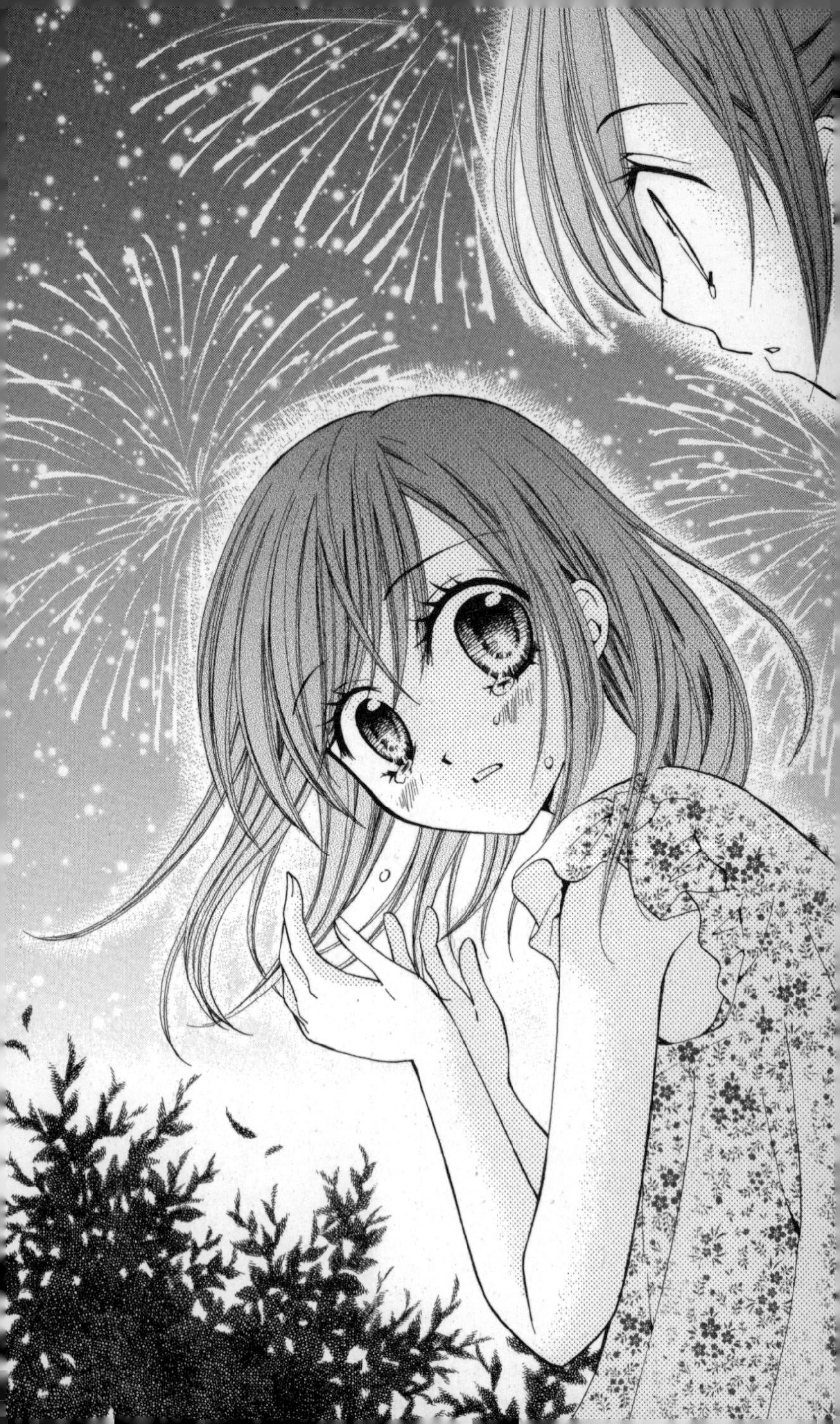

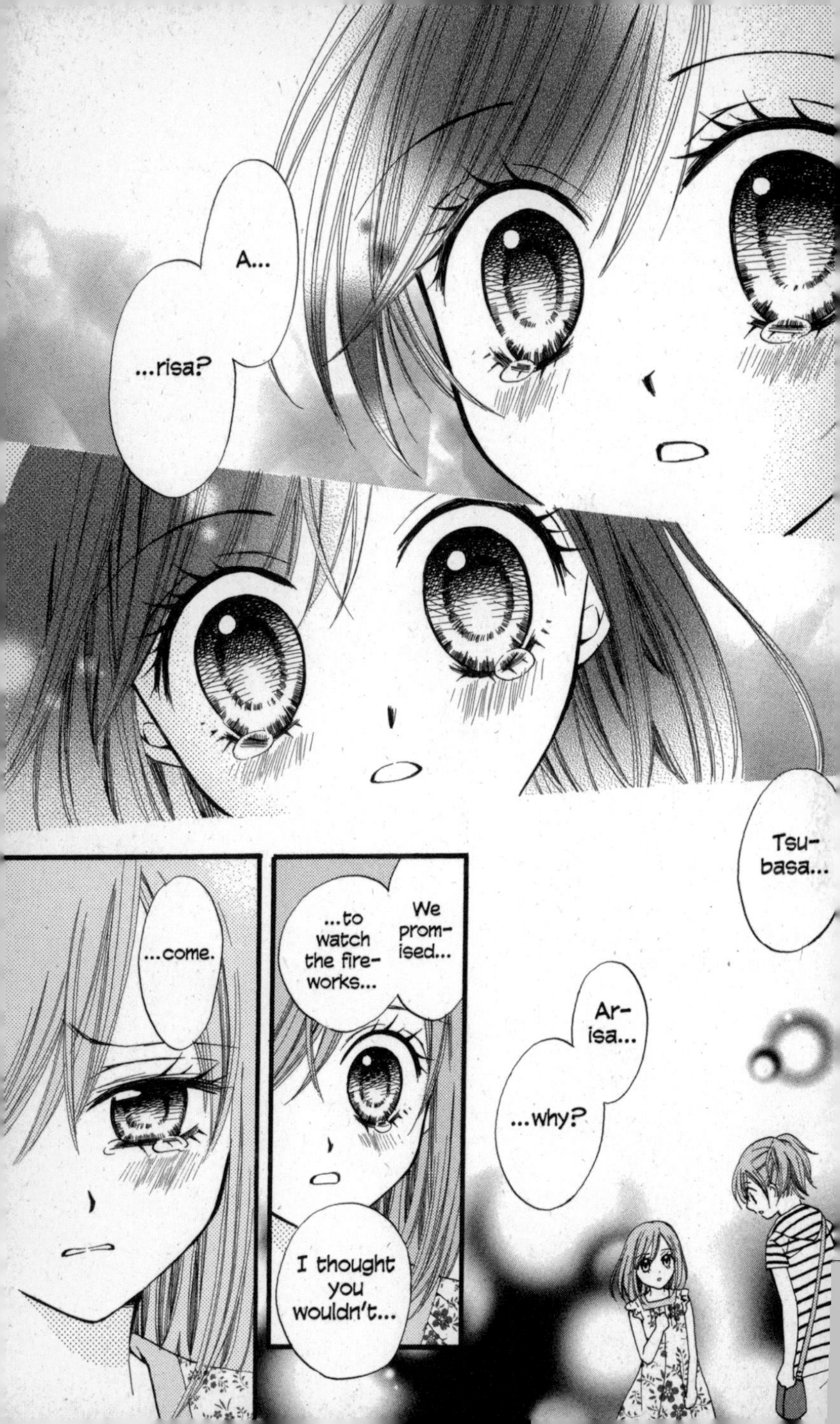
A...
...risa?
Tsu-basa...
Ar-isa...
...why?
We prom-ised...
...to watch the fire-works...
I thought you wouldn't...
...come.

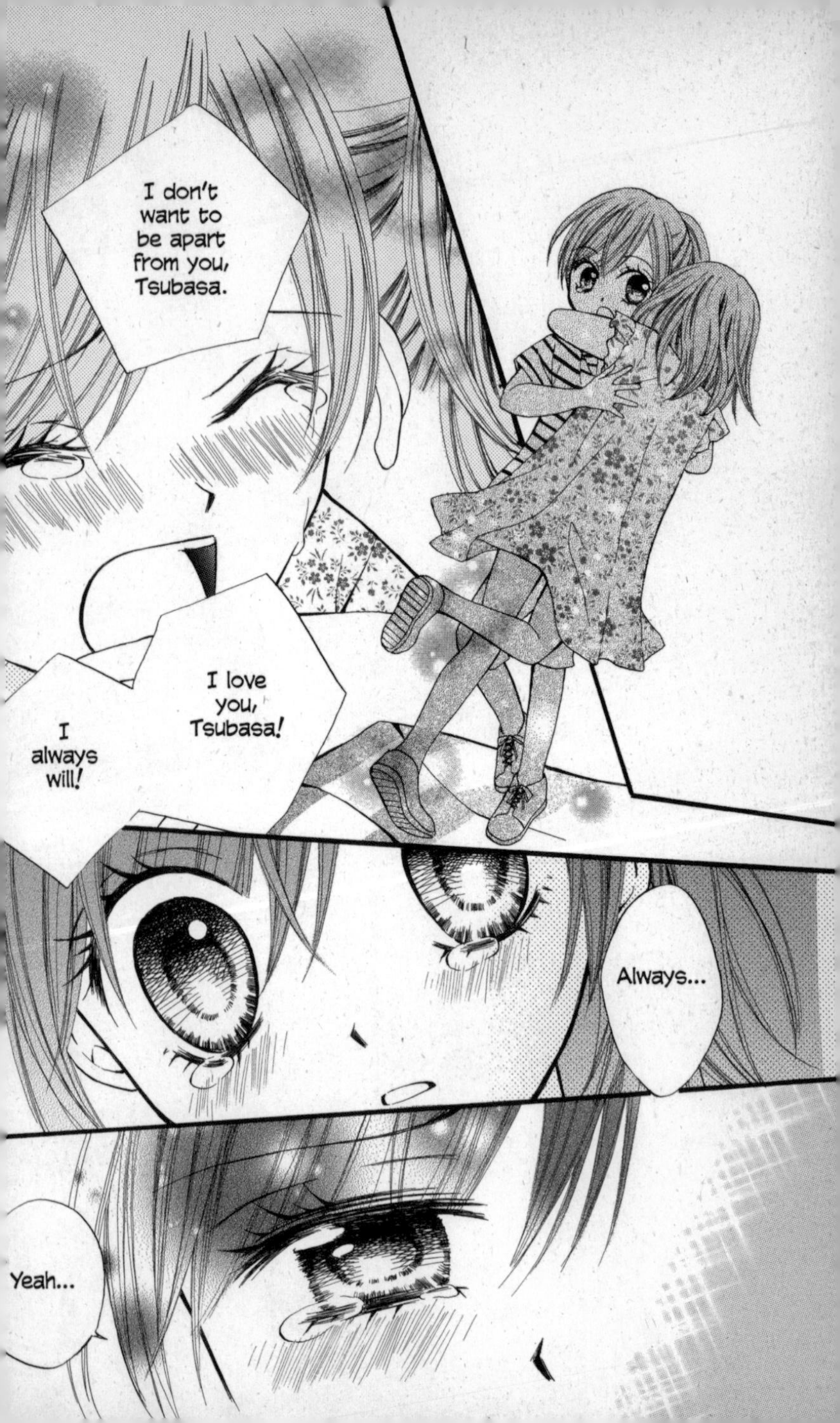
I don't want to be apart from you, Tsubasa.
I love you, Tsubasa!
I always will!
Always...
Yeah...

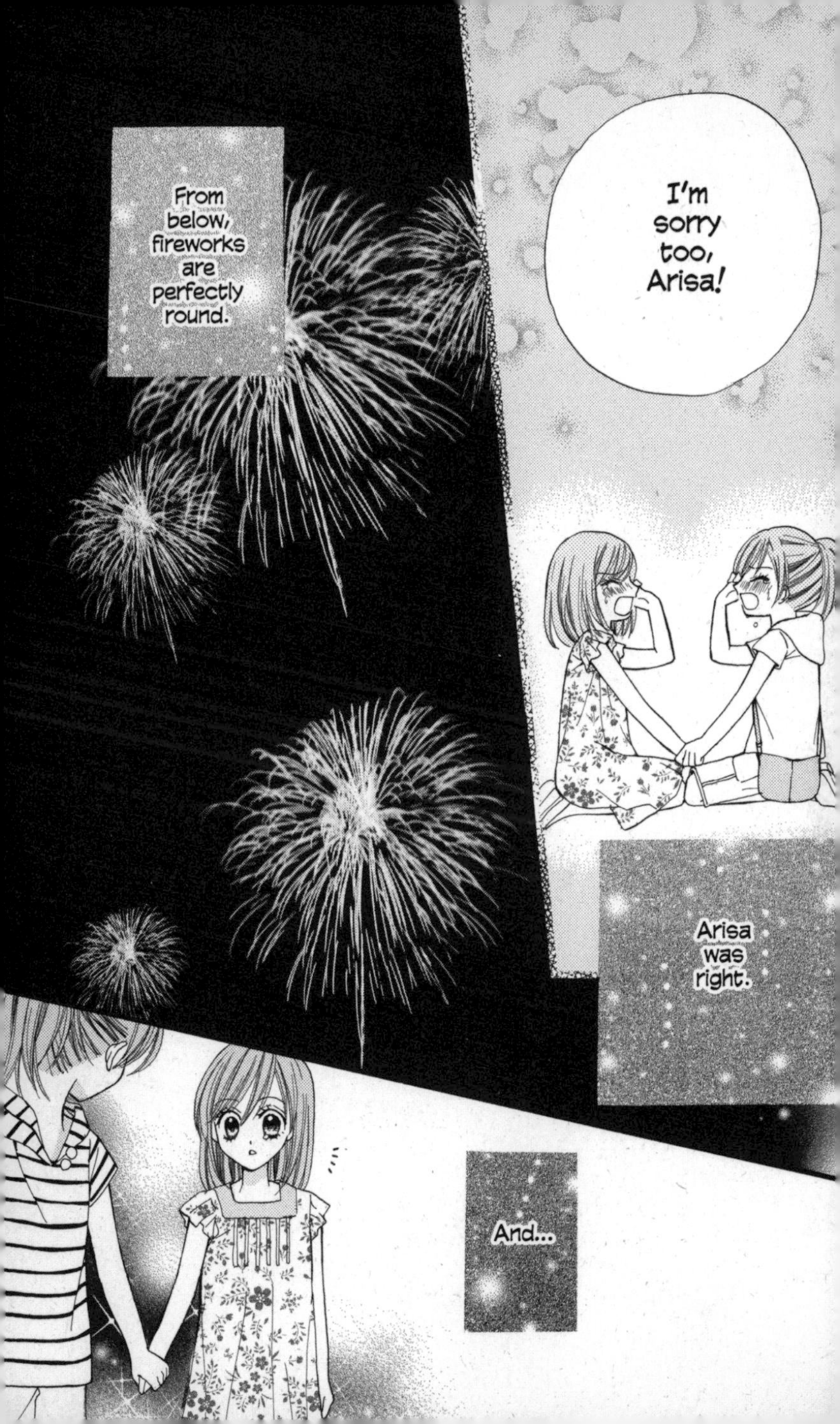
I'm sorry too, Arisa!
Arisa was right.
From below, fireworks are perfectly round.
And...

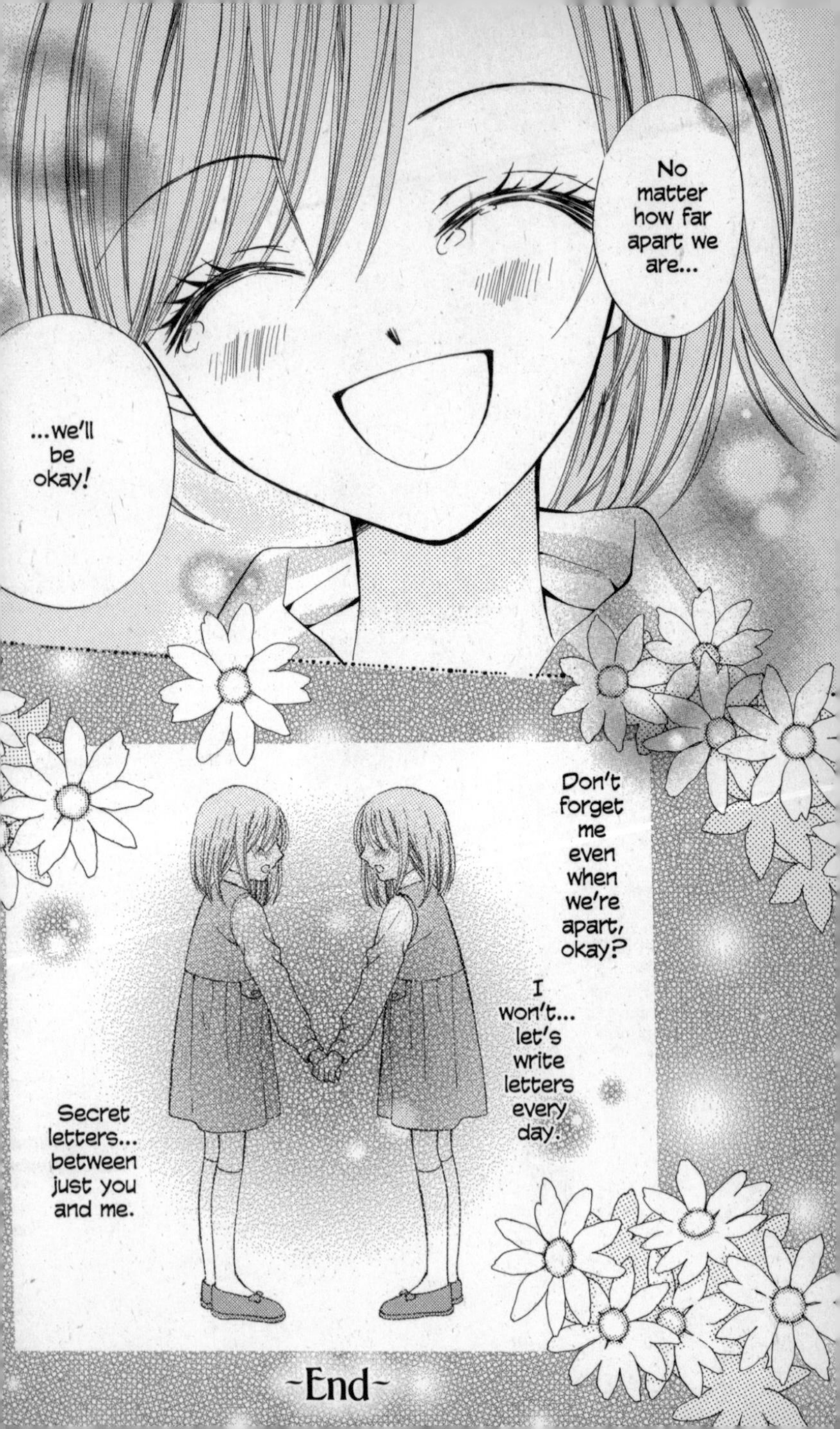
No matter how far apart we are...
...we'll be okay!
Don't forget me even when we're apart, okay?
I won't... let's write letters every day.
Secret letters... between just you and me.
-End-

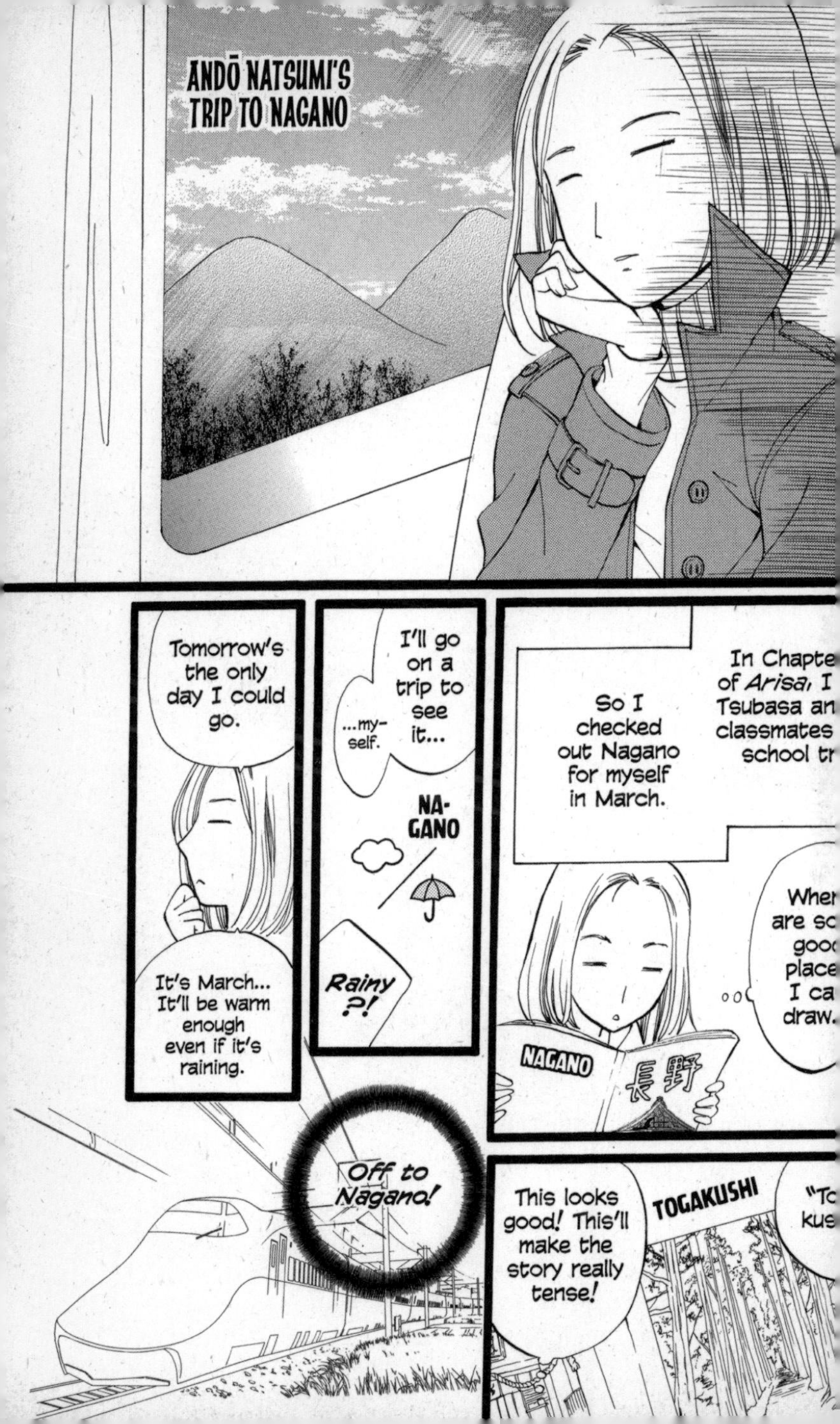

ANDŌ NATSUMI'S TRIP TO NAGANO
In Chapte of Arisa, I Tsubasa an classmates school tr
So I checked out Nagano for myself in March.
Wher are sc goo place I ca draw.
NAGANO
I'll go on a trip to see it...
...myself.
NA-GANO
Rainy?!
Tomorrow's the only day I could go.
It's March... It'll be warm enough even if it's raining.
"To kus
TOGAKUSHI
This looks good! This'll make the story really tense!
Off to Nagano!

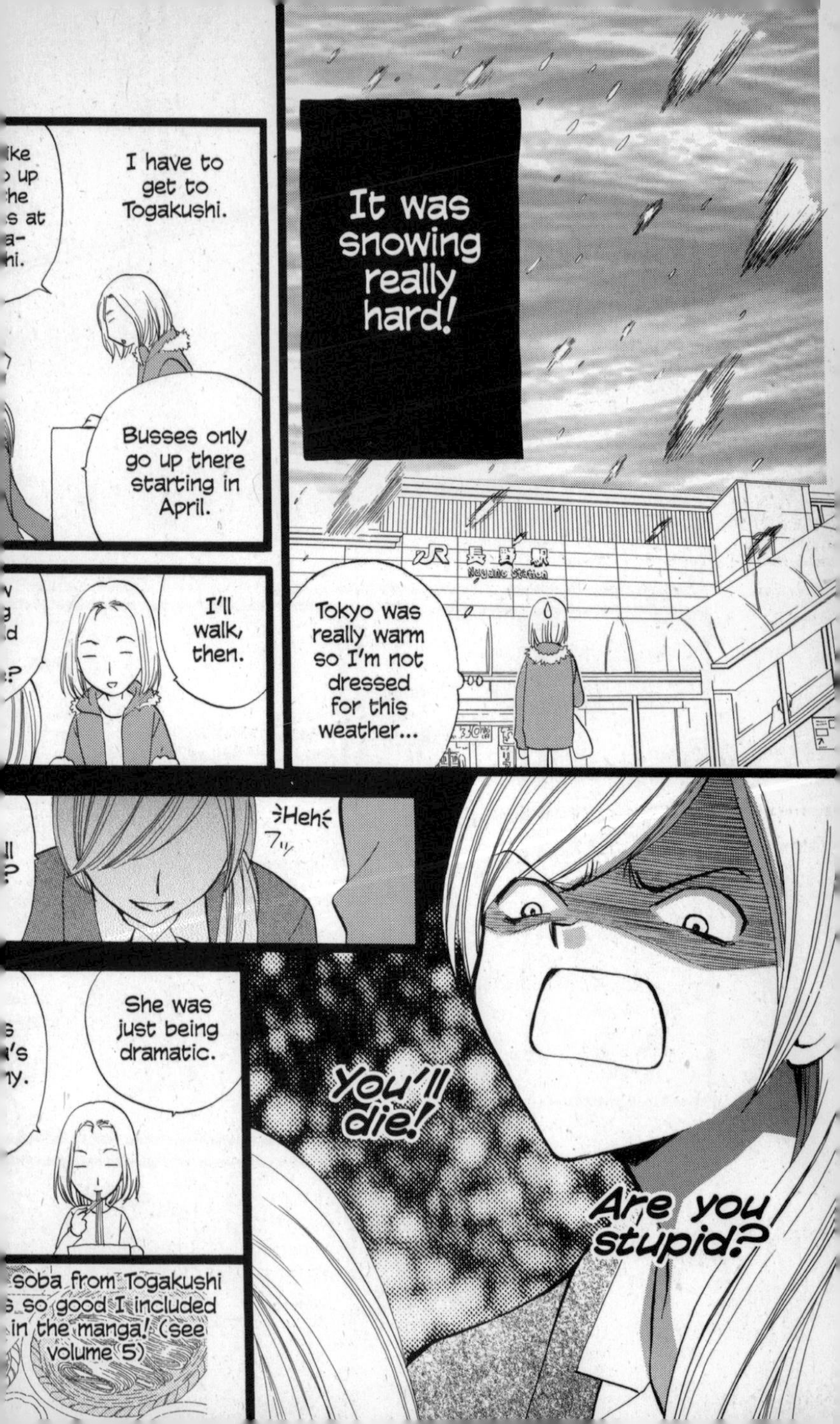
It was snowing really hard!
長野駅
Nagano Station
Tokyo was really warm so I'm not dressed for this weather...
I have to get to Togakushi.
Busses only go up there starting in April.
I'll walk, then.
You'll die!
Are you stupid?
Heh
フッ
She was just being dramatic.
soba from Togakushi s so good I included in the manga! (see volume 5)

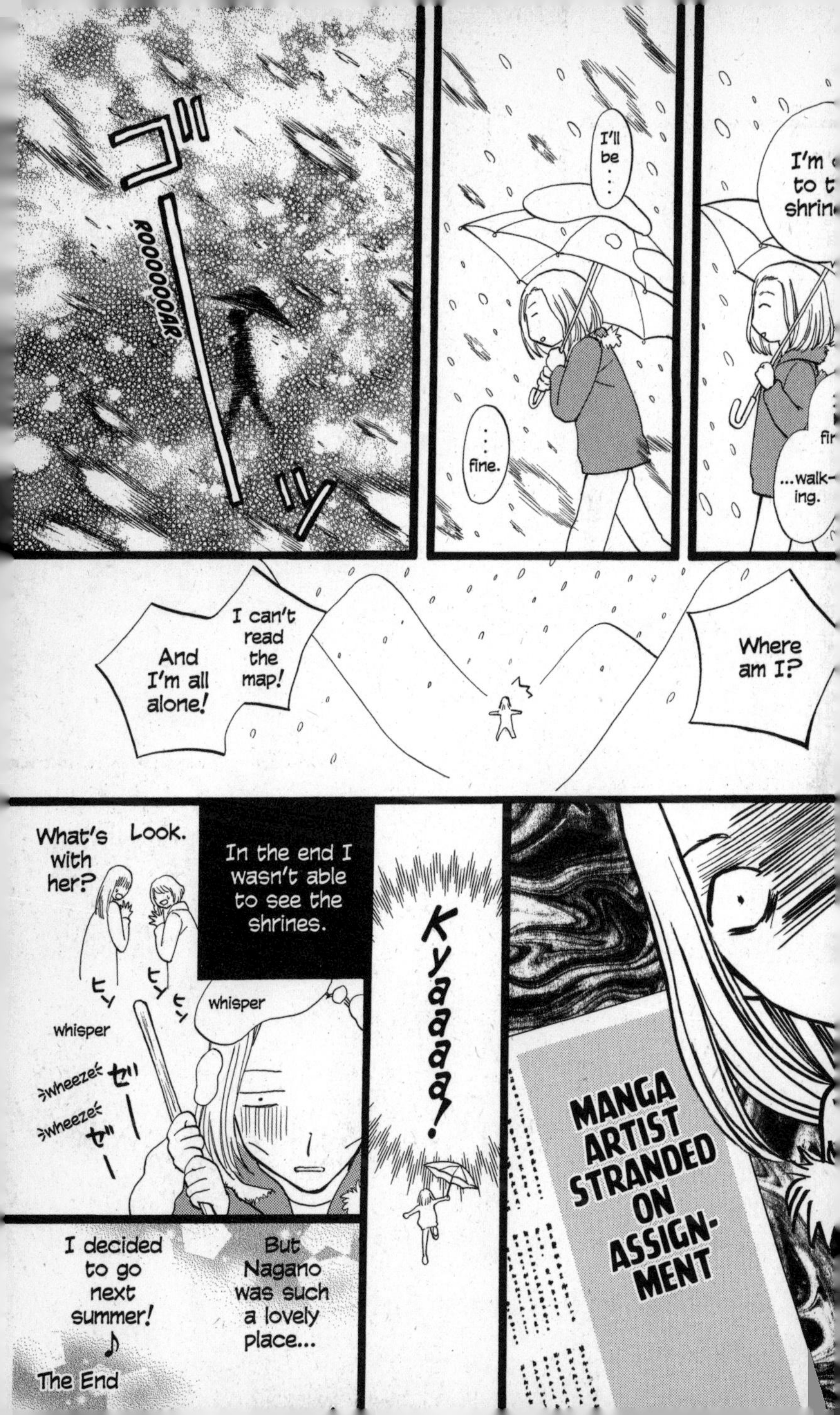
I'm
...walk-ing.
I'll be...
...fine.
ROOOOOOAR
Where am I?
I can't read the map!
And I'm all alone!
MANGA ARTIST STRANDED ON ASSIGNMENT
Kyaaaaa!
In the end I wasn't able to see the shrines.
Look.
What's with her?
whisper
whisper
wheeze
wheeze
But Nagano was such a lovely place...
I decided to go next summer! ♪
The End

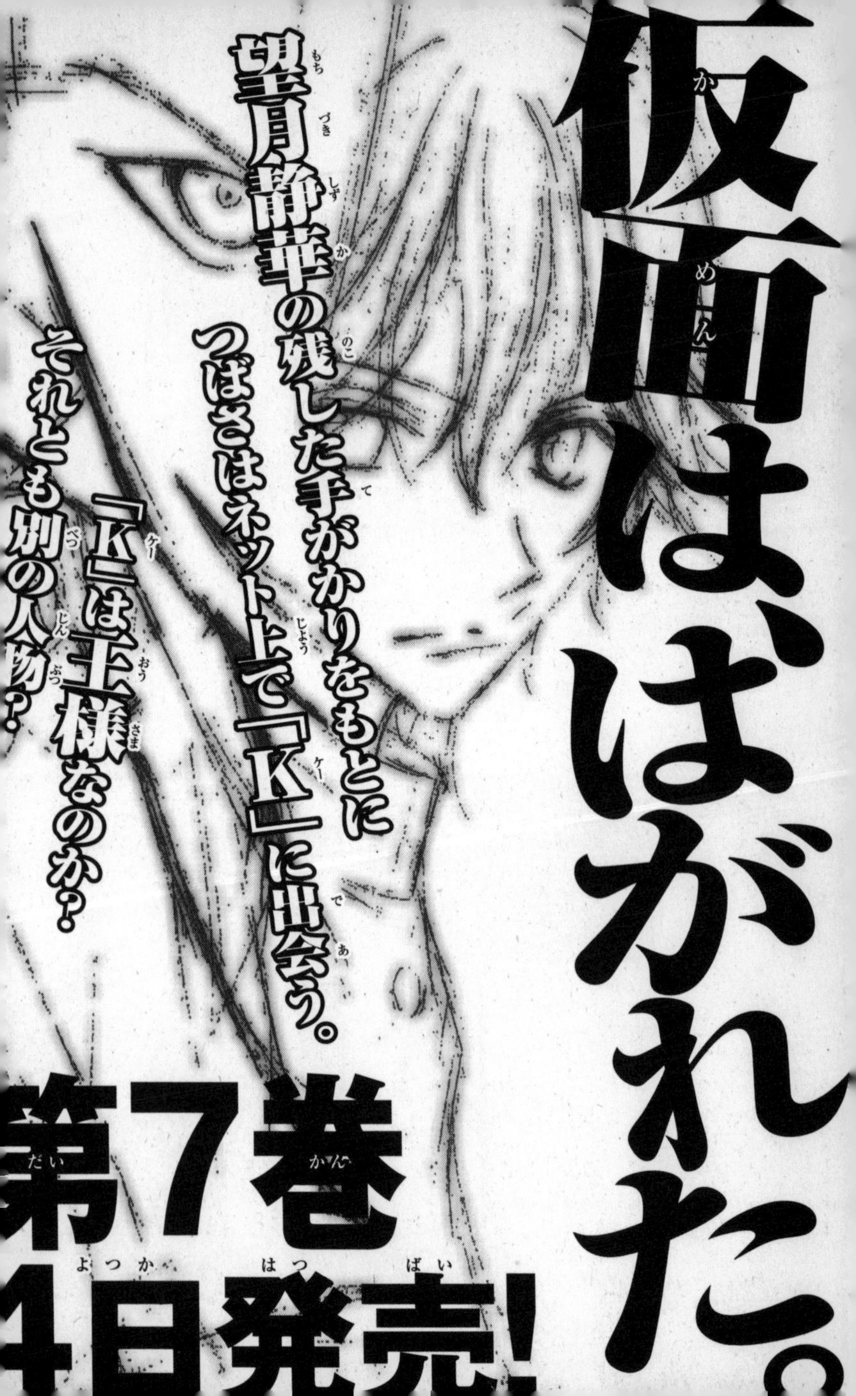
仮面ははがれた。
望月静華の残した手がかりをもとに
つばさはネット上で「K」に出会う。
「K」は王様なのか？
それとも別の人物？
第7巻
4日発売！

次巻予告

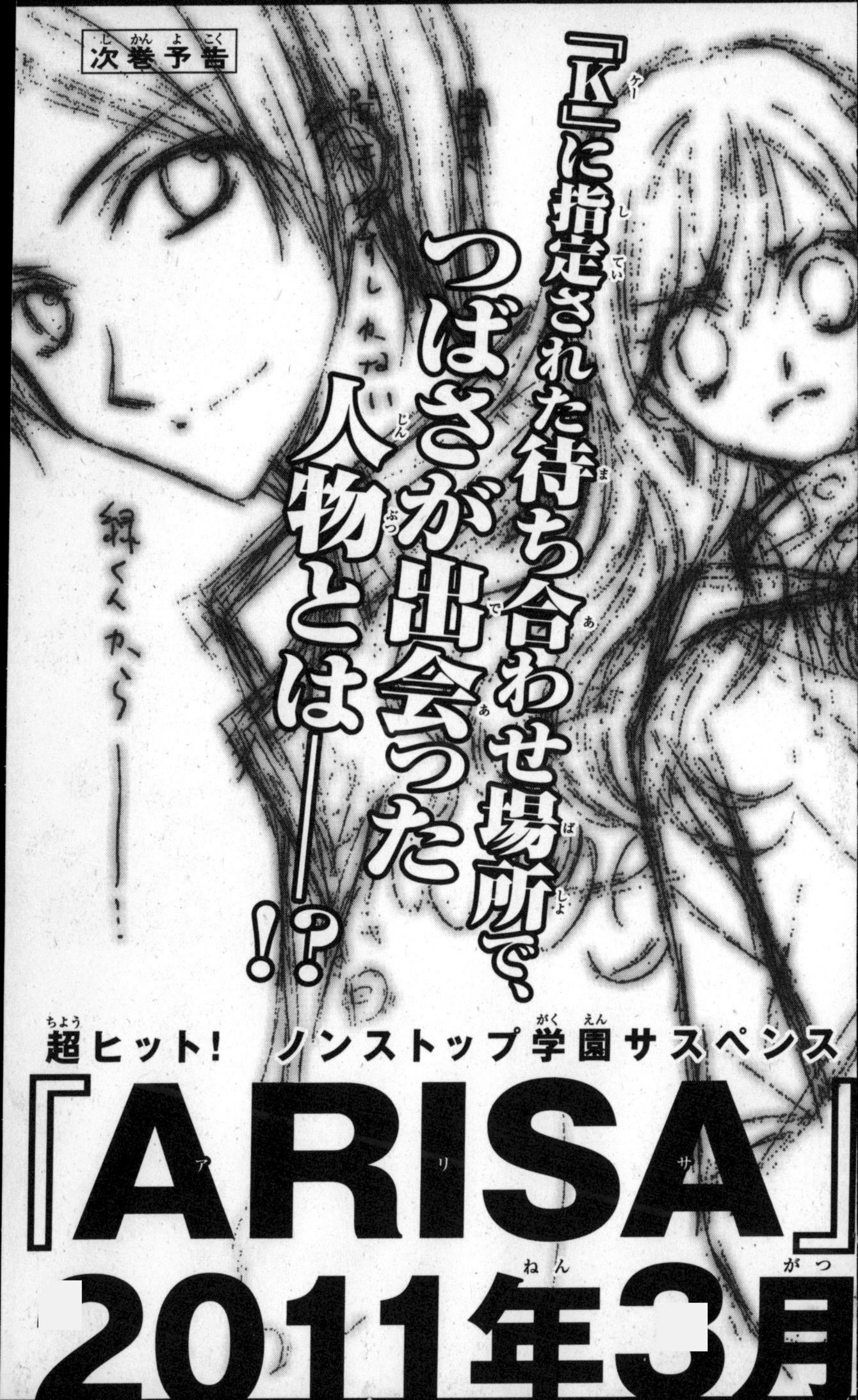
絹くんから――…

『K』に指定された待ち合わせ場所で、つばさが出会った人物とは――!?

超ヒット! ノンストップ学園サスペンス

『ARISA』

2011年3月

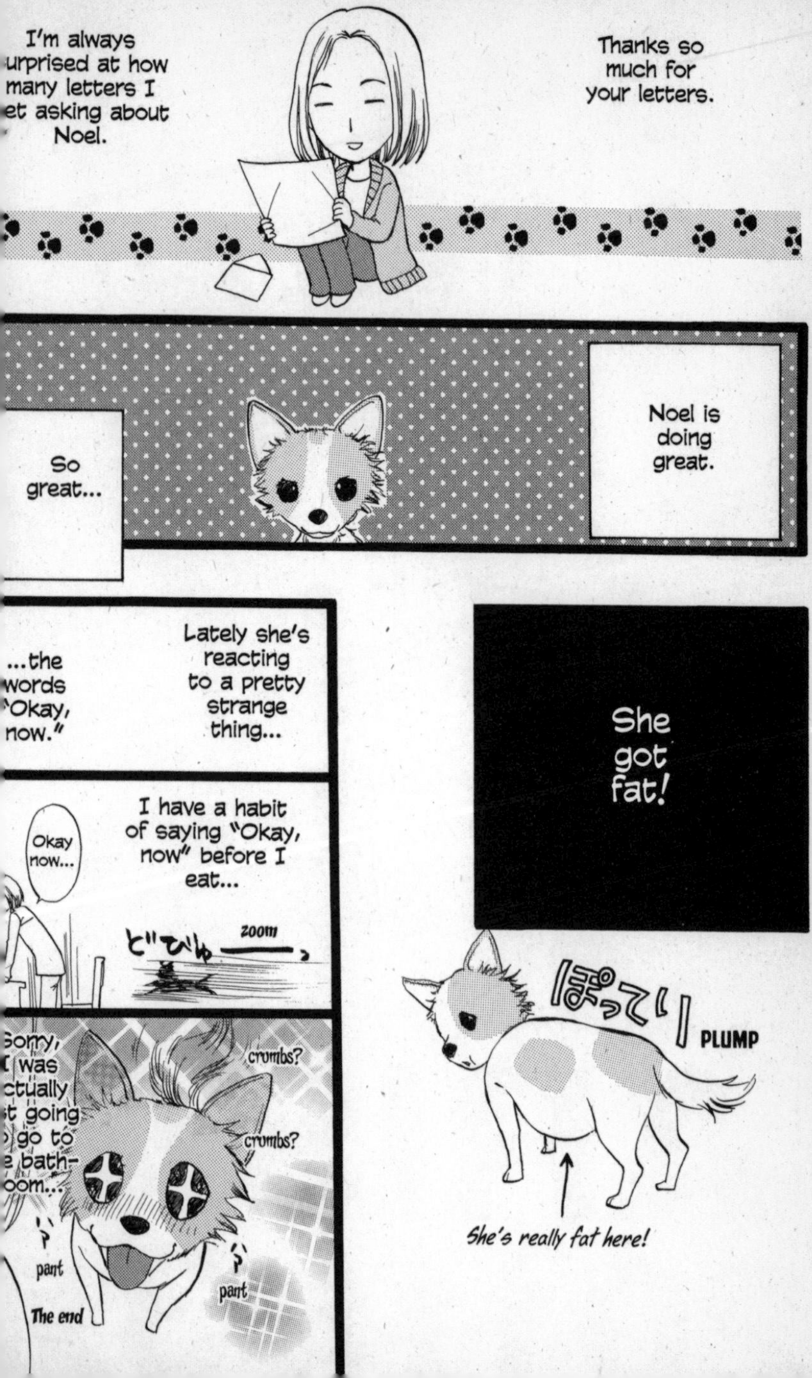
Thanks so much for your letters.
I'm always urprised at how many letters I et asking about Noel.
Noel is doing great.
So great...
She got fat!
PLUMP
She's really fat here!
Lately she's reacting to a pretty strange thing...
...the words "Okay, now."
I have a habit of saying "Okay, now" before I eat...
Okay now...
zoom
crumbs?
crumbs?
Sorry, I was ctually t going go to e bath- oom...
pant
pant
The end

Words from the Author

Thanks for everyone who have sent letters guessing the King's true identity.

Please keep reading until the answer is revealed!

—Natsumi Ando

Profile

Birthday: January 27
Blood type: B
Hometown: Aichi Prefecture
Zodiac Sign: Aquarius

Other series by Natsumi Ando:
Kitchen Princess

Translation Notes

Japanese is a tricky language for most Westerners, and translation is often more art than science. For your edification and reading pleasure, here are notes on some of the places where we could have gone in a different direction with our translation of the work, or where a Japanese cultural reference is used.

The King

In Japanese, there is no pronoun used to refer to the King. It is not clear in the Japanese whether the King is male or female. This is more difficult in English, so the King is referred to as "he" in this translation. Keep in mind this does not necessarily mean the identity of the King is a male (or isn't).

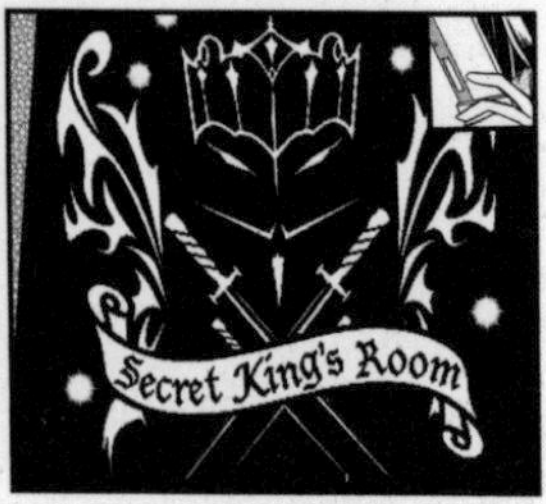
Secret King's Room

Soba, page 160

Noodles made from buckwheat.

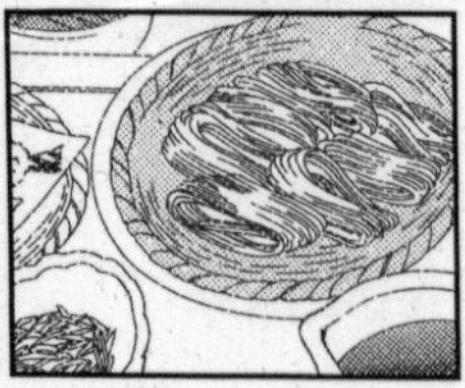

Preview of *Arisa* Volume 7

We're pleased to present you a preview from volume 7. Please check our website, www.kodanshacomics.com, to see when this volume will be available in English. For now you'll have to make do with art!

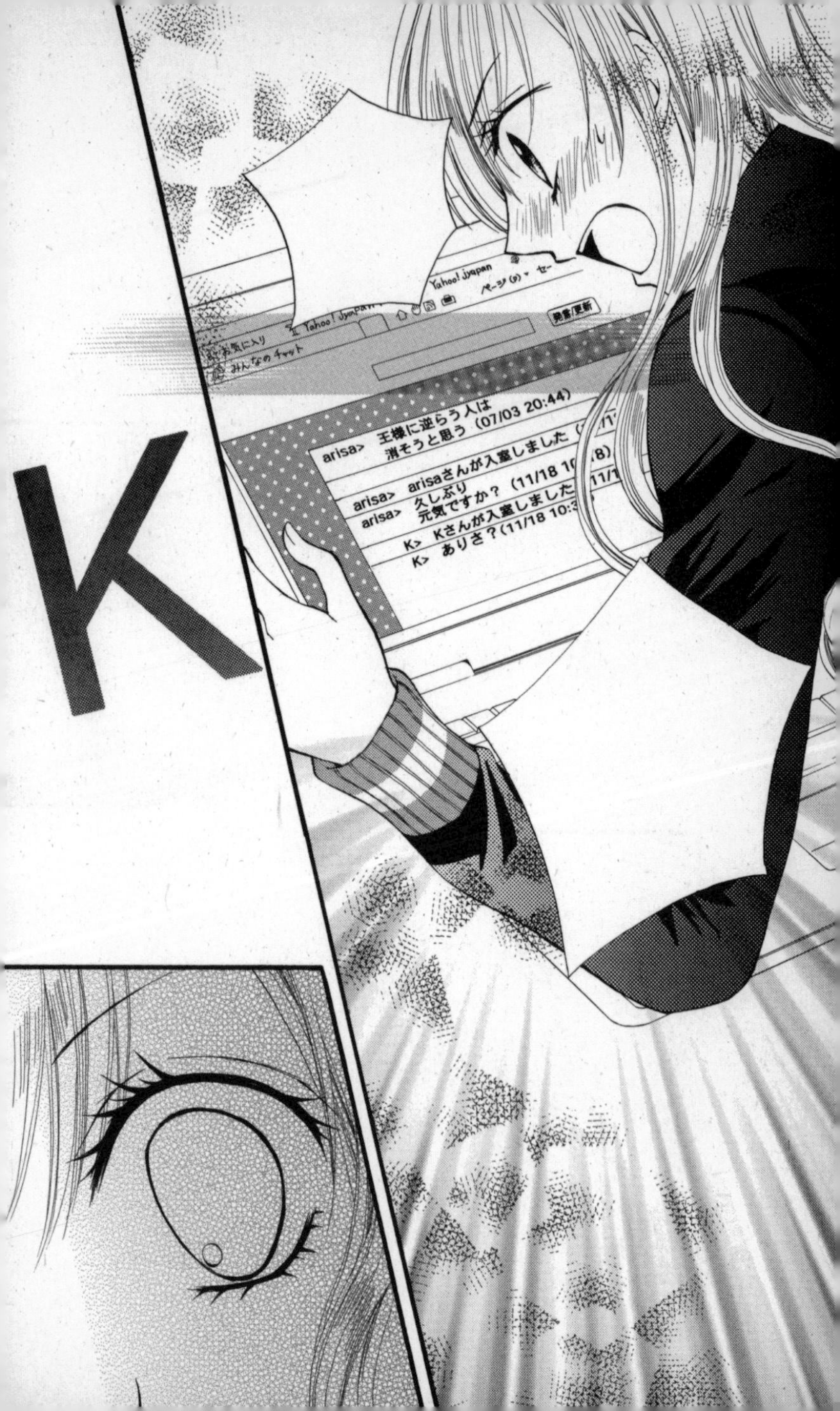
Yahoo! jyapan
ページ(P)
発言/更新
お気に入り
みんなのチャット
arisa> 王様に逆らう人は
消そうと思う (07/03 20:44)
arisaさんが入室しました
arisa> 久しぶり
arisa> 元気ですか？
Kさんが入室しました
K> ありさ？
K

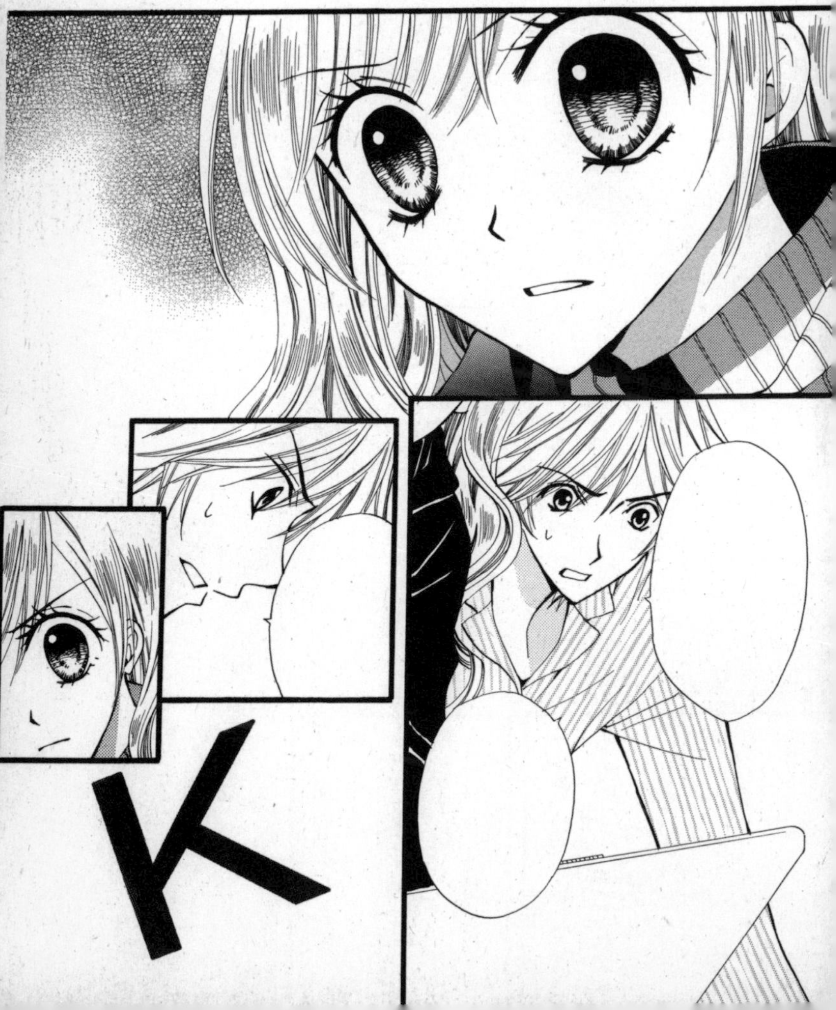
K

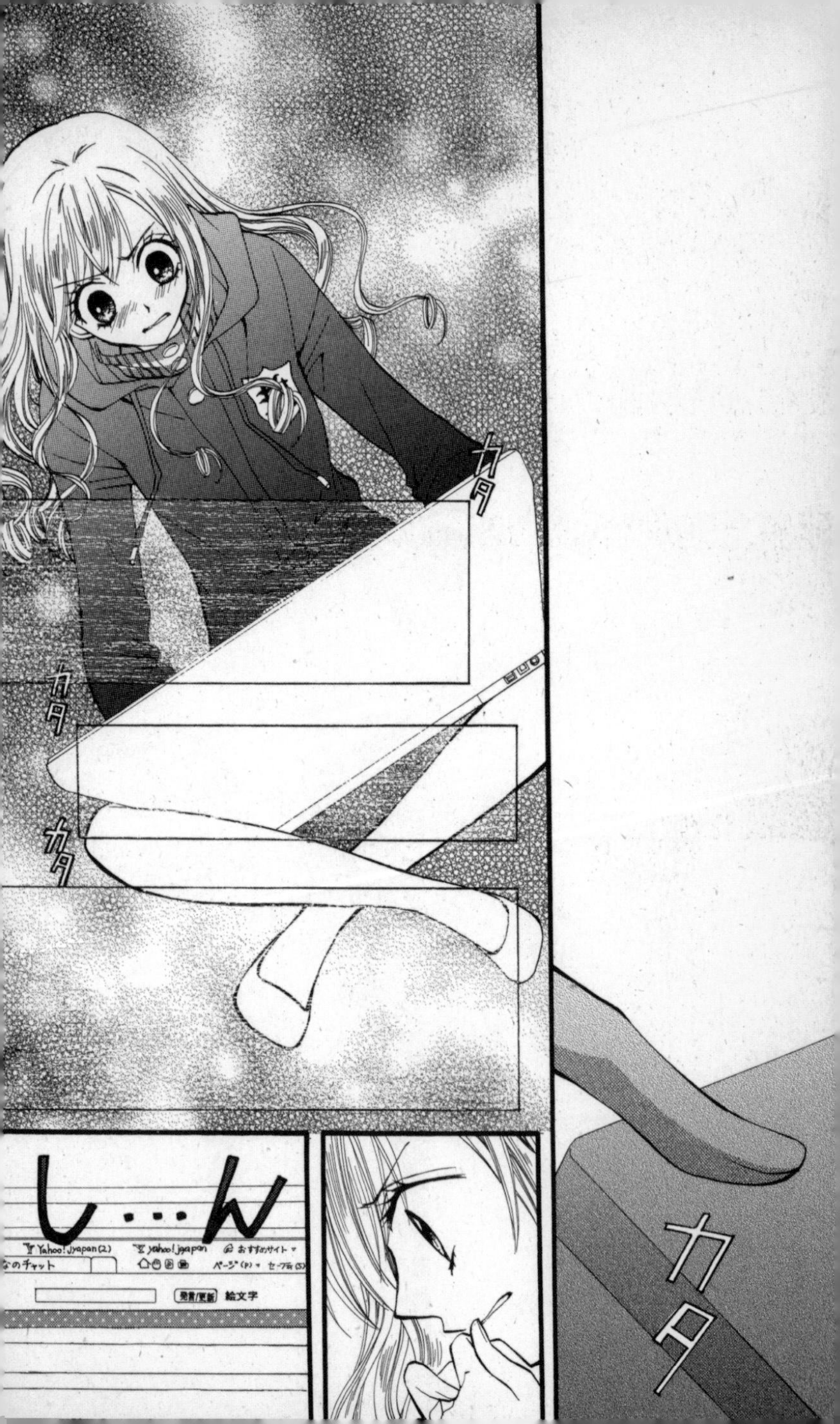
カタ
カタ
カタ
カタ
し…ん
Yahoo! Jyapan(2)
yahoo! jayapan
おすすめサイト
なのチャット
ページ(P)
セーフティ(S)
発言/更新
絵文字

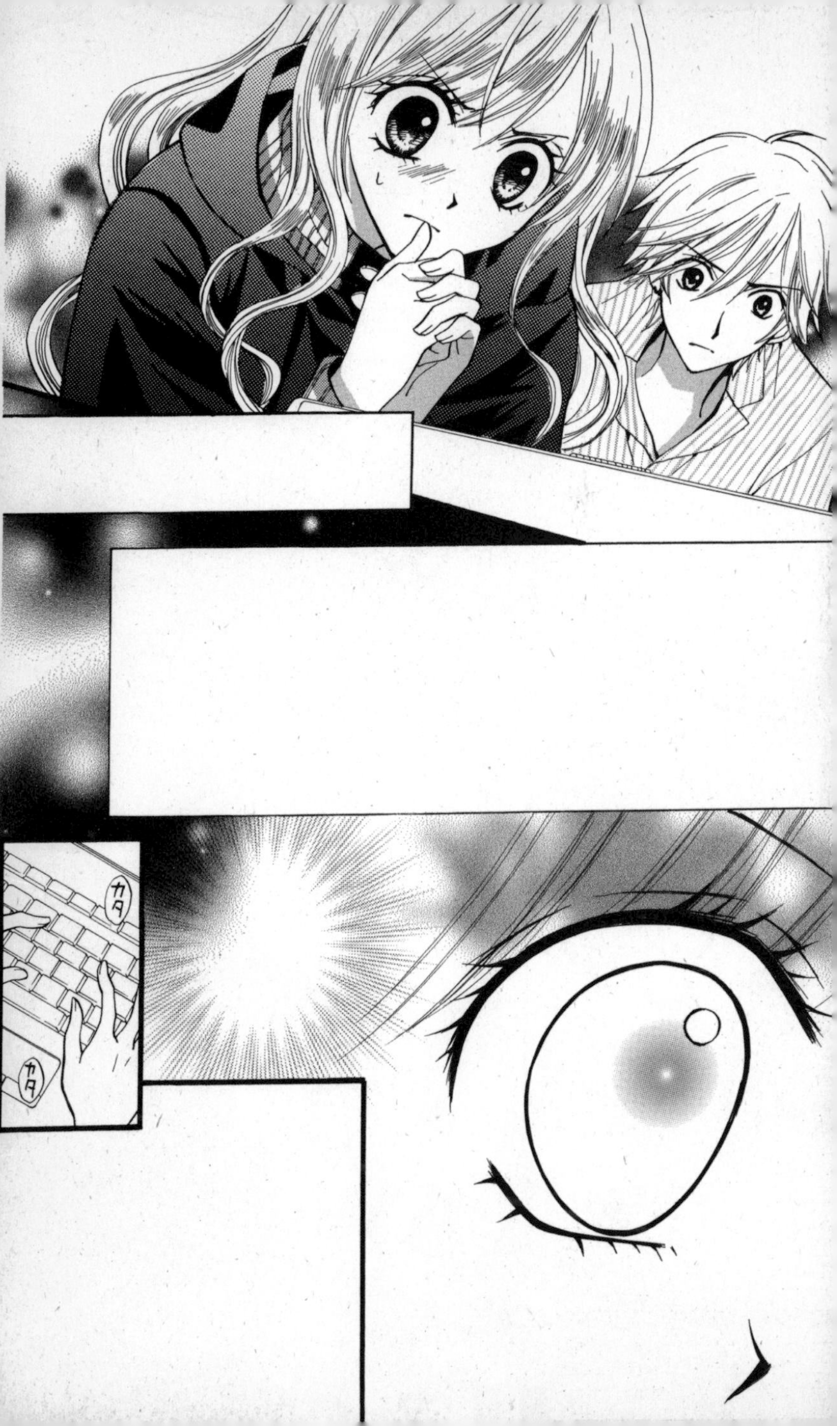
カタ
カタ

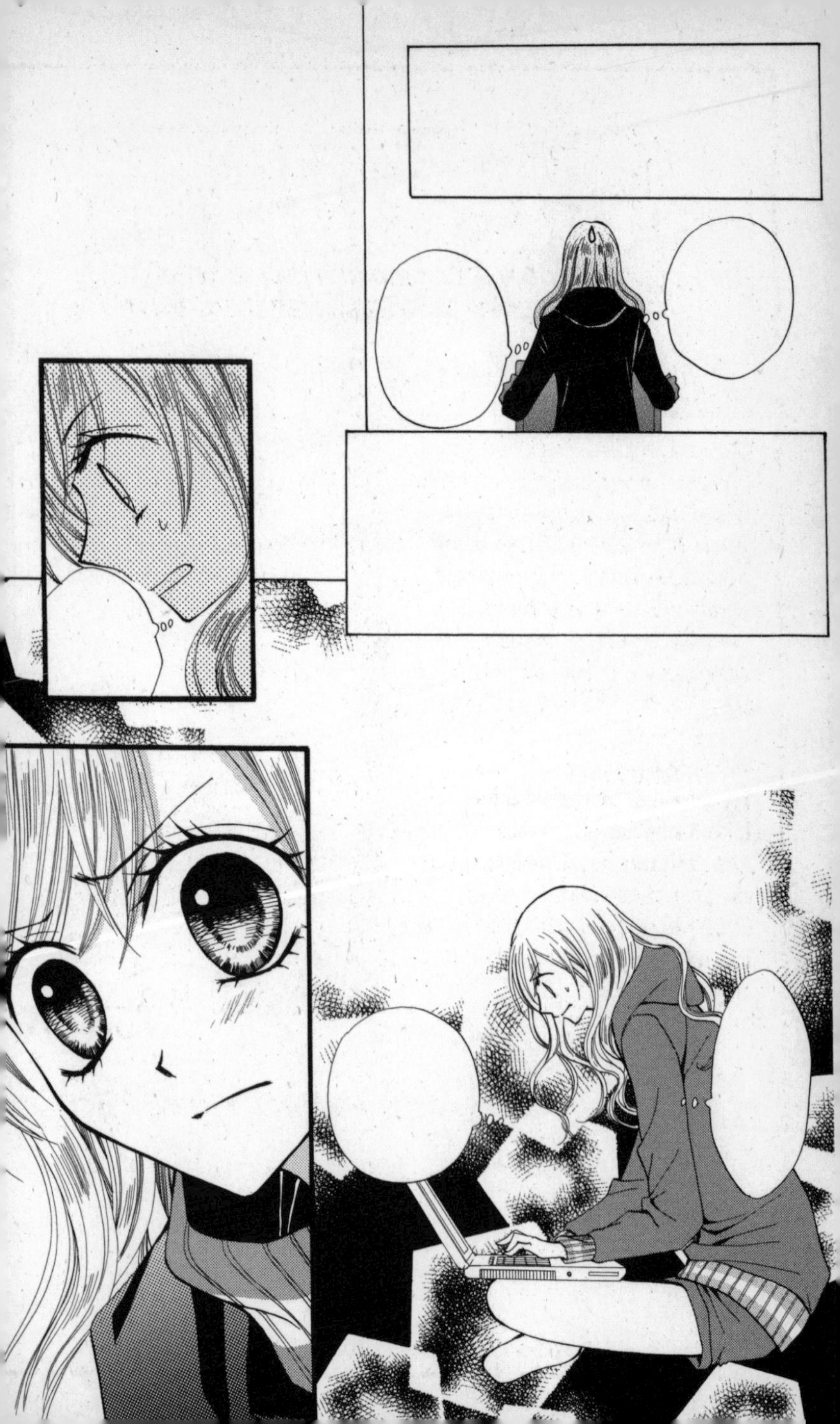

THE wallflower
YAMATONADESHIKO SHICHIHENGE

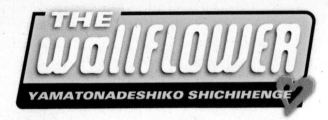

BY TOMOKO HAYAKAWA

1
THE wallflower
YAMATONADESHIKO SHICHIHENGE
TOMOKO
HAYAKAWA

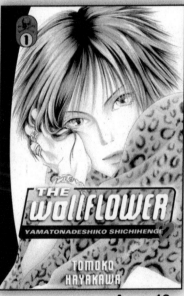

It's a beautiful, expansive mansion, and four handsome, fifteen-year-old friends are allowed to live in it for free! But there is one condition—within three years the young men must take the owner's niece and transform her into a proper lady befitting the palace in which they all live! How hard can it be?

Enter Sunako Nakahara, the horror-movie-loving, pock-faced, frizzy-haired, fashion-illiterate hermit who has a tendency to break into explosive nosebleeds whenever she sees anyone attractive. This project is going to take far more than our four heroes ever expected; it needs a miracle!

Ages: 16 +

Special extras in each volume! Read them all!

KC KODANSHA COMICS

VISIT WWW.KODANSHACOMICS.COM TO:

- View release date calendars for upcoming volumes
- Find out the latest about new Kodansha Comics series

The Pretty Guardians are back!

*

Kodansha Comics is proud to present *Sailor Moon* with all new translations.

For more information, go to **www.kodanshacomics.com**

PEACH-PIT
CREATORS OF *DEARS* AND *ROZEN MAIDEN*

Everybody at Seiyo Elementary thinks that stylish and supercool Amu has it all. But nobody knows the real Amu, a shy girl who wishes she had the courage to truly be herself. Changing Amu's life is going to take more than wishes and dreams—it's going to take a little magic! One morning, Amu finds a surprise in her bed: three strange little eggs. Each egg contains a Guardian Character, an angel-like being who can give her the power to be someone new. With the help of her Guardian Characters, Amu is about to discover that her true self is even more amazing than she ever dreamed.

Special extras in each volume! Read them all!

VISIT WWW.KODANSHACOMICS.COM TO:

- **View release date calendars for upcoming volumes**
- **Find out the latest about new Kodansha Comics series**

Arisa volume 6 is a work of fiction. Names, characters, places, and incidents are the products of the author's imagination or are used fictitiously. Any resemblance to actual events, locales, or persons, living or dead, is entirely coincidental.

A Kodansha Comics Trade Paperback Original

Published in the United States by Kodansha Comics, an imprint of Kodansha USA Publishing, LLC, New York.

Publication rights for this English edition arranged through Kodansha Ltd., Tokyo.

First published in Japan in 2010 by Kodansha Ltd., Tokyo.

ISBN 978-1-61262-039-8

Printed in the United States of America.

www.kodanshacomics.com

9 8 7 6 5 4 3 2 1

Translator/Adapter: Andria Cheng
Lettering: Scott O. Brown

TOMARE!

[STOP!]

You're going the wrong way!

Manga is a completely
different
type of reading experience.

To start at the *beginning*,
go to the *end*!

That's right! Authentic manga is read the traditional Japanese way—from right to left. Exactly the *opposite* of how American books are read. It's easy to follow: Just go to the other end of the book, and read each page—and each panel—from the right side to the left side, starting at the top right. Now you're experiencing manga as it was meant to be!